CHRISTIAN EXISTENCE TODAY

To
Adam John Hauerwas
Son and Friend

CHRISTIAN EXISTENCE TODAY
Essays on Church, World, and Living In Between

Stanley Hauerwas

THE LABYRINTH PRESS
Durham, North Carolina

Library of Congress Cataloging-in-Publication Data

Hauerwas, Stanley, 1940-
    Christian existence today : essays on church, world, and living in between / Stanley Hauerwas.
        p.   cm.
    Includes bibliographies and index.

    1. Theology.   2. Christian ethics–Methodist authors.   3. Christianity–20th century. 4. Church and the world.   5. United States–Church history–20th century.   I. Title.
BR50.H34 1988
230–dc19
                                                                    88-18774
                                                                    CIP

Printed in the United States of America

CONTENTS

III. SERVING IN THE WORLD

PREFACE

Contrary to popular opinion I do not have a compulsion to write. On the contrary, I find writing and thinking, which is probably the same thing, as hard now as when I began. I write because people ask me to read a paper about this or that for this or that amount of money and since I always need money I write. I believe that Samuel Johnson was right that anyone who does not write for money is a fool.

That I write in response to requests also helps explain the occasional nature of my essays. I do what people ask me to do. I make no apology for this as I do not believe that thinking is self-generating. If I have any "creativity" it comes from forcing myself to meet others' agendas while trying to be true to what I care about. In the process I discover that what I have been doing "occasionally" turns out to have a kind of unity or perspective that sometimes justifies collecting the essays as a book. Of course, that does not mean this collection of essays amounts to a coherent position, but I do think it results in an interesting perspective that I hope will challenge and provoke.

Most of these essays have been written since I came to teach at the Divinity School at Duke University. I was apprehensive about my move to Duke since, as I indicated above, I do what people ask me to do. I was unsure how what I was asked to do here might change me. I feel sure I have been changed as I not only discovered new people with new challenges and ideas, but I rediscovered the Protestant world. I am extremely grateful for the former and I remain ambivalent about the latter.

I am sure, however, that I owe much to the faculty at Duke, both in the Divinity School and University, for their extraordinary hospitality. I am particularly grateful to Dennis Campbell, my Dean and friend, as well as Geoffrey Wainwright, Harmon Smith, Tommy Langford, John Westerhoff, Will Willimon, and Rich Lischer for their willingness to engage me in conversation. The graduate students at Duke have been an unfailing source of help and challenge.

I owe a particular debt to Mr. Greg Jones, who has been my graduate assistant for the years I have been at Duke. He has not only corrected the grammar in most of what is written here, but he has substantively made the book better by suggesting how my arguments fail or by calling my attention to books I should have but had not yet read. Such students are gifts which make me better than I am. I also owe a special debt to my colleague, David Steinmetz, who quite literally made this book possible. David is a scholar so committed to enlarging the world of theological scholarship, he has taken time to create The Labyrinth Press that the classics of Christian theology will not be lost. I am sure he knows that this book is no "classic," but I am indebted to him for suggesting that I might bring these essays together to be published by Labyrinth. Though I hated to leave out an essay on Trollope, as well as a few others, David rightly suggested the book should be a "bit" shorter. He made valuable suggestions as well about the shape of the book. I am also grateful to Ms. Debra Weiner for her excellent editing of the text.

Of course, I continue to owe much to my many friends and colleagues beyond Duke. The debt I continue to owe to Alasdair MacIntyre and John Howard Yoder is evident in these pages. David Burrell, Robert Wilkin, Tom Shaffer and Jim McClendon remain good friends and teachers. Richard Neuhaus and Paul Ramsey refuse to give up on me even though I hold all the wrong views. The endnotes to this book testify to the many old and new friends that make my work possible. I am deeply grateful to them.

One of the greatest debts I owe, however, is to Mrs. Gay Trotter, secretary to the Graduate Program in Religion at Duke. I became Director of Graduate Studies at Duke because, as I said, I do what I am asked to do—no one seeks these jobs as they inevitably involve much responsibility with no power. But with the job came Mrs. Trotter, who not only does most of the work of the Director, but who has done or has seen to it that all the typing for this book was done. I am deeply grateful for her and her co-workers, as they not only work well but with unfailing good cheer.

In 1974 I published my first collection of essays, called *Vision and Virtue: Essays in Christian Ethical Reflection*, which I am pleased to say is still in print, thanks to the willingness of the University of Notre Dame Press to republish them in 1981. I dedicated the book to Adam and his mother because I thought it might be the only book I would ever write or be able to get published. Adam is now grown, in college, and learning to find his own way. I dedicate this book to him not only in celebration of his maturity, but because, in spite of what Aristotle rightly says about the unlikely possibility of true friendship between fathers and sons, he is my good friend. That is a gift I had no right to expect in this life but it is one for which I praise God daily.

ACKNOWLEDGMENTS

The author and publisher are grateful to the following for permission to reprint:

Perkins Journal for "A Tale of Two Stories: On Being a Christian and a Texan," reprinted from vol. XXXIV (Summer, 1981), pp. 1–15.

Fortress Press, publishers of *Scriptural Authority and Narrative Interpretation*, edited by Garret Green, 1986, for "The Church as God's New Language."

D. Reidel, publishers of *Moral Theory and Moral Judgment*, edited by Baruch Brody, 1986, for "Reconciling the Practice of Reason: Casuistry in a Christian Context."

The Furrow for "Peacemaking: The Virtue of the Church," reprinted from vol. 36 (October, 1985), pp. 605–614.

Theology Today for "The Gesture of a Truthful Story," reprinted from vol. XLII (July, 1985), pp. 181–189.

Word and World for "Clerical Character: Reflections on Ministerial Morality," reprinted from vol. VI (Spring, 1986), pp. 181–193.

Pilgrim Press, publishers of *The Pastor as Prophet*, edited by Earl Shelp and Ronald Sunderland, 1985, for "The Pastor as Prophet: Ethical Reflections on an Improbable Mission."

The Cresset for "A Christian Critique of Christian America," reprinted from vol. L (November, 1986), pp. 5–16.

Soundings for "Hope Faces Power: Thomas More and the King of England," reprinted from vol. LXI (Winter, 1978), pp. 456–479.

Katallagete for "How Christian Universities Contribute to the Corruption of Youth: Church and University in a Confused Age," reprinted from vol. 9 (Summer, 1986), pp. 21–28.

Religion and Intellectual Life for "Taking Time for Peace: The Ethical Significance of the Trivial," reprinted from vol. III (Spring, 1986), pp. 87–100.

INTRODUCTION

1. On Representing "Something New"

The theologian's task is faithfulness, not the creation of the new. Yet I am told the position represented in these pages and in earlier work strikes many as new and even challenging. I hope those making such observations mean that I have thrown fresh perspectives on traditional commitments. I certainly have not tried to be "creative" and/or do something "new" as if that were worth doing in and of itself. Rather, I began my work wanting to do no more than recapture the significance of the virtues for understanding the Christian life and in the process perhaps even help us live more faithfully.

Closely connected with that project was my concern to understand how Christian convictions can be said to be true or false. As a result, my work appears to many as a strange mix of philosophy, literature, a few historical asides, theology, and ethics. That, no doubt, contributes to the impression that I am doing something that is at least strange, if not new. I am not inclined to apologize for crossing so many disciplinary lines, however, as I simply do not see how any genuine investigation can avoid doing so. When I began my work I had no idea I would believe the church to be as important as I now think it is for understanding the nature and truth of Christian convictions. Even less did I think that Christian nonviolence might be crucial for the epistemological status of Christian belief. Of course, I do not pretend I have said the last word on any of these matters, but I rejoice that this process of discovery for myself has begun to attract the attention of others who, I hope, will be able to develop these themes better than I have.

Such a hope is not my attempt at false modesty, as neither true nor false modesty is my strong suit. Rather, I am simply indicating my increasing awareness of how much I depend on others in my work. That is one of the reasons I am so hesitant to claim that my work is "new" or "creative" because such a claim betrays the existence of that "cloud of witnesses" that has made it possible. For example, I am aware I often appear to make excessive use of footnotes, yet my footnotes indicate my indebtedness to others both past and present without whom I literally could not write or think. Writing and thinking, which are often the same thing, are a conversation with an ongoing community. Those who disagree with me are as precious as those who are supportive (though I prefer the latter), for without disagreements I would have little sense of what I really think. For example, I am sure my views on the significance of the church as a social ethic would lack critical edge if I did not always have Reinhold Niebuhr in mind.

I have chosen, therefore, to introduce this book by discussing the considerable disagreement between Jim Gustafson and myself. I suspect Gustafson's critique of my work gives voice to the disquiet many feel about the "newness" of my perspective. By responding to his criticisms I hope to advance my constructive proposals by challenging the dominant philosophical and theological assumptions shared by those who make criticisms such as Gustafson's. Gustafson's great virtue is his willingness to make those assumptions explicit.

By responding to Gustafson I hope to help some readers understand better what I am about. I think many interpret me as having reminded us of the importance of virtue or the church for ethics in a manner that leaves everything else as is. But that simply is not the case. One cannot understand what I am about if one continues to presuppose the dominant philosophical and theological intellectual habits of the last hundred years. For example, though I have learned much from both Niebuhrs, the way I think cannot be easily joined with their work. As a result, I do not pretend that coming to understand me is easy or without risk but only that such a rethinking is required. I do not expect that those who make the effort will necessarily agree with me, but I do hope that having made the effort they will have learned something which they value.

To introduce a book with a report on a disagreement as well as a determination to continue it may seem odd. But "Introductions" are often rather boring if the author only tells the readers what they are going to read; or, as an alternative, new lines of analysis are developed which usually only result in confusing matters. By beginning in controversy, however, I hope to make the reading of this book more interesting, as the reader can test my response to Gustafson through the essays in the book. Moreover, I hope that reading in that manner will help the reader see the book for what it is—a continuing conversation I am fortunate to have with myself, friends, and critics in the hope of better understanding the nature of Christian existence.

2

2. On a Representation of "The Sectarian Temptation"

James Gustafson began his critique by reporting that he discovered at the 1984 meeting of the British Society for the Study of Christian Ethics some enthusiasm for my work among theologians from the Church of Scotland and the Church of England, as well as the Roman Catholic Church.[1] Gustafson described this enthusiasm as a "seduction" and advised that anyone tempted to follow me give some consideration to the incongruities between the sectarian ecclesiology I represent and the ecclesiology represented by their more traditional churches. Moreover, he suggested that some thought be given to the tension between the adherence to the classic creeds on the Incarnation and the Trinity made by these churches and my historicist portrayal of Jesus. In short, Gustafson found it surprising that theologians who should know better are accepting a position that would require them to abandon their most cherished commitments. I find all this a little odd, since Gustafson's most recent work argues that Christians should abandon their traditional understanding of Christ as an unwarranted form of anthropocentric theology.

Though I am of course pleased that my work has had some influence, even in England, I cannot be happy that Gustafson sees that influence in such a negative light. I understand myself neither to represent the kind of sectarianism he describes nor to deny the doctrines of the Incarnation and Trinity. It is my hope that this book will help make clear that such charges are oversimplifications. Contrary to Gustafson's characterization, I stand in the catholic tradition that both affirms the universality of the church and confesses God's trinitarian nature. Yet, how then am I to explain the vast difference between how Gustafson and I understand my work? By exploring that question through an analysis of Gustafson's critique, I hope to suggest the main lines of the position developed in this book.

Gustafson reported that the strange influence I have had in Britain was explained to him a few days later by a Scottish theologian at a conference on Reinhold Niebuhr. It was suggested that my "sectarianism" was attractive "because it made clear a historic confessional basis on which Christian morality could be distinguished from the culture, and how Christians could stand prophetically as Christians on matters of nuclear armaments and the like" (p. 85). That such a stance might be attractive in England, where the churches have lost so much influence that they have nothing more to lose, is not surprising to Gustafson. From his perspective the situation of the churches in England is but a dramatic example of the contemporary state of Christianity in general. As he says,

> Christianity is a beleaguered religion. In the secularization of Western culture we have many alternative interpretations of how things really and ultimately are—that is, functional equivalents to theology. We have, even in the West, a variety of moralities, many of which are defended by modern ways of interpreting the nature of persons and the nature of morality itself . . . Religious pluralism is an inexorable fact. In this situation every *aggiornamento* in the Christian community poses threats to its historic uniqueness and identity, every such move stimulates a conservative reaction. Pastors engaged in care of their parishioners are informed by theories of psychotherapy and begin to wonder what distinguishes them as Christians from their competitors down the street. Moralists become engaged in practical problems and social policy questions and wonder whether they are being faithful to their Christian commitments. Theologians take account of the learning provided by various non-theological disciplines in the university and are criticized for too much revisionism in their writing (pp. 83–84).

Therefore, Gustafson understands why a "sectarian withdrawal" is a temptation, but that is what it is—a temptation—for to give into it, Gustafson argues, is to betray the church and the theologians' task. According to Gustafson, a theology formed by this temptation cannot but result in a fideistic stance that legitimates a tribalistic understanding of Christianity. While such sectarianism may provide Christians with a clear identity and insures distinctiveness of belief, it has the unfortunate effect of "isolating Christianity from taking seriously the wider world of science and culture and limits the participation of Christians in the ambiguities of moral and social life in the patterns of interdependence in the world." (p. 84)

Gustafson develops this broadside by suggesting that my sectarianism reflects the position of certain "Wittgensteinian fideists," such as Paul Holmer and George Lindbeck, who hold that the language of science and the language of religion are totally incommensurable. They do so in the interest of making theological claims incorrigible, such that persons are socialized into a particular form of life so thoroughly that they are not open to other ways of viewing the world that might challenge their religious categories. Drawing on hermeneutical theory, this position simply adopts a text, viz. the Bible, without justifying that text as worthy of interpretation (p. 87). From such a position it is hard to see what prevents doctrine from becoming ideology, since it is not clear how one can criticize the tradition so construed, either internally or externally.

In opposition to this view, Gustafson argues that insofar as religion and science are rational activities, it must be possible in principle to subject theological claims to correction and revision in terms of what we have learned from social and physical sciences. Any attempt to maintain that knowing religiously and theologically is radically distinct from other ways of knowing can only result in making Christianity unintelligible in a world in which fewer and fewer people are formed by the "Christian language." The alternative is for theologians to relativize the Christian tradition by drawing on other sources of knowledge so that we can construe God's relation to the world in the light of our modern knowledge.

Gustafson, moreover, argues that my "theological fideism" is correlative to a "sociological tribalism," resulting in a truncated ethic unable to deal adequately with contemporary challenges. In particular, the emphasis on "narrative theology" and sectarianism go hand in hand. Thus, he characterizes my emphasis on narrative in the following manner:

> . . . We grow up in communities in which we share narratives, the stories of the community. This, I would agree, is partly true in a descriptive sense. The narratives and our participating in the community, in his [Hauerwas] case the "Church" (very abstractly), gives shape to our characters. Our characters are expressed in our deeds and actions. Further, the narratives of the community give shape to the way in which we interpret life in the world. So far this is a description. A turn to the normative takes place. Since we belong to the Christian community its narratives *ought* to shape the lives of its members. In Hauerwas' case, for example, this means that Christian morality is not based on a concern to be responsible participants in the ambiguities of public choices. It is based on its fidelity of the biblical narratives, and particularly of the Gospel narratives. Thus the principal criterion for judging Christian behavior is its conformity to the stories of Jesus. For Hauerwas this means, for example, that Christian morality must be pacifist because he reads the Gospel narratives as pacifist. In this example, we have wedded a way of doing theology—narratives—to an ecclesiology—classical sectarian—and to an ethic which is also classically sectarian (p. 88).

Gustafson argues that by succumbing to this sectarian temptation I assume wrongly that the church is socially and culturally isolable from the wider society and culture. As a result Christians are turned into a kind of tribe living in a ghetto, unable to participate in universities or to be called to serve in the professions and making no contribution to "critical ambiguous choices" necessary in political and public life (p. 91). Such a tribalism, however, is based on a false sociological assumption which cannot help but lead to failure. "Because of the power that other institutions in society and culture have to furnish symbols and constructs that interpret the same reality that Christian faith and theology does, the parish and congregational life of churches necessarily have to take these matters into account as it seeks to educate and form persons in Christian faith and life" (p. 91). In short, Christians are never just members of the church but must rightly live in the world. As long as people have to make a living, there is no way to withdraw.

But the unrealistic sociology of my tribalizing is not nearly as serious an error as the theological presuppositions that underlie it. For my sectarian tendencies are based on the theological assumption

> . . . that God is known only in and through history, and particularly the history of the Biblical people culminating in the events of Christ and their effects. Insofar as this describes an assumption it ignores a great deal of the Biblical witness itself. In Christian sectarian form God becomes a Christian God for Christian people: to put it most perjoratively, God is assumed to be the tribal God of a minority of the earth's population. Or, if God is not a tribal God there is only one community in the world that has access to knowledge of God because God has revealed himself only in the life of that community. Or still another possible assumption, and worse from my perspective than the other two, Christian theology and ethics really are not concerned so much about God as they are about maintaining fidelity to the biblical narratives about Jesus, or about maintaining the "Biblical view" as a historical vocation that demands fidelity without further external justification, or idolatrously maintaining a historic social identity (p. 93).

Gustafson seems to suggest I have fallen into the last mistake because I have argued that any attempt to move beyond the "particularistic historical tradition" (as defined, in the end, by him), either to justify it or to criticize and possibly alter it, is to move to what he calls "universalism" (p. 89). But since I supply neither a doctrine of revelation (as Barth does) nor a way that the revelatory power of the biblical material can be confirmed in human experience (as the Niebuhrs do), my position can only be a defensive effort "to sustain the historical identity of the Christian tradition virtually for its own sake." (p. 89).

In particular, Gustafson faults me for omitting any doctrine of creation as a basis for ethics, for only on the basis of creation can contemporary ways of knowing nature be appropriated. Moreover, it is only on the basis of such knowledge that an ethic adequate for our times can be mounted. "Faithful witness to Jesus is not a sufficient theological and moral basis for addressing the moral and social problems of the twentieth century. The theologian addressing many issues—nuclear, social justice, ecology, and so forth—must do so as an outcome of a theology that develops God's relation to all aspects of life in the world, and develops those relations in terms which are not exclusively Christian in a sectarian form. Jesus is not God" (p. 93).

3. In Defense of "Temptation"

Because of the story Christians tell about our first parents and their run-in with a subtle serpent, we tend to think temptations are necessarily to be resisted. Yet if I represent a temptation, even to the British, I hope they will give in to it. I equally hope neither they nor others will accept Gustafson's characterization of that temptation, as I certainly do not recognize in his depiction of my work a position I defend. I have taken the time, however, to spell out his criticism, not only because his views will have added weight due to his well-deserved stature in the field but also because they bring together often-made characterizations and criticisms of my position.

Consider first the allegation that I am a "sectarian." What I find disconcerting about that claim is the assumption that the one making the charge has the argumentative high ground, so that the burden of proof is on me. But where is the generally agreed criterion for the use of this term, "sectarian"? Too often those making the charge assume epistemological (as well as sociological) positions that are question begging. Has it not been long recognized that Ernst Troeltsch's typology presumed the normative status of the "church type"?[2]

That I have been critical of the moral limits of liberalism is certainly true, but I do not understand why that makes me a ready candidate for being a sectarian. Indeed, I have argued earlier (and will again in this book) that insofar as the church can reclaim its integrity as a community of virtue, it can be of great service in liberal societies.[3] Moreover, the fact that I have written about why and how Christians should support as well as serve the medical and legal professions,[4] Christian relations with Judaism,[5] how we might think about justice,[6] as well as an analysis of the moral debate concerning nuclear war[7] seems to have no effect on those who are convinced I am a "withdrawn" sectarian. To be sure, I have made no secret of my indebtedness to John Howard Yoder, as will again be evident in these pages, but I do not understand why that association is sufficient to make me a sectarian, unless one assumes uncritically that a Mennonite must be a sectarian. At the very least those making that charge should attend to Yoder's arguments concerning the Christian's positive duties to wider society and the state.[8]

I am certainly aware that the position I have developed is not in the recent mainstream of Christian ethical reflection. To be candid, I often am a bit surprised by some of the implications that arise as I continue to try to think through the course on which I am set. So I do not blame anyone for approaching my work (or Yoder's) with a good deal of caution and skepticism. What I find unfair, however, is the assumption that my critic has a hold on my task by calling me "sectarian." Show me where I am wrong about God, Jesus, the limits of liberalism, the nature of the virtues, or the doctrine of the church—but do not shortcut that task by calling me a sectarian.

Gustafson's criticisms must still be addressed, if for no other reason than that they have the virtue of interrelating the theological, epistemological, and ecclesiological (sociological) themes in my work. Gustafson is surely right to suggest that these themes are interrelated, for I have never tried to make neat distinctions between theology, philosophy, and ethics in the interest of disciplinary security. That does not mean I have any ambition to develop a grandiose system. I simply do not think so systematically, as is clear from the unsystematic and occasional nature of my work. Rather, I try to respond, for example, to epistemological questions only as is necessary in terms of the argument I am making at the time. That I do so, of course, reflects my conviction that there is no way to deal with the question of "truth as such" but only with the question of the truth of this or that claim. That said, however, I will now try to respond as directly as I can to Gustafson's claims: (1) that I am a fideist, (2) that I justify an irresponsible attitude of Christians toward worldly involvement, and (3) that I either lack a theological doctrine of creation or that I am an idolator.

3.1 On Questions of Truth Versus "Fideism"

Gustafson suggests that those representing the "sectarian temptation" are responding to the "beleaguered" state of contemporary Christianity in a secular world. In the name of narrative we make a virtue of our inability to free ourselves from our parochial starting points by underwriting the assumption that every position is ultimately parochial. While this may be an effective survival tactic, Gustafson charges that such a strategy necessarily gives up on the central Christian claim setting all things relative to God.

I suspect few of us are able to know or account for all the presuppositions with which we work, but I have never thought myself working out the agenda Gustafson attributes to me. Though I am convinced that

Christianity has wrongly tried to underwrite foundationalist epistemologies, at times perhaps in the interest of justifying the imperialistic political strategies of the West, I have not argued in the manner I have because I think the culture of the West is beginning to fail. Nor have I tried to justify Christian belief by making Christian convictions immune from challenge from other modes of knowledge, particularly science.

Indeed, as I have argued elsewhere[9] as well as here, theological convictions inextricably involve truth-claims that are in principle open to challenge. The claim that our existence has a teleological character that requires narrative display is a "metaphysical" claim. I take it that such claims might well be challenged, but I cannot predict what all such challenges will look like. Thus, while I certainly believe that Christian convictions make claims about our existence, I do not believe that the veridical status of those claims can be or should be based on the questionable assumption that all possible challenges have been anticipated and taken into account or defeated.

Indeed, I have avoided all appeals to a Kuhnian-like position (with which Kuhn may unfairly be identified) designed to protect theological convictions from possible scientific challenge. But rather than asserting that material theological convictions *must* be revised in the light of science, should not Gustafson indicate which scientific conclusions should be considered and why? Certainly I see no reason why the central affirmations of the Christian faith need to be surrendered or denaturalized in terms of the mere activity of science, and I am unaware of any scientific conclusion that would now require such revision—particularly those about the ultimate end of the human life or even the world that so impress Gustafson. The history of modern theology is littered with the wrecks of such revision done on the basis of a science that no longer has any credence; which is but a way of saying that while I have eminent respect for scientific work, I am less confident than is Gustafson that it is meaningful to assign to science qua science an overriding veridical status. Certain kinds of science, and particularly the presuppositions of some scientific research agendas, may present theological challenges— e.g., that humans are completely explicable in terms of mechanistic chemical reactions—and nothing I have said is meant to protect theology or Christians from such challenges. Of course, I do not assume that such confrontations will necessarily result in victory for the challenger.[10]

I cannot hope to address here the many questions involved in assessing the truthfulness of theological claims. Indeed, I do not believe that all theological language works at the same level or takes out similar drafts about the way the world is. Suffice it to say that, as I try to suggest in several of the essays in this book, I assume that Christian theology has a stake in a qualified epistemological realism.[11] I certainly do not believe, nor did Wittgenstein, that religious convictions are or should be treated as an internally consistent language game that is self-validating. What Wittgenstein has taught me, however, is that if we attend to the diversity of our language we learn to appreciate what a marvelously diverse world we inhabit and how complex claims about the way the world is will inevitably be.

There is, however, one characteristic of Christian convictions that, while not unique to Christians, is nonetheless a stumbling block to many who would assess whether Christian convictions are true. Moreover, it is an aspect that I have repeatably emphasized; it may be the ultimate issue troubling Gustafson. For I have argued that the very content of Christian convictions requires that the self be transformed if we are adequately to see the truth of the convictions—e.g., that I am a creature of a good creator yet in rebellion against my status as such. Talk of our sin, therefore, is a claim about the way we are, but our very ability to know we are that way requires that we have already begun a new way of life. That is why the Christian doctrine of sanctification is central for assessing the epistemological status of Christian convictions. Assessing the truthfulness of religious convictions cannot be separated from the truthfulness of the persons who make those claims.

Therefore, the most important knowledge Christian convictions involve, and there is much worth knowing for which Christians have no special claim, requires a transformation of the self. Christianity is no "world view," not a form of primitive metaphysics, that can be assessed in comparison to alternative "world views." Rather, Christians are people who remain convinced that the truthfulness of their beliefs must be demonstrated in their lives. There is a sense in which Christian convictions are self-referential, but the reference is not to propositions but to lives. While such a view has similarities to some pragmatic theories of truth, I suspect that the Christian sense of "fruitfulness" involves a "realism" that might make some advocates of those theories uneasy.

Putting the matter this way, however, is still too formal, for it may appear that Christians are left with nothing to say other than "Try it—you will like it." As a result, Christians are epistemologically in the same position as Nazis and/or Moonies. Yet such a conclusion is false because the content of the convictions of those communities cannot stand challenge scientifically, metaphysically, or morally. However, that does not mean that disputes between all communities can be resolved by applying such tests. For example, I do not think the differences between

Jews, Christians, or Muslims can be settled in terms of what we now know.[12] To realize that is to begin to appreciate what it means to live eschatologically.

Yet this objection is a crucial reminder that the subject of transformation for Christians is not the isolated individual, but a community living through time. For the convictions that Christians hold about the way things are entail the existence of a people, since what we know can be known only through witness. Moreover, contrary to Gustafson's claim that such a community lacks any means to criticize its tradition, its worship of God requires it be open to continual "reality checks." God comes to this community in the form of a stranger, challenging its smugness, exposing its temptations to false "knowledge," denying its spurious claims to have domesticated God's grace. Thus, one of the tests of the truthfulness of Christian convictions cannot help being the faithfulness of the church.

3.2 On Christian Social Engagement Versus "Irresponsibility"

I hope I have made clear that there are no epistemological grounds to keep one holding views such as mine from participating in the cultural, intellectual, and political life of society. Indeed, I share with Gustafson his concern about the over-specialization of disciplinary fields legitimized by the modern university. I do, after all, continue to teach in a university that while not unfriendly to religion certainly gives it no special status. Such a position seems appropriate for theological work, since as theologians we are put in a position of engaging critically other perspectives as well as remaining open to the challenge of other perspectives without the outcome of those challenges being predetermined by legal or social power. It may be that some universities at present or in the future may for political reasons find it difficult to support the teaching of Christian theology as a university subject, but I know of no reasons intrinsic to the canons of scholarship and thought of the university why such an excommunication would be necessary.

In that respect I find Gustafson's attitude odd, as he seems to assume that the only option for Christians is either *complete* involvement in culture or *complete* withdrawal. I see no reason why such a stark alternative is necessary. The issue is how the church can provide the interpretative categories to help Christians better understand the positive and negative aspects of their societies and guide their subsequent selective participation. Moreover, such categories cannot be developed in the abstract, since they depend on the actual societies in which Christians find themselves. The gospel does not simply contain a theory of society and/or legitimate government. All we know as Christians is that government will exist—not what form it will or must take.

That does not mean that Christians, along with others, will not try, through the study of history and social and political thought, to gain wisdom about how societies, the law, and government best work. Such knowledge, however, lacks the status of "gospel truth," as we are too much the product of accidents of geography, climate, and history to speak with certainty about what society ought to look like. Every society has its strengths and weaknesses which change through time. How Christians relate to those strengths and weaknesses will and should also change through time.

It is certainly true that I have been critical of liberal social and political presuppositions, particularly as these are played out in American society. Indeed, part of my concern has been with liberalism's presumption, linked to the peculiarity of its origin in America, that people can create a society and government de novo. The ahistorical character of liberal social and political theory strikes me as particularly pernicious, as in the name of freedom manipulative social relations are legitimated.

Moreover, I have emphasized the importance of a recovery of the integrity of the church as an alternative political community. That I have done so, however, does not commit me to a sectarian ecclesiology, unless it is assumed that the secular state has the right to determine what will and will not count as political. Unless the church and Christians are trained first to understand their community's language, they will lack resources to notice times when the language of the state is not their own. To be sure, there may also be continuities between those languages, but those continuities cannot be recognized unless Christians first know that their community's language is determined by what Walter Brueggemann has called the "singular holiness of God."[13]

Drawing on the wonderful exchange at the city wall between the Assyrian ambassador, Hezekiah, and Isaiah in II Kings 18–19, Brueggemann notes that without Israel having a language behind the wall there would have been no way to resist the seduction of the language at the wall with its claim that Israel's God had been defeated. As Brueggemann puts it,

> . . . the Assyrian negotiators at the wall are not offering a policy in the general interest, but under such a guise are pursuing Assyrian policy at the expense of all those behind the wall. Then the dominant conversation partner acts and speaks only from a narrow interest that is sectarian. We are not accustomed to thinking of the voice of the empire as a sectarian voice. But so it is when it

serves only a narrow interest. *Empire as sect* is a theme worth pursuing in our own situation because it may be suggested that the voice of American power, for example, claims to be the voice of general well-being and may in a number of cases be only the voice of a narrow range of economic and political interest. The ideological guise is effective if large numbers of people can be kept from noticing the narrow base of real interest. That narrow base will not be noticed unless there is another conversation behind the wall which gives critical distance and standing ground for an alternative assessment. In ancient Israel, the prophets are the ones who regularly expose the voice of the empire as a sectarian voice not to be heard as a comprehensive, disinterested voice.[14]

To this I can only add that the church is a prophet only when it is capable of remembering it has a history that is neither that of nations nor empires—and is in its own way finite.

Such a position does not commit me to believing we live socially and politically in a night when all cats are grey. For example, Richard Neuhaus chides me for suggesting in "A Christian Critique of Christian America" (Chapter 9 of this book) that we are lucky if we live in regimes that justify themselves in the name of consent of the governed. He argues such a view is inconsistent, since I also maintain that democracy is not different in kind from other forms of states.[15] Drawing on the latter claim he attributes to me the view that it makes no difference to Christians whether rulers are just or unjust. I certainly do not believe that nor do I think the views I have defended require me to believe it.

It obviously makes all the difference whether rulers are more nearly just if they are to receive support from Christians. I do not believe, however, that we know beforehand for all times and all places what set of procedures or practices will insure such justice. For example, if the "consent of the governed" is constitutionally insured it makes all the difference what kind of people the governed are. I certainly do not believe that consent in itself insures just government, as it is clear that even before the beginning of the war Hitler commanded the widespread support of the German people. As I have suggested earlier and again in these pages, the most important political service the church does for any society is to be a community capable of developing people of virtue. Thomas More, I believe, was not speaking ironically when he avowed he died as the king's good servant. Kings are poorer when they command subjects who have compromised their virtue in the interest of being influential.

My call for Christians to recover the integrity of the church as integral to our political witness does not entail that Christians must withdraw from the economic, cultural, legal, and political life of our societies. It does mean, however, that the form of our participation will vary given the nature of the societies in which we find ourselves. For example, in one of the essays in this book I support a Mennonite attempt to avoid using law courts to sue, but that does not entail that Christians are to avoid all contact with the law or are in principle prevented from practicing law. Rather, I understand the kind of restraint shown in not suing to be the condition necessary to help us find the means to be a more cooperative, virtuous, and peaceful polity.

In that respect I am sympathetic with what Robert Rodes calls a jurisprudence of aspiration. He understands the law to be an expression of what we aspire to as a community

> which is not necessarily what we can realistically hope to accomplish. If as a community we aspire to live virtuously, to deal virtuously with one another, to encourage and support one another in leading virtuous lives, then the law must bear an effective witness to the whole of that aspiration rather than merely coerce or manipulate a measure of compliance with some part. It was no sentimentalist or visionary, but the ever-practical Justice Holmes who said that "The law is the witness and external deposit of our moral life. Its history is the history of the moral development of the race. The practice of it, in spite of popular jests, tends to make good citizens and good men." If we concern ourselves only with what can or should be enforced, we overlook this function of our law, and, as a consequence, badly attenuate the moral life of our society.[16]

Ironically, exactly because liberal societies have tended to undercut the moral aspirations of the law in the name of individual freedom, the law has become increasingly coercive in the interest of maintaining order. As a result, the Christians who presently serve as lawyers may find themselves in greater tension with their profession.

There is one final issue that must be addressed if I am to meet Gustafson's criticism fairly. In a paper written for *Theology Today* Michael Quirk perceptively observes that though I have drawn on as well as aligned myself with critics of liberalism such as Alasdair MacIntyre, Michael Sandel, Charles Taylor, and Michael Walzer, I am not of them.[17] For, as Professor Quirk notes, even if we were able to move to some form of civic republicanism in America, I would still consider that society but a form of humanism. According to Professor Quirk, my position on the church commits me to holding that "Christianity entails allegiance to a story which is inevitably alien to all forms of secular political institutions however 'humanistic' they may be."[18]

That is accurate but I do not believe it entails an indiscriminate rejection of the secular order. Rather, I maintain that Christians must withdraw their support from a "civic republicanism" only when that form (as well as any other form) of government and society resorts to violence in order to maintain internal order and external security. At that point and that point alone Christians must withhold their involvement with the state. Such an admission, however, hardly commits me to a sectarian stance, unless one assumes, as some do, that every function of the state depends on its penchant for violence. Indeed, I believe it to be the responsibility of Christians to work to make their societies less prone to resort to violence. Surely one of the ways they can do that is by using the law as a means to settle disagreements short of violence.

I am aware that such a response will not satisfy those who believe a disavowal of violence requires a withdrawal from politics. In contrast, it is my contention that politics only begins with such a disavowal, for only then are we forced genuinely to listen to the other, thus beginning conversations necessary for discovering goods in common. From my perspective, far from requiring a withdrawal from the political arena, pacifism demands strenuous political engagement, because such a commitment forces us to expand our social and political imaginations. Christians therefore stand ready to be citizens, even if we finally must remain in Rowan Greer's memorable phrase "alien citizens."[19] If my work appears sectarian in our time I suspect it is because in the name of being responsible too many Christians are under the illusion we live in societies in which we can be at home because the societies are our creations. To reclaim alien status in contexts which were once thought home requires transformation of social and intellectual habits that cannot help but be a wrenching process.

Because I have been intent to help Christians rediscover our alien status I may have left the impression that the only community in which Christians can or should live is the church. No such view is either descriptively or normatively defensible. Christians rightly find themselves members of many communities. Thus I am not only a Christian but a university teacher, a Texan, a United States citizen, and a devoted fan of the Durham Bulls. Neither the general position I have developed nor my stance as a pacifist requires a general withdrawal from these communities. The essays on virtue and politics as well as those on the university should help make this point. What is required for Christians is not withdrawal but a sense of selective service and the ability to set priorities. This means that at times and in some circumstances Christians will find it impossible to participate in government, in aspects of the economy, or in the educational system. Yet such determinations can only be made by developing the skills of discrimination fostered in and through the church.

3.3 On a Theology of Creation and Redemption vs. A-theological "Tribalism"

I am sure these last remarks only reinforce Gustafson's conviction that I lack an adequate doctrine of creation. Such a charge actually involves two separable issues: (1) whether I have a doctrine of creation, and (2) whether my purported lack of a doctrine of creation, and my corresponding emphasis on Jesus, result in my failure to have an adequate theological and moral basis for addressing the moral and social problems of the twentieth century—i.e., nuclear weapons, social justice, ecology. I note these are separable criticisms because Gustafson does not indicate what is wrong with what I have written about nuclear war or show that the problem results from my Christocentric perspective. Moreover, he does not say why a doctrine of creation in and of itself is superior for dealing with these issues.

I suspect the assumption underlying his criticism is that without a doctrine of creation we have no way to underwrite the natural orders— and in particular the givenness of our social and political orders—as self-validating. Yet I have not denied the place of the state—even the coercive state—as part of God's "order." Rather, what I have refused in the name of an autonomous created order is to legitimate the state as an end in and of itself.

Admittedly, these are murky matters, but I think Gustafson exhibits a rather doubtful theological alternative by suggesting we need an independent doctrine of creation as a basis for ethics. Why doesn't Gustafson simply say that what is needed is a morality in which all people can agree? To appeal to doctrines of creation is only to make such agreement less likely. That is especially the case if we recognize, as Gustafson seems not to do, that Christian affirmation of God as creator is, because of God's trinitarian nature, a Christological claim.

Gustafson's call for a doctrine of creation, I suspect, involves a method not unlike that of H. Richard Niebuhr in *Christ and Culture*. In that book Niebuhr judges each of the various types, except "Christ the transformer," by how well it maintains the proper relation between creation and redemption. Yet creation and redemption are treated in such an abstract manner they almost become ciphers, especially since no reference is made to Israel and/or Jesus to explicate their content. Yet by appealing to some unspecified relation that should be maintained between these concepts, Niebuhr is able to make criticisms of every position without revealing his own material theological convictions; or put more argumentatively, in the name of creation Niebuhr in effect accepts "culture" as an independent norm that determines the significance of the work of Christ.[20]

This is but a way of saying that I doubt whether the issue is really a question of the doctrine of creation at all. I certainly have never denied the Christian affirmation of God as creator, but rather I have refused to use that affirmation to underwrite an autonomous realm of morality separate from Christ's lordship. The issue is not creation, but the kind of creation Jews and Christians continue to affirm integral to God's being. What allows us to look expectantly for agreement among those who do not worship God is not that we have a common morality based on autonomous knowledge of autonomous nature, but that God's kingdom is wider than the church.

Gustafson suggests that I believe that God is known only through history and in particular that small tribe we call the church. Certainly I believe that God as savior is known in Israel and Jesus in a way not available anywhere else. But I see no other basis for affirming God as creator if we mean anything more by that claim, as I assume we must theologically, than the hypothesis or hunch that something must have started it all. For creation in Christian theology is an eschatological act that binds nature and history together by placing them in a teleological order. Indeed, from a theological perspective nature and history are both abstractions when considered in the light of God's redemption. In Christ's bodily resurrection nature and history are made forever inseparable.[21] I certainly would not deny the natural order as a manifestation of God's kingdom.

I am aware that this response will hardly allay Gustafson's concern but instead will only reinforce his views that I represent a form of Jesus idolatry. Hence, Christology is the issue, though not in the way that Gustafson seems to think. To assert as Gustafson does that "Jesus is not God" is simply not a very interesting claim. It is not interesting because we have no context or speaker to know what is being denied and so lack any way to know what the denial means.

Classical Christian theologians have never, in fact, made so blunt a statement as Gustafson seems to think worth denying. Of course Jesus is not God if you mean, for example, God is no longer eternal by being identified with Jesus. It is just such worries that have made the Christian people careful about how they say God is present to us in the life, death, and resurrection of Jesus. That God was peculiarly at work in Jesus there is, for us, no doubt. How that work is to be explained is quite another matter—Jesus, very God and very man, is not a bad place to start.

One issue that can be overlooked in Gustafson's jeremiad against my "tribalism" is that the criticism he makes against me applies equally against the Jews. After all, affirmations of God's redemption through Jesus are not different in kind from the claim that "Israel is God's promised people." Yet Jews as well as Christians believe that insofar as we are faithful to God's call the world has an opportunity to be freed from such tribes as "the West" or "Europe" or "oppressed people of the world." So rather than being a justification for tribalism, my emphasis on Jesus as the first form of the new age is, I believe, our best hope to stand against contemporary tribalism.[22]

4. The Character of This Book

When Barth was writing *Theological Existence Today*, the challenges confronting Christians seemed clear and dramatic. After all, Hitler was the enemy, and who could miss the threat of that? The answer is that most people, religious or not, did. I cannot pretend that I have in these essays rightly read our challenge, but I have tried to suggest the kind of people we must be as Christians to be able to understand our situation— in short, people of virtue, forgiveness, hope, and peace. In other words, if Christians are not being sanctified, our affirmations of our belief in God mean little, and we lack the power to stand against the powers of the world.

Therefore, this is a book on the church, its ministry, the kind of virtues integral to the Christian life, and how those virtues make possible service in the world. It would, however, be presumptuous of me to claim any great unity for the book or a clearly developed argument through the arrangement of the essays. I have made no attempt to disguise the fact that these essays were written over a period of time—though most have been written in the last three years—as well as for diverse contexts and subjects. Yet I think it equally true that the book has a unity of perspective that makes the essays interrelate in a coherent and sometimes surprising manner.

Though I have arranged the essays in three sections to give a sense of order to the book, I would not want the reader to think that too much hangs on the arrangement. The first section deals more with methodological issues, but since I think it a mistake to separate methodology from content, I have also included a more "pastoral" essay in that section, "Peacemaking." The middle grouping of essays brings together those that deal more internally with the nature of the church and its ministry. The final section is composed of those essays more directed at the issue of church and world. That two of the essays are concerned with the university may indicate an overemphasis because of my own biographical situation. I hope the reader will find, however, that they also develop the theme of the relation of virtue and service to the world.

Theology, and even Christian ethics, is not generally at the top of people's reading lists, whether the person be church member or minister. I am sure there are many reasons for this, some good and some weak. I am equally sure that there is little that can be done about this state of affairs. Yet I try to write interestingly by using material that is not strictly "theological." I do not, I should say, consciously try to use nontheological literature, I just find that often I cannot say what I want without it— thus the use of William Humphrey, lemurs, and Robert Bolt's *A Man For All Seasons*. It is my hope, however, that some will find the essays not only interesting but at times entertaining. Christians today will be less absorbed with questions of our relevance and power, or lack of it, when we take the time to enjoy who we are. If these essays help to accomplish that to some small extent, I will be deeply gratified.

NOTES

1. James Gustafson, "The Sectarian Temptation: Reflections on Theology, the Church, and the University," *Proceedings of the Catholic Theological Society*, 40 (1985), pp. 83–94. Further citations will be in the text.

2. For Troeltsch's account see his *The Social Teachings of the Christian Churches* (New York: Macmillan, 1931).

Troeltsch says a "sect is a voluntary society, composed of strict and definite Christian believers bound to each other by the fact that all have experienced 'the new birth.' These 'believers' live apart from the world, are limited to small groups, emphasize the law instead of grace, and in varying degrees within their own circle, set up the Christian order, based on love; all this is done in preparation for the expectation of the coming Kingdom of God" (II, 993). For a judicious criticism of Troeltsch, see Duane Friesen, "Normative Factors in Troeltsch's Typology of Religious Association," *Journal of Religious Ethics*, 3, 2 (Fall, 1975), pp. 271–283.

3. Stanley Hauerwas, *Vision and Virtue* (Notre Dame: University of Notre Dame Press, 1974), pp. 222–260. See also my *Community of Character: Toward a Constructive Christian Social Ethic* (Notre Dame: University of Notre Dame Press, 1981).

4. Stanley Hauerwas, *Suffering Presence* (Notre Dame: University of Notre Dame Press, 1986).

5. Stanley Hauerwas, *Against the Nations* (Minneapolis: Winston-Seabury, 1985), pp. 61–90.

6. Stanley Hauerwas, "Should Christians Talk So Much About Justice?," *Books and Religion*, 14, 6 (May–June, 1986), p. 5ff as well as "On the Right To Be Tribal," *Christian Scholars Review*, XVI, 3 (March, 1987), pp. 238–241. Though these essays are more recent, they expand themes I was developing as early as *Truthfulness and Tragedy: Further Investigations into Christian Ethics* (Notre Dame: University of Notre Dame Press, 1977), pp. 132–147.

7. Hauerwas, *Against the Nations*, pp. 132–208.

8. John Howard Yoder, *Christian Witness to the State* (Newton, Kansas: Faith and Life Press,

1964). It is not clear to me why Gustafson did not criticize Yoder in his article since Yoder has argued about these matters more extensively and conclusively than I. Moreover, in his *Ethics From a Theocentric Perspective, I* (Chicago: University of Chicago Press, 1981) Gustafson avows that Yoder represents the most compelling alternative to his position (pp. 74–76).

Gustafson's suggestion that I can offer no internal critique of the Christian tradition is surely odd in the light of my defense of non-violence. From such a perspective the mainstream of the Christian tradition has been at odds with itself.

9. Stanley Hauerwas, *The Peaceable Kingdom* (Notre Dame: University of Notre Dame Press, 1983), pp. 1–35.

10. As I argue in "How the Christian University Contributes to the Corruption of Youth" (Chapter 13), it may be that how Christians approach certain modes of investigation may be different from non-Christians. Contrary to Gustafson, I suspect the most serious challenges to Christian convictions of truthfulness come not from science but from (extrascientific) modern morality.

11. Sabina Lovibond in her *Realism and Imagination in Ethics* (Minneapolis: University of Minnesota Press, 1983) developed with philosophical rigor the kind of epistemological realism I have only asserted. See also Alasdair MacIntyre, "Objectivity in Morality and Objectivity in Science," in *Morals, Science, and Society*, edited by Tris Engelhardt and Dan C. Callahan (New York: The Hastings Center, 1978), pp. 21–47. As MacIntyre puts it, "History has primacy over semantics and the continuities of history are moral continuities, continuities of tasks and projects which cannot be defined except with reference to the internal goods which specify the goals of such tasks and projects. Those tasks and projects are embodied in practices, and practices are in turn embodied in institutions and in communities. The scientific community is one among the moral communities of mankind and its unity is unintelligible apart from commitment to realism. . . To be objective is to understand oneself as part of a community and one's work as part of a project and of a history. The authority of this history and this project derives from the goods internal to the practice. Objectivity is a moral concept before it is a methodological concept, and the activities of natural science turn out to be a species of moral activity." (pp. 36–37) For a decisive critique of those who would seek to use Wittgenstein's reference to "language games" or "forms of life" to avoid testing religious language, see Joseph Incandela, "The Appropriation of Wittgenstein's Work by Philosophers of Religion: Towards a Re-Evaluation and An End," *Religious Studies*, 21 (1986), pp. 457–474. For a defense of Lindbeck against the charge of relativism see Michael Root, "Truth, Relativism, and Postliberal Theology," *Dialog*, 25, 3 (1987), pp. 175–180.

12. That does not mean that all discussion is useless. For example, see David Burrell's *Knowing the Unknowable God: Ibn-Sina, Maimonides, Aquinas* (Notre Dame: University of Notre Dame Press, 1986).

One simply cannot deny, however, questions about God transform, or better, challenge our epistemological paradigms. As Nicholas Lash suggests, "We are gravely mistaken if, in our attempts to sustain our awareness of the difference between 'God' and 'the world,' we construe the quest for God or one particular quest upon which we may be sometimes engaged alongside the quest for domestic happiness, unified field theory, social justice, a cure for cancer, or whatever. All attempts to construe the difference between God and the world fall into the trap of supposing 'God' to be one of a number of actual or possible objects of experience, expectation and discourse. But *such* a 'God' would be merely a 'feature' of reality, a part of the world, not the incomprehensible mystery of its origin, significance and destiny. If God were one of a number of actual or possible objects of experience and discourse, then the concept of God would have immeasurably more restricted range than the concept of 'truth.' If however, the God whom we seek, the God whose truth sustains and infinitely transcends all projects and all imaginings is, in fact, the imcomprehensible ground and goal of all reality and all significance, the creator and redeemer of nature and history, then each and every aspect of the human quest—in all of its bewildering, uncontrollable and often conflictual diversity—is an aspect of the quest for God, even when it is not so named or characterized. There is no truth, no reality, 'outside' the truth and reality of God and his grace." *Theology on the Way to Emmaus* (London: S.C.M. Press, 1986), pp. 13–14.

13. Walter Brueggemann, "II Kings 18–19: The Legitimacy of a Sectarian Hermeneutic," *Horizons in Biblical Theology*, 7 (1985), p. 15.

14. Brueggemann, pp. 22–23.

15. Richard Neuhaus, "Democratic Morality—A Possibility," (Unpublished paper delivered at University of Indiana, March, 1986), p. 11.

16. Robert Rodes, "On Law and Virtue," in *Virtue: Public and Private*, edited by Richard Neuhaus (Grand Rapids: Eerdmans, 1986), p. 35. I should say on the same grounds I assume the church necessarily must develop a law internal to herself. See, for example, Rodes' "The Church as a Liberating Judicial Presence," in his *Law and Liberation* (Notre Dame: University of Notre Dame Press, 1986), pp. 16–18.

17. Michael Quirk, "Stanley Hauerwas' *Against the Nations*: Beyond Sectarianism," *Theology Today*, XLIV, 1 (April, 1987), pp. 78–86. See also my response in the same issue, "Will the Real Sectarian Stand Up," pp. 87–94.

18. Quirk, p. 79.

19. Rowan Greer, *Broken Lights and Mended Lives: Theology and Common Life in the Early Church* (University Park, Pennsylvania: Pennsylvania State University Press, 1986), pp. 141–161.

20. I owe this way of putting the matter to John Howard Yoder who has developed it at length in his still unpublished paper, "How Richard Niebuhr Reasons: A Critique of Christ and Culture."

21. Oliver O'Donovan, *Resurrection and Moral Order* (Grand Rapids: Eerdmans, 1986). O'Donovan notes, "The sign that God has stood by his created order implies that this order, with mankind in its proper place within it, is to be totally restored at the last. This invites a comment on a debate which has occupied too much attention, the debate between the so-called 'ethics of the kingdom' and the 'ethics of creation.' This way of posing the alternatives is not acceptable, for the very act of God which ushers in his kingdom is the resurrection of Christ from the dead, the reaffirmation of creation. A kingdom ethics which was set up in opposition to creation could not possibly be interested in the same eschatological kingdom as that which the New Testament proclaims. At its root there would have to be a hidden dualism which interpreted the progress of history to its completion not as a fulfillment, but as a denial of its beginnings. A creation ethics, on the other hand, which was set up in opposition to the kingdom, could not possibly be evangelical ethics, since it would fail to take note of the good news that God had acted to bring all that he had made to fulfillment. In the resurrection of Christ creation is restored and the kingdom of God dawns. Ethics which start from this point may sometimes emphasize the newness, sometimes the primitiveness of the order that is there affirmed. But it will not be tempted to overthrow or deny either in the name of the other." p. 15.

22. I suspect behind Gustafson's use of "tribalism" is the Enlightenment presumption that tribes are regressive since they do not represent "open and tolerant communities"—i.e., they fail to acknowledge universal rights. Of course, it was exactly such an ideology that justified American treatment of the Indians as well as European policies in Africa. Christians do not have a stake in the denial of tribal identity as such, but rather for us "tribalism" is only a problem if it threatens the new unity of creation in Christ Jesus which we believe is most nearly embodied in the church.

I

THE PRACTICE OF THE CHURCH'S STORY

A TALE OF TWO STORIES

On Being a Christian and a Texan

1. On Entertainment and Analysis

Stories, whatever else they may do, should entertain. We rightly love to be entertained; therefore, we all love a good story—indeed, exactly what makes a story good is its capacity to entertain. We want to be drawn out of ourselves and literally rejoice in the lives of others which can be discovered through stories. By calling this essay an "entertainment," I am inviting the reader to judge it by the exacting standard of whether it illumines by being entertaining.

While entertaining is my first interest, I also want to clarify some of the critical issues associated with the recent interest in narrative and its relation to theology. "Story theology" is currently one of the growth industries in theology. This development has every sign of being one of those fads that commands widespread attention and then is quickly forgotten under the onslaught of rigorous criticism and/or replacement by some new titillation. I think, however, that narrative is too important a conceptual tool for this to be allowed to happen. It is particularly important, therefore, for those of us employing the idea of narrative to spell out both its limitations and possibilities for helping us understand better the nature of Christian conviction.

We certainly ought not to salute every flag run up the pole that bears the inscription "story." For example, I have little interest in trying to develop a "theology of story" or "story theology." The former I associate with those attempts to show that story is an unavoidable aspect of our lives—we all need interpretative frameworks—and therefore Christianity has a story for you. In this sense, story simply becomes a new word for myth and trades on the dishonest strategy that tries to compel belief by

25

making all "stories" count equally. Yet my own interest in narrative, as I hope to show in this essay, is how it helps us show how knowledge of God provides critical purchase on the many stories that unwarrantedly seek to claim our lives.

Nor am I trying to do "story theology" if that means theology is thought to consist primarily of telling stories. I do not wish to deny that theology involves the critical telling of a story, but that is not all it is meant to do. This is especially the case if "story telling" is used as a substitute for the development of critical skills and analysis that is a responsibility of the theologian to develop.

In short, my own interest as a theologian is not in trying to provide a general account of the human condition by exploiting the ubiquity of stories in our lives. I have no doubt, as I have tried to argue elsewhere, that narrative is a crucial category for understanding the continuity of the self we associate with character.[1] Yet it has not been my purpose to suggest thereby that theology is primarily reflection about the significance of the narrative quality of human experience. As Ralph Wood has recently suggested, it is simply not licit to try to generate a theology from a genre.[2]

The proper object of theology is not stories but God. Our task is not to try to show how stories save but rather how God saves. To be sure, the latter involves a story, and a story that is meant to form the self, but we cannot forget that the means of God's salvation cannot be separated from the fact that it is God who is doing the saving. Again, as Wood has suggested, "to argue for the Christ story as definitive of other stories does not require any demonstration that gospel as a genre is unique but that He whom it proclaims is utterly singular."[3]

2. On "Choosing" a Story

In this essay I want to try to illustrate these claims, as well as entertain, by juxtaposing two quite disparate stories that are bound together in my own life—namely, the story of being a Christian and the story of being a Texan. However, in doing so I want to issue a warning at the beginning. Though I have written much about autobiography, I have never written autobiographically (at least not directly). In other words, I have used the nature of autobiographical literature to try to enliven the grammar of religious convictions, but I have studiously avoided any suggestion that the strength or weakness of theological argument was in any manner relative to the limits or richness of my or any theologian's biography.

Indeed, I find those theologians who argue about what they are prepared or not prepared to believe in accordance with their peculiar experience, which they often claim represents what it means to be a "modern man," take their own subjectivities far too seriously. The important question is not what I do or do not believe but the convictions I should have if I am to have the skills to deal with this existence in a truthful manner.

Of course, I have chosen to focus on the story of Texas because it is the one I know best, and like most Texans, I assume it is infinitely entertaining. Yet I have also chosen to talk about it for what I hope are more substantive reasons. For Texas, like the South, generally continues to represent a unique cultural experience which places its stamp on you forever. You may come to view its influence negatively or positively, but you know it has forever marked you.

Indeed, some suggest that the storytelling propensities of Southerners, and in particular, Texans, can be attributed to the loss of the experience of being so marked. As Flannery O'Connor observed, "The anguish that most of us have observed for some time now has been caused not by the fact that the South is alienated from the rest of the country, but by the fact that it is not alienated enough, that every day we are getting more and more like the rest of the country, that we are being forced out, not only of our many sins but of our few virtues."[4] We tell our stories, therefore, as the only means we have of remembering a culture and a time that once had the courage or the presumption to mark us. To say that one is "from Texas" is never meant just to indicate where one happened to be born, but represents for many of us a story that has, for good or ill, determined who we are.

Therefore, my use of the story of Texas is meant to be both a challenge and an argument against some of the dominant assumptions associated with our modern and liberal culture. For one of the oddities of the contemporary situation is that what it means to a person, to be free and/or autonomous, is to be capable of creating or "choosing" our "identity." Thus, we do not think of ourselves as inheriting a family tradition or a group identity with which we must learn to live. Rather, our particular story is that we have no history and thus we can pick and choose among the many options offered by our culture. I suspect that this may account for the tremendous pressure many feel today in choosing a vocation— for it is our vocations, or perhaps better our jobs, that provide us with the basic account of who we are—teacher, doctor, lawyer, and so on.[5] And since it seems we "choose" to undertake one of these tasks rather than another we have the presumption that we have created our own

27

story or "self."

But at least part of the burden of this essay is to dispel this assumption. For I will try to suggest that all of us are more fundamentally formed by stories we did not create than those we have chosen. There are many problems with being a Texan, but at least the Texan does not have the illusion he is a person without a history. I did not choose to be a Texan, but simply in the process of coming to myself—that is, in the realization that I am who I am and cannot be other—I discovered I was and am unavoidably Texan. It is not a "role" that I have chosen, any more than I have chosen to talk with the kind of accent I do, but rather it is simply part and parcel of who I am. In this sense the kind of story that "being a Texan" entails is closer to being like the story "male" and "female" than doctor or lawyer—for "Texan," male, and female are more like stories that we are born with, that we must come to terms with in some way, than stories that we have chosen.[6]

There is an obvious objection to this, for it is clear that no one is forced to be a Texan—any more than one is forced to be an Oklahoman, New Yorker, or New Englander. It is perfectly possible to free ourselves of the particularities of our birthplaces and where we were raised. Accents can be changed, as can habits and manners.

Moreover, some may even wish to argue more strongly that one should try to be free of the limits of the accidental and arbitrary nature of our nurturing. Exactly what it means to be free is to throw off the shackles of our history. For we know such histories contain much injustice. We Texans have told a glorious tale of the conquest of the land, often forgetting to include the injustices perpetrated on Indian and Mexican alike, that this land and history be ours. As Reinhold Niebuhr reminds us, "No society ever achieved peace without incorporating injustice into its harmony."[7] To be human today means to accept no such story with its inevitable injustice but to identify with a story or stories that provide a fresh start.

Or perhaps a more existential question for many is how we should accept the physiological designation of male and female with the corrupting social roles associated with each of them. The jarring fact has been made obvious that there is no necessary reason why women should be associated with the mothering role, at least when it comes to caring for the child, and men understood only as breadwinners. Thus, in the name of freedom we are urged to throw off the arbitrariness of the societal expectations and look for new forms of relationships in which no one's self-fulfillment will be delimited or stunted.

It is not my purpose in this essay to defend or criticize the charges made by those working for women's liberation. Generally, I think most of the charges made against male-dominated culture are both fair and just.[8] My interest is not that particular issue but the assumption that lies behind the recommendation that freedom means rejecting the limits of our birth—either culturally or sexually. Put more strongly, I want to argue that there is something very misleading and self-deceiving about the description many have accepted that they are or should try to become free from all stories except those they have "freely" chosen. For I will try to suggest that freedom comes not by choosing our stories, but by being formed by a truthful narrative that helps us appreciate the limits and possibilities of those stories we have not chosen but are part and parcel of who we are. Moreover, we will have some hint as to the truthfulness or falsity of the stories that grasp us just to the extent that they provide us appropriate skills to accomplish that task.[9]

It may be that I take this position because for me it has been impossible to be other than who I am—Texan is written in my voice, in my manners, and even more in my soul—I cannot be other than I am. But as I suggested, I think that each of us, in our own way, is equally bound—not by the same story by which I happen to be bound—but nonetheless storybound. The question is, finally, what we should do about being so bound.

Moreover, I hope to show that juxtaposing the stories of being Texan and Christian in this manner will also enliven aspects of the Christian story that are often overlooked. For example, it is often assumed that the Christian story is primarily one of the overcoming of limits—i.e., being a Texan, male (there is neither Jew nor male), and even the limit of death. Christianity is assumed to be the universal story that supplants all particularistic stories with their specific drawbacks. It thus becomes the super-story that is true because it gives a more complete explanation of every matter that we all confront as human beings.

But I am going to suggest that it is our particular stories that provide us the training to understand how the Christian story may fit over our lives. For the story we find in the Gospels is as particular as that involved in the name "Texan," and it comes into our lives in as particular a fashion. It is not a universal story about all human existence (though it involves aspects of our existence with which we all must deal) but a story of a man who came to a designated people. It does not provide us, therefore, with a philosophy of life but rather with a story that is offered as one to be made our own.

For example, H. R. Niebuhr tells us in the Introduction to *The Responsible Self*:

29

I call myself a Christian though there are those who challenge my right to that name, either because they require a Christian to maintain some one of various sets of beliefs that I do not hold or because they require him to live up to some one of various sets of moral standards, including those of my own conscience, to which I do not conform. I call myself a Christian simply because I also am a follower of Jesus Christ, though I travel at a great distance from him not only in time but in the spirit of my traveling; because I believe that my way of thinking about life, myself, my human companions and our destiny has been so modified by his presence in our history that I cannot get away from his influence; and also because I do not want to get away from it; above all, I call myself a Christian because my relation to God has been, so far as I can see, deeply conditioned by this presence of Jesus Christ in my history and in our history. In one sense I must call myself a Christian in the same way that I call myself a twentieth-century man. *To be a Christian is simply part of my fate*, as it is the fate of another to be a Muslim or a Jew. In this sense, a very large part of mankind is today Christian; it has come under the influence of Jesus Christ so that even its Judaism and Mohammedanism bears witness to the fact that Jesus Christ has been among us. But I call myself a Christian more because I have both accepted this fateful fact and because I identify myself with what I understand to be the cause of Jesus Christ. That cause I designate simply as the reconciliation of man to God . . . Jesus Christ is for me, as for many of my fellow Christians, the one who lived and died and rose again for this cause of bringing God to men and men to God and so also of reconciling men to each other and to their world. The establishment of this friendship is to me the key problem in human existence. Because through Jesus Christ—his fate—as well as by him—that is, his ministry—this has become evident to me; because in him I see the prospect of my own reconciliation; because I have been challenged to make this cause my own—therefore I call myself a Christian.[10]

I have for many years tried to understand this passage, as there seem to be as many things strikingly wrong about it as there are right.[11] It finally occurred to me that perhaps part of the reason I was having difficulty is that Niebuhr calls himself a Christian in the same way he calls himself a twentieth-century man, but I do not think of myself as a twentieth-century man—my "fate" is to be a Texan. Following Niebuhr, therefore, I want at least to investigate the possibility that the relation between these two stories—these two "fated" aspects of my own existence—will at least give me some clues about what it means to claim the story of Jesus Christ as my own and as true.

3. Is "Being a Texan" a Story?

An appropriate question at this point is whether I have not been making an unwarranted assumption that "being a Texan" in fact constitutes a story. Generally we do not think of the designation "Texan" as a story but rather as a description which indicates where a person is from or perhaps even a set of odd behavioral characteristics—"What kind of funny accent is that?" Or sometimes "Texan" is used to call forward the image of bigness or unwarranted pride, but such an image is still too sparse to constitute a genuine story.

But "Texan" cannot be limited to being a description or an image, as it also functions for many as a story. For to claim that I am a Texan is to appeal to a narrative account that helps me bind together a series of contingent events that create an intelligible pattern for my life. "Being a Texan" is a story because it helps me to say who I am. So used, it cannot be just a description or image, for I use it as the means to tie together parts of my life—a use I suspect shared by many others who find themselves to be "Texan."

"Being a Texan," however, is not a story simply because it binds the events of our lives together, but more importantly because it supplies a way to form our future. A narrative must not only provide an intelligible pattern that links the contingent events of our lives; it must also provide us a way to go. A story of who we are must give us the power to make our actions consistent with our identity—it must, so to speak, shape the world. It is just such a power that at once is the significance and danger of stories, for if our stories are false or limited then so will be our world and lives.

3.1 The Story of Texas and Being a Texan

But here we seem to run on an inescapable difficulty, as there is not one, but many, stories of Texas or of what it means to be a Texan. Most Texans know vaguely, of course, our early history, the story of the homesteaders and Austin's courageous efforts to keep the first settlements going. We also know the struggle to win independence from Mexico, which we associate with names such as Houston and with events such as San Jacinto and the Alamo. But we also know, and as the historians take pleasure in reminding us, this way of telling the story of Texas often distorts the complex history of Texas' beginning as well as serving as an ideology for Texas chauvinism.

The issue of telling accurately the history of Texas, however, is not central for the question of what it means to be a Texan. I am not suggesting that it has no importance, but simply that its importance can be easily overestimated. For example, there are at least four different stories that comprise what my "being a Texan" means: (1) the official story of

Texas (whether the story is told by historians or not), (2) the story of my family in Texas, (3) my story of being a Texan, and (4) my story as a Texan who no longer lives in Texas.[12] Moreover, as these stories are related and told they require a narrator with a particular point of view and context.[13]

I am not going to try to provide an analysis of how these various stories interrelate or from what point of view they are being told, for if I did so I would never get around to telling the story. Rather, I am going to try to elicit what it means for me to be a Texan by drawing on William Humphrey's novel, *The Ordways*.[14] This novel traces the history of a family—the Ordways—as they are forced by the wounding of Thomas Ordway at Shiloh to move from Tennessee to Clarksville, a town just over the Red River in upper eastern Texas. They move in the hopes that a better life awaits them on the edge of the prairie. The story is told by Thomas Ordway's great grandson and thus comprises the account of several generations' struggle to survive and flourish in that land.

It may be objected that it seems odd to use a piece of fiction to tell what it means to be a Texan. But remember that my object is not to tell the story of Texas but to tell what it means to be a Texan. And I can find no better means to do that than Humphrey's novel, for what he tells shows clearly that it is not the accuracy of stories of Houston or the Alamo that makes a Texan but how the Texan values those stories as they provide the background necessary for recounting his family's history.[15]

Thus, Humphrey's novel begins, not with stories of the official or unofficial history of the great events of Texas but with graveyard day—the community's yearly cleaning and remounding of the graves of their families. For it was on that day that Texans learned who they were by learning who their ancestors were.

> The great stone faces of my ancestors—how clearly I see them still! Bearded with moss, freckled with fungus, bathed in tears when the rain fell, inclined this way and that as though in whispered conversation with one another. Each had, for me, taken on the aspect of its owner: here a high bald dome, pinched features formed by the cramped and scanty epitaph, here a crack like a scar across a cheek, a pair of small round old-fashioned spectacles formed by a double O in the text: my family album in stone. Barely legible by now, I suppose; even in my childhood some of the older ones could scarcely be made out, effaced by those prairie winds which, laden with grit, are like a sand-blast—yet carved upon the tablets of my memory as with a chisel. My people, my dead, with each of whom, I was taught to believe, and in those days still did, I should one day sit down and converse. To them I owed my features, my voice, the strengths and weaknesses of my mind and body. Their migrations had determined that I was born where I was and not some other place. Before

32

I could become myself, as according to the biological law, ontogeny recapitulates phylogeny, I would first have to live through the lives of those who had produced me. With each was associated some story, which, as his or her mound was raked, the weeds cleared away, the fallen stone set upright, was once again retold. Yearly repetition did not dull these tales; on the contrary, we looked forward to them as, seated in the concert hall with program in hand, one anticipates the opening notes of a favorite piece of music, and we would have been disappointed if, for instance, the tending of Great-uncle Hugh's grave had not elicited from my grandfather the story, known to us all by heart, of Uncle Hugh and the lady's corncobs. Honest, blunt, plainspoken Hugh Ordway, the enemy of all pretense and pose, whose epitaph stated not that he had "passed away" or "fallen asleep" but that he had died on a day in March 1858, had once been among the guests at a supper party, back in Tennessee. The menu included roasting ears, and to the problem of what to do with the unsightly cobs, the hostess had worked out this delicate solution: the white-gloved Negro butler (borrowed for the occasion) would go around the table with a big silver platter (likewise) and collect them from the guests between servings. From right to left he went, and as our Uncle Hugh happened to be seated on his hostess's left, by the time it got to him the platter was piled high. As he had done with the dishes of food all evening, the butler stood with his platter at Uncle Hugh's elbow. Noticing him at last, Uncle Hugh inspected his soggy offering, and in his broadest back-country accent said, "No, thank you just the same, don't believe I'll have any" (pp. 19–21).

Or then there was

Bachelor Great-granduncle Giles was extremely absent-minded. Once he bought himself a horse and buggy, the first he had ever owned, to go on a trip to Knoxville, a three days' ride. His business there concluded, he took the train home. About a week later he remembered his horse and buggy, and went to the depot and bought a round-trip ticket to go and get them. Uncle Giles was never known to refuse a chew, yet he never became a slave to the weed. A heavy chewer once marveled at this. "I like tobacco," Uncle Giles responded. "There's nothing I like better, and I wish I could get the habit. But unless somebody reminds me I just can't seem to remember it." However, it was not really absent-mindedness: Uncle Giles had a lifelong preoccupation. When he was young he had overheard someone assert that the lifetime of man was not long enough for him to count to one million. "What!" he had snorted. "Well, we'll just see about that!" and commenced counting. "Giles, how's it coming? How far along are you now?" people would ask. "Three hundred and eighty-six thousand, four hundred and twelve—make that thirteen," Uncle Giles would reply—until, latterly, he became secretive about his total. Just how far he did get no one ever knew. For though he was vouchsafed twelve years more than his allotted three score and ten, and did hardly anything else towards the

33

last, his dying words were, "Tell them that fellow was right. It can't be done. I only got up to—" And there Uncle Giles stopped counting (p. 21).

It is of course true that we no longer have graveyard days, but we are the people produced by the people who had graveyard day. Thus, rather than telling their stories, some of which we still remember—you remember old nutty Uncle Jack—we tell the story of graveyard day. And in telling it we find ourselves, as Humphrey suggests, at another place:

> The Southerner is like those ancient Hebrews who preserved and recounted and gloried in the stories of double-dealing and in his own rather frequent outbreaks he is emulating the exploits of his family heroes whom he has heard about all his life, who lived in freer and more manly times. When a Southerner sighs and says, "We are not the men our fathers were" (an expression often on his tongue), he means to say we are more civilized; he is lamenting the fact. Undoubtedly the Southerner clings to certain outmoded social attitudes and resists changes, which for his own part he knows he could learn to live with, because they are unacceptable to Great-grandfather, whose voice, should he think one moderate thought, hears accusing him of capitulation, of cowardice, of betrayal, of unworthiness of the name he bears in trust. To appeal to his reason does no good: he admires foolishness above all qualities—in the same sense one intends when saying, a fool never changes his mind, a fool never knows when he's licked. "That's the kind of fool I am! A damn fool!" he will proudly assert. This is why telling him that the old cause, Great-grandfather's old cause is doomed, already lost, is the surest way to harden his resistance: those are precisely the odds which appeal to his imagination, the odds which Great-grandfather fought against, which are calculated to win Great-grandfather's esteem. Tell him he is on the winning side, he loses interest and quits the field. This is not because he does not like to win, but because he does not like to have a side. He sees himself a stubborn lone remnant, conquered but unsubdued, unreconstructed, he and Great-grandpa, ready to grapple with the very winds of change (p. 39).

"Being a Texan" is therefore not necessarily identifying with the official history of those who helped make this geography country and nation but rather it is a designation to remind us that we are inextricably tied to our forebearers. Thus, a Texan is not a man who has the presumption he is without a story; he has a story that he accepts as it locates him on a land and within a people without whom he would not be at all. For example, Humphrey suggests that Southerners are accused of living in the past,

But what can we do? The past lives in us. And not just that single episode

34

which those who accuse us have in mind: the Civil War—but all of the past. If the Civil War is more alive to the Southerner than to the Northerner it is because all the past is, and this is so because the Southerner has a sense of having been present there himself in the person of one or more of his ancestors. The War forms merely a chapter—the most vivid single chapter, it is true, but still just one chapter—in his book of books, the bible of his family—which is not to say the family Bible, but rather that collection transmitted orally from father to son of proverbs and prophecies, legends, laws, traditions of the origins and tales of the wanderings of his own tribe. For it is this, not any fixation on the Civil War, but this feeling of identity with his dead (who are the past) which characterizes and explains the Southerner, which accounts for his inflexible conservatism, his lawlessness and love of violence, his exaggerated respect for old age, his stubborn resistance to change, his hospitality and his xenophobia, his legalism and his anarchy. It is with kin, not causes, that the Southerner is linked. Confederate Great-grandfather lived in stirring and memorable times, but he is not remembered by his descendants for his (probably undistinguished) part in the Battle of Bull Run; rather, the Battle of Bull Run is remembered because Great-grandfather was there (p. 36).

Of course, for many the past no longer lives so vitally in us. As a result, and in our hunger to be like our forebearers, the official stories assume a primacy that they were not meant to have. As a result they too easily become an ideology, no longer qualified by the reality of an actual family, and thus distort as much as display our lives.

3.2 The Vitality and the Limits of the Story of "Being a Texan"

Yet for many of us the story of "Being a Texan" has remained vital. Perhaps more so even for those of us who no longer live in Texas, as by being away we do not see the changes that in fact make the story increasingly irrelevant.[16] It is vital because it continues to give us a place to be—an identification—that prevents us from being lost in a world where the story is that we have no story.

For example, why should I take being a Texan so seriously? I am only a second-generation Texan. My grandfather came to Texas via Alabama from Wisconsin, of all places. My forebearers on my father's side never fought in the Civil War, having come too late from Germany. Of course, the reality of that was forever burned into me through my father's marriage to a woman from the dirt-poor backwoods of Mississippi. But that hardly seems sufficient to create the deep identity I feel with the South and, in particular, Texas.

I think the clue is to be found in the stories that Humphrey tells about the Ordways. For their story reminds me of the stories my grandfather told me of his early struggle to make it in this tough land. Like the Ordways, I have been taught through the stories of and about my family that I am heir of a lively but often cantankerous group of folk. I like the story of how my grandfather left behind his Catholicism to marry my grandmother—a Coffee of Alabama who took such pride in her faded family's doubtful achievements that she made my father bear that name as his given name. I loved to hear my grandfather talk about buying a new pair of patent leather shoes, getting on a riverboat in St. Louis, and wearing them out dancing by the time he reached New Orleans. I take pride in my father's accounts of his cowboy past as he participated in one of the last of the cattle drives. And I identify deeply with the energy and work required for my mother to escape from some of the worst aspects of being raised in a "poor white" family. Yet at the same time I know how to continue to bear the marks of such a background as I try to avoid losing the freedom of spirit that comes only from being "poor."[17] Moreover, that background, as well as watching and participating in my grandfather's and father's hard life as bricklayers, has taught me that the great gift of hard work is independence and pride.

Therefore I identify with, or better put, I am a Texan because it is the context that makes intelligible the stories of my people. I am a Texan, and I even know that the story of the war (and, of course, even to this day that means the "War Between the States") is my story, because its tragic nature also is part of my story. For being part of my people also means the experience of prejudice, fear, and hate that has marked me as deeply as has the good.

Yet still the story of being a Texan provides me, and I expect many others, with the skills to find the boundaries between ourselves and other stories that would claim our lives. For example, even though a Texan may know his state is part of the United States, he is not overly impressed by the fact. For he knows that he has a story that is not replaceable by the larger story of America, for his story may even be in conflict with this larger story. We pay a price for this, of course, as often we feel that because we know we do not belong we must justify our strangeness by emphasizing our differences more than is warranted or by trying to be excessively loyal. But "being a Texan" is for many of us one of our most valuable lessons, as it has taught us how to be different. Indeed, I sometimes think that without this I would have no idea what it might mean to be a Christian, as I would have no idea what it might mean to belong to a separate society.

But at the same time that "being a Texan" has provided me with a place to be, it has also imposed its limits. For the story of Texas is a story of overcoming hardship, but such a story often requires us to forget parts of our past that must become part of us if we are to be whole. We Texans have little ability to know how to admit our failures, and cruelty, and our tragedies. We thus make a virtue out of some of our worst sins—like the sign that hung over the main street of Greenville for years: "Welcome to Greenville: The Blackest Land, the Whitest People."[18] The way we hide our sins is to turn them into a banner. Our inability to know how to integrate into our lives some of our less noble practices means that our souls are not capable of facing the full reality of this existence. Thus, to the extent "being a Texan" functions as our primary story it determines us more than it makes us capable of action, in that it inextricably functions as an ideology that denies that injustice is part and parcel of our history.

Like the reaction of the narrator of *The Ordways* on coming to the realization that the South lost the (Civil) War, we tend not to know how to face our defeats and tragedies. He says,

Lee surrendered to Grant on April 9, 1865. The news was two months reaching Texas. I did not hear about it until 1931. I learned by reading on to the end of my school history book. Before that time I had sensed that we were in for a long struggle, but I had no idea that things were going that bad. We had suffered setbacks—that was war; but we had given as good as we had gotten, and, no one having told me any different, I supposed that the fighting was still going on. Suddenly at the age of ten I not only had snatched away from me any chance ever to avenge my great-grandfather and redeem our losses and cover myself with glory on my country's battlefields, I had to swallow down my pride and learn to live with the chronic dyspepsia of defeat. Nothing had prepared me for this. My knowledge of American history up to that point had conditioned me to the habit of success and leadership. I had theretofore identified myself with my country's eminence and expansion, and as a Southerner I had belonged to the dominant party. The founding fathers, the early generals, the great presidents, were Southerners. In the War, as presented to me, we had fought the better fight. At the point at which the account of it had always previously left off, we were winning. Now all of a sudden it was over, and we had lost. For me, a Texan (which is just another word for "proud"), this was even harder to accept than for most Southerners. I say that, yet is it true? The moment when he discovers that the Civil War is lost comes to every Southern boy, and proud Texan though I was, it was perhaps less shattering for me than for most. I had, right on my doorstep, another myth to turn to. When the last bugle call went echoing off into eternity and the muskets were stacked and the banners lowered and that star-crossed flag hauled down—in short, when Appomattox came to me and I was demobilized and disarmed and returned home, filled with wounded pride and impatient with peacetime life—like many another veteran—I began to face about and look the other way, towards Blossom Prairie, where the range was open and the fancy free to roam. In my fashion I was repeating not only the history of my family, but of the country. For the West provided America with an escape from the memory of the Civil War (pp. 88–89).[19]

But there is no escape, and just this is the lesson that the Texan has such a hard time accepting. Like most, we cannot acknowledge the injustice we have perpetrated or benefited from unless we think we can make it a right. As a result we cannot face the fact that there are some things that cannot be made up for, cannot be made right.[20] The more we try to use the story of Texas to deny or escape the knowledge of this fact the more we become determined by what we fear and captured by our own false accounts of righteousness. By denying the reality of the tragic the Texan, and all of us, lose the skills to free ourselves from the self-deceiving stories we tell to avoid the truth.

It is, of course, true that we do not feel this dilemma because our lives are also bound by so many other stories—husband, teacher, liberal. Yet each of these stories, like that of being a Texan, has the same difficulty—they cannot within their own framework account for their own limits and the tragedies that result from that. This becomes especially troublesome as one of them, as it must, takes the form of a central story that gives our life coherence. For such a story becomes indispensable to us, as without it we have no place to be.

As a result such stories must ultimately rely on violence to secure themselves against other competing stories in the world. For people do not fight for selfish gain so much as they fight to preserve the good bound up in their limited stories. Violence is the natural outcome of making a story such as "being a Texan" central to our lives, because it is necessary to defend it against those other stories that would challenge it. For example, our great problem, I suspect, with the integration of black Americans into the story of America is that they carry a story that cannot easily be accommodated within the story of white Americans. I am not referring to the story of slavery itself, which simply reminds us that we have been less than decent people. Rather, I am referring to the story of pointless suffering that the black man carries which simply is not part of our story as Texans or Americans. The only way finally to deal with such a challenge is violence—namely, to refuse to recognize such people until they become like us.

It is thus my suggestion that one has an indication of one of the ways a story might be false exactly at the point where it must appeal to violence in order to protect itself. I am not referring simply to the glorification of violence that the story may or may not contain, and certainly the story of "being a Texan" contains a great deal of that, but rather the sense that the only way to preserve the story, that is, ourselves, is by force. For it is the characteristic of a true story that it can grasp the tragedy occasioned by its being lived and told without the defensiveness of violence.

4. On "Being a Christian"

I have spent so much space talking about "being a Texan" I have little left to talk about "being a Christian." At least part of the reason for this is that I feel more at ease talking about the former than I do the latter. I think I have every right to claim I am a Texan, but I feel less sure to claim I am a Christian. Indeed, I think this has always been characteristic of my relationship to Christianity. Raised in an evangelical Methodist church where we knew it was not sufficient simply to be a member of the church—you had to be "saved" (preferably at a revival or at least on Sunday night)—I was never saved. Indeed, I think that one of the reasons I dedicated my life to the ministry at the mature age of fifteen, on a Sunday night and at the tenth singing of "I Surrender All," is that it was the only way I could think of to insure I was really among the blessed.

Though my understanding of what it means to be a Christian might come as a considerable surprise to many who witnessed the profession of my "calling," it is nonetheless true I remain a Christian (though unordained). But then one of the things I have learned as a theologian is not to take too seriously "my understanding" of what it means for me to be a Christian. For by claiming to be a Christian, I am declaring my allegiance to those people, past, present, and future, who continue to struggle to live faithful to the God we find revealed in Israel and Jesus Christ. That, however, is also the primary reason I find myself hesitant to declare myself "Christian," for I have increasingly learned how difficult it is to be faithful to such a God.

The story of being a Christian involves claims on our lives which few of us feel able to avow we have fulfilled. Who among us feels free to affirm that we are or have been faithful disciples of the man who died on the cross? Who among us is able to say, much less live, what it means to claim that every moment of our lives should take the form of a thankful attitude to the God we believe is the beginning and end of our existence? Therefore, we are hesitant to claim our being "a Christian," as we know such a claim involves more than simply believing this or that about

God, Jesus, or the world.

Yet that is exactly why it is important that we not lose sight of the fact that "being a Christian" involves, no less than does being a Texan, a story. Moreover, it is a story that is every bit as concrete and particular as the story of Texas. The difference is that it is not just a story of a land or a family, but the story of a man whose deeds and life are claimed to be as crucial to our lives as the story of being a Texan. Unlike the story of Texas, we are told this is a story that we literally cannot do without, for without it we have no means to know wherefore lies our salvation.

That this story involves such a grand claim and theme, however, does not mean that it subsumes or makes unnecessary all other particular stories that form our lives. Indeed, the story of Jesus, which we Christians affirm is nothing less than the story of God's action on our behalf, is not simply a particular instance of a more universal truth that can be known separate from the story. The story of Jesus is as unsubstitutable for Christians as the story of Texas is for Texans.

But we cannot push the similarity too far, as not all are asked to become a Texan, but those who have made the story of Christ their own are told they should be witnesses to the power of this story to all people.[21] Such a universal invitation, however, is not based on an assumption that the story is really but a way of talking about common human characteristics. Rather, such an invitation is offered because Christians believe that the story of Jesus, when told and lived rightly, witnesses to the God who is the creator and redeemer of all people yet who chooses to be known through the calling of the people of Israel and the life and death of Christ.

Therefore, the story of "being a Christian" is no less concrete than the story of being a Texan. However, Christians believe they have a much better account of their official story than Texans do of the story of Texas. This does not mean that we are able to claim greater historical accuracy for our story than the story of Texas—though questions of historical truth are not irrelevant— but rather that we know the stories we find in Scripture are crucial for living our lives truthfully.[22]

But we can no more learn what it means to be a Christian simply by attending to Scripture than we can learn to be Texan by reading about the history of Texas. Rather, we learn that story, like the way we learn the story of Texas, by caring for the tombstones of the saints. It is from them, as we see what the story of Jesus has done to their own stories, that we begin to understand what that story requires and means. For the truth of the story we find in the gospels is finally known only through the kind of lives it produces. If such lives are absent then no amount of hermeneutical theory or manipulation can make those texts meaningful.

Because we attend to the lives of our ancestors in the faith, we know we cannot claim that this is simply one story among others. To make such a claim dishonors their willingness to sacrifice and even die rather than deny the truthfulness of this story. By learning the story from them, however, we also learn that what it means to call this story true should prevent this story from ideological perversion. This story is about a God who is capable of forgiveness—indeed, whose very nature is forgiveness—and thus we have no reason to seek to hide from others and ourselves in the sinfulness of our fathers and our own history. Unlike the story of Texas, therefore, the story of Jesus provides the skills for us to make our lives our own—in short, to be free from our self-imposed fears.

Ironically, however, exactly because the gospel is such a story, we are given the skill to make the story of being a Texan our own. I have tried to suggest how our particular stories, such as being a Texan, provide us with the training to understand how the Christian story is meant to construe and fit over our lives. But the point is also reversible. By teaching us what it means to be forgiven, the Christian story gives us the freedom to understand our particular stories as Texans. As Augustine shows in the *Confessions*, our own particular history seems like a chicken yard full of patternless tracks until, in Jesus' redemption, we come to see that the maze is in fact a story of grace which we can affirm despite its suffering and sin.[23]

We must learn to live in a world where injustices and scandals cannot be made right. Our task is not to downplay or deny the evil that we or our forefathers have done, especially when it has been done in the name of the very God we worship, but rather to acknowledge it by learning to live the life of the forgiven. Nor are we called upon to attribute especially evil intentions to ourselves or others which perpetuated such wrongs, though some may deserve such judgment, but rather we must recognize that some of the worst crimes are committed by people who are very much like us—that is, moderately good. By learning to understand ourselves in this manner we can perhaps begin to understand that the story we learn in the gospels demands more than moderate goodness—it demands faithful holiness.

In this respect, the most decisive difference and challenge the story "being a Christian" entails for "being a Texan" is its prohibition on the use of coercion to sustain its truth.[24] The followers of Jesus can attract others to the way of Jesus only by living faithful lives. Indeed, they must learn to make the story of Jesus their own in a manner that makes clear they would rather lose their lives than sustain that story through violence. Not to live in such a way would deny the very character of that story as the story of a God who we believe is the truth of our existence. If he is such, then violence in the name of truth cannot help but deny that it is the truth we have come to know.

To live in this manner strikes at the heart of our illusions, underwritten by many of the stories that grip our lives (not the least of which is that we have no story) and are thus necessarily sustained by violence made righteous in the name of cause, country, family, or ideal. It is the terrible truth of the story we find in the gospel that there are worse things than dying, and indeed the truth is not present in those who would kill for it. For it requires a powerful story that would train us to live in a world of competing and limited stories, trusting only in God to be our protection and provider.

That we make such a claim for the story we find in Christ is but a reminder what an entertaining story it is. It is the ultimate adventure story, as it invites us to contribute to God's kingdom through our living faithful to it. Only such a story could have the power to break our fatal self-absorption and fascination by directing our attention to how marvelously the Lord of the universe has grasped our attention through the cross and resurrection of Christ.[25]

NOTES

1. For my own work on narrative, see my *Truthfulness and Tragedy: Further Investigations in Christian Ethics* (Notre Dame: University of Notre Dame Press, 1977) and *A Community of Character: Toward a Constructive Christian Social Ethics* (Notre Dame: University of Notre Dame Press, 1981).

2. Ralph Wood, "Narrative Art and Theological Affirmation: Why, for All Their Affinity, the One Cannot Be Reduced to the Other," (unpublished, Wake Forest University), p. 1.

3. Wood, p. 17.

4. Quoted by Lisa Alther in "Will the South Rise Again?," *New York Times Book Review* (December 16, 1979), pp. 7, 34.

5. This, I think, helps account for the tyranny of the professions over lives. For in the absence of any other story that might determine the self we in fact become our profession — we are a doctor, lawyer, etc. Of course, such a tyranny may be voluntary, but that makes it no less tyrannical. We are dominated by our self-imposed necessities.

6. Of course, I do not mean to suggest that male and female are not in many respects culturally determined roles. However, I think it can hardly be doubted that they find expression in more fundamental ways than most "roles" our or any society offers. In that respect, I think it may be misleading to think of male and female as "roles" at all.

7. Reinhold Niebuhr, *Moral Man and Immoral Society* (New York: Charles Scribner's Sons, 1932), p. 129.

8. There is a particular ambiguity, however, in much of the rhetoric surrounding women's liberation that is worth mentioning in this connection. Much of the moral basis for women's liberation derives from the liberal assumption that everyone ought to be treated equally — as persons. Thus the claim is made that there is no fundamental difference between men and women. Yet at the same time women argue that what it means to be a woman is special

and unique and should be appreciated more fully by male-dominated societies. At a philosophical level it may well be possible to show that such claims are not incompatible, but they at least suggest the deep confusion of our culture's moral presumptions.

9. I will not try to spell out the philosophical issues involved in this kind of project, as I have tried to do that more fully in the works noted in note 1. In particular, my object has been to challenge those accounts of morality that try to ground the moral life in "rationality" in a manner that avoids what Julian Hartt has called the "historicality" of our existence. In his *Theological Method and Imagination* (New York: Seabury Press, 1977), Hartt suggests that to have a history "is to participate in lives and events that have chosen 'me'; I have not chosen them," p. 190. Or again, "To be a historical subject, to have a history, means to participate personally in the storied past of one's people. But that is also to live out the destiny pushed ahead by achievements and hopes of that community," p. 195.

10. H. Richard Niebuhr, *The Responsible Self* (New York: Harper & Row, 1969), pp. 43–44.

11. The problem is not just Niebuhr's confessionalism, which seems to make unclear how questions of truth and falsity are raised about religious convictions, but also his understanding of "fate." There are, perhaps, some senses of that notion that are perfectly accessible, but it is not clear in what sense Niebuhr is using the term. Indeed, given some of Niebuhr's views the term could involve a more Stoic sense than I am prepared to accept. However, I think Niebuhr is right to point us to the fact that most of us are simply "fated" to be Christian, or Texan, but as I will try to show, the former, unlike the latter, provides us with skills to turn our fate into destiny. Both stories "fate" us, but the story of God involves, in the way the story of being a Texan does not, a painful training that enables me to make my life my own.

12. I am particularly grateful to Professor Richard Bondi for helping me clarify this.

13. For an analysis of the nature of narrative which I find extremely instructive, see Seymour Chatman, *Story and Discourse: Narrative Structure in Fiction and Film* (Ithaca: Cornell University Press, 1978). Chatman argues that narrative, because of its transposability, is a structure independent of any medium. As such, narrative is constituted both by story and discourse. Story is the content of the narrative expression, while discourse is the form of that expression. Story is the content or chain of events that includes character, actions and happenings; discourse is the means by which that content is communicated, which involves point of view.

14. William Humphrey, *The Ordways* (New York: Alfred Knopf, 1965). Pagination will be in text.

15. Of course, some may object that this is not what it means for them to be a Texan and, therefore, I am distorting the story. (In particular, I suspect the way blacks and Mexicans tell it will be quite different. The "story of Texas" finally requires the telling of each of these stories.) I do not deny that my story of what it means to be a Texan involves normative claims— i.e., the significance of family—but I am not suggesting that my telling of the story is the way anyone must tell it. Rather, it is the way I must tell it. Yet I expect that the way I tell it, or better, the way Humphrey tells it, will ring true to the experience of many that have been born or raised in Texas (and the South, North, or anywhere). Indeed, that is why I have employed Humphrey's account, as like most master storytellers he has told his story in a manner that helps me better tell and understand mine. As Hartt argues, the status of the truth of such stories is more that of verisimilitude, for what good stories do is enable us to identify "real characters interacting with the other real characters in situations recognizably mundane no matter how heavily charged with importance they may be. To identify with such a character in such a situation does not mean that we empathize with him or otherwise put ourselves in that situation; though we may come to do both. What is first of all at stake in identification is recognition of real individuality whether or not it is admirable" (p. 237). Equally important, according to Hartt, is the "shape of the story—that in those devices which draw individualities up out of a dense background and the progression of events in which characters express themselves, whether or not they control those events or are borne away by them. So a story may be truthful, that is authentic, whether

or not it is factually accurate. This does not mean that we ought to be patient with careless transpositions of events or with dogmatic denials of fact. But the story is out to shape and verify our perceptions rather than to prove that the barn we remembered as red was really yellow" (*Theological Method and Imagination*, pp. 238–239). Hartt goes on to suggest, rightly I think, that the New Testament, while certainly involving verisimilitude, is a "reality intending story" that involves claims about God and the world (pp. 241–248).

16. For example, Alther in her article "Will the South Rise Again?" wonders if there will be a new generation of Southern writers that can compare with the Southern Renaissance begun in the 1920s and still present in such voices as O'Connor and Percy. It is her view that one of the reasons for this renaissance was the necessity of the Southern writer, as O'Connor suggests, to have a dual citizenship—in particular, when at least part of that citizenship involved a section of the country that had experienced the humiliation of losing a war. But Alther thinks if that is the case, then we may not expect a new batch of Southern writers. For as she says, "Lots of young Southerners are writing interesting books these days, but they aren't usually thought of as 'Southern' writers however they think of themselves. Often they and their characters don't live in the South or deal with issues of Southern identity. For me the South of the Southern Renaissance writers—the rural and small-town South—represents some kind of vanished Golden Age. My South is one of bustling industrial cities with crammed franchise strips. Southerners used to have to go North to confront the wonders of urban civilization but now we don't have to budge. The values of the Southern Renaissance South seem sadly inapplicable now. But the acquisitive values of this New Improved South seem repulsive. Whether or not books that attempt to resolve this tension will be written, whether or not heirs to the Southern Renaissance will emerge remains to be seen. The tools, the tradition and the turmoil are still there, but are the potential writers? One bunch has decamped for the North, and the others are busy running Burger Kings" (p. 34). Larry MacMurtry's work makes particularly interesting reading from this perspective.

17. One of the great tragedies of being poor and white in the South, beyond the condition itself, is that the poverty is of the sort that people are not produced who are able to say later what it means. The struggle out of that kind of poverty in our society does not produce writers, but entrepreneurs or sometimes preachers. However, for a notable exception see Harry Crews, *A Childhood: The Biography of a Place* (New York: Harper & Row, 1978) and Will Campbell, *Brother to a Dragonfly* (Philadelphia: Seabury Press, 1978). Campbell was raised just a little way from where my mother grew up, only his family was just a mite better off.

18. This was a common phrase in North Texas, as Humphrey uses it as a slogan in a political rally in Paris, Texas, in *The Ordways*, p. 199. I have a postcard from Greenville showing the sign existing at least till 1963. I use the postcard as a bookmark in *Church Dogmatics*, III/4.

19. I suspect this is the major difference between being a Southerner and a Texan. Texans often did not nor do not have the tragic sense of the deep South as the very magnitude and underdeveloped nature of their land offered them new opportunities. The Southerner, unlike the Texan, could only turn inward. This may partly account for why the better novelist still comes from the deep South.

20. This is, of course, the theme that George Eliot explored so profoundly in *Adam Bede* (New York: Signet Classic, 1961). In particular see p. 442.

21. Again as Julian Hartt suggests, "The New Testament faith is not just a story. It is also a strenuous effort to show how the import of the story must be made out; not only understood but, above all, appropriated. That requires theological work. Moreover, both as story and as theology, the Christian faith has now, and has always had, to compete with other stories and other theologies. So I think it a fundamental and far-reaching mistake to suppose that telling the story is the whole thing. What one makes of the world and of one's own existence on the strength of the story: that is the pay-off. That is what real and decisive case-making is" (*Theological Method and Imagination*, p. 254). That is why I have emphasized that "ethics" is not what is done at the end of systematic theology, but at the beginning.

44

Professor Hartt has written an extremely interesting essay raising the metaphysical issues involved in the emphasis on story: "Theological Investments in Story: Some Comments on Recent Developments and Some Proposals", *Journal of American Academy of Religion*, LII, 1 (Spring, 1984), pp. 117-130; also see my reply, "Why the Truth Demands Truthfulness: An Imperious Enjoyment with Hartt" in the same issue, pp. 141-156.

22. For a particularly informative account of what sense it makes, for example, to say the resurrection is historical, see Christopher Morse, *The Logic of Promise in Moltmann's Theology* (Philadelphia: Fortress Press, 1979), pp. 97-108. For example, Morse rightly suggests that the resurrection cannot qualify as historical narrative insofar as it involves an event not totally located in space and time, is not consistent with what we know of other events in our world, and does not stand in necessary relation to evidence since the materials out of which it is formed does not have a requisite "public." But the resurrection does function historically insofar as it makes "events which do conform to the conditions for historicality—the events of the fact and death of Jesus and the beginning and perseverance of the witnessing mission—historically significant in a manner which otherwise would not allow, 'the best narrative that we can get' in the sense of one that is 'consistent, plausible, and in accordance with all the evidence.' (W. B. Gallie) If the point can be granted that not all narratives which properly may be said to provide historical significance contain only historical references, then it is difficult to see how in principle there can be any necessary reason in the logic of narrative for denying that the story generated by the resurrection may properly be said to create history" (p. 105).

23. I am indebted to Ralph Wood not only for helping me see this but for the wording itself.

24. Though I am personally committed to a stance of Christian nonresistance, the point made here does not entail Christian pacifism. All I imply is that it is impermissible to use violence to compel others to believe or to defend the gospel from those who would seek to destroy it through violence. One might hold that and yet think it permissible for Christians to use violence for protection of the nations in which they live, though I think such a position a mistake.

25. I would like to thank Mark Sherwindt and Ralph Wood for their criticism of an earlier draft of this paper. I would also like to thank those at Southwestern University, where I first delivered the paper, and at Hendrix College, for their response and criticism were extremely helpful in revising this paper. The paper was in fact occasioned by my being asked to lecture at Southwestern, which is my alma mater. It was the only way I had to thank the many people there who so decisively shaped my life.

THE CHURCH AS GOD'S NEW LANGUAGE

It is a bit unusual to begin a putatively scholarly essay with a sermon — particularly when one is writing in honor of a theologian as scholarly as Hans Frei. I have, however, begun with a sermon partly because I did not think the world needed from me yet another formal and methodologically oriented essay about the significance of narrative theology for theology and ethics.[1] Too often many of us who have written about narrative end up using that emphasis to talk about how we should do theology if we ever get around to doing any. So I thought I would try to do a little by writing a sermon. Of course, since I was trained at Yale I am too insecure to let the sermon stand on its own, so it is followed by methodological commentary. Yet I believe if I have anything of value to say on these matters it is said in the sermon. In particular, I hope the sermon suggests why questions of the veridical character of Christian convictions cannot be abstracted from their ecclesial and moral context.

1. A Pentecost Sermon

Genesis 11:1–9
Acts 2:1–21
John 15:26–16:11

At Pentecost we celebrate the birth of the church by the Holy Spirit. Pentecost is the climax of the Christian year as only now are we able liturgically to tell the whole story of God's redemption of his creation. All is finally summed up through God's new creation of the church. By creating this timeful people God has storied the world, as now we have everything necessary to know the time in which we live. For God saves by making possible the existence of a people who are formed by God's time

47

so that the world can know that we are creatures of a good creator, formed by God's time.

The grand sweep of the texts for today reminds us that the salvation wrought by God in the death and resurrection of Jesus of Nazareth is cosmic in scope. All nature has now been renewed—returned to its ordered relation to God. The mighty wind that gave birth to the church involves the affairs of nations and empires. That wind created a new nation that was no longer subject to the constraints of the past. Salvation cannot be limited to changed self-understanding or to insuring meaningful existence for the individual. Salvation is God's creation of a new society which invites each person to become part of a time that the nations cannot provide.

For we believe that at Pentecost God has undone what was done at Babel. In Genesis we are told that originally the whole earth had one language, though few words. That such was the case allowed for unusual cooperativeness as people migrated together seeking a good place to live. Finding the land of Shinar they discovered how to make bricks and became builders. As the son of a bricklayer I think I have a deep appreciation for that achievement. Making bricks, while simple enough, makes possible shelter, the home, and that wonderful, complex phenomenon we call the city. Please note that God does not object to people using their creative energies to embellish creation—he wants us to make bricks. We are invited to plant vineyards and cultivate the soil that our lives might be less subject to chance. Equally important is our capacity for concerted effort through which community is formed in the effort to discover the goods we share in common.

The problem at Babel is not human inventiveness; it is when our forebearers used their creative gifts to live as if they need not acknowledge that their existence depends on gifts. Thus the people said, "Come, let us build ourselves a city, and a tower with its top in the heavens, and let us make a name for ourselves, lest we be scattered abroad on the face of the earth." It is not technology that is the problem but the assumption that God's creatures can name themselves—insuring that all who come after will have to acknowledge their existence. They thus erect a tower, an unmistakable edifice, so they will never have to fear being lost in this vast world. God acknowledges our extraordinary power, as seeing the accomplishments of this united people he feared they would think that now nothing they proposed would be impossible. Such is the power of human cooperativeness.

So, God confused their language such that people could no longer understand one another. So confused they were scattered across the earth, abandoning all attempts to build the one city of humanity. Condemned to live as separate peoples isolated into homes, lands, and histories and no longer able to cooperate, people lost their ability for the concerted action so necessary for the grand project of "making a name for themselves."

God's confusing the people's language as well as his scattering of them was meant as a gift. For by being so divided, by having to face the otherness created by separateness of language and place, people were given the resources necessary to recognize their status as creatures. God's punishment was the grace necessary to relearn the humility that ennobles.

But our parents refused to accept this gift as gift and instead used their separateness as a club, hoping to force all peoples to speak their tribe's language. Thus, at Babel war was born, as the fear of the other became the overriding passion which motivated each group to force others into their story or to face annihilation. The killing begun in Cain was now magnified as humankind's cooperative ability unleashed a destructiveness that is as terrible as it is irrational. Humans became committed to a strategy of destroying the other even if it meant their own death. Better to die than to let the other exist. To this day we thus find ourselves condemned to live in tribes, each bent on the destruction of the other tribes so that we might deny our tribal limits. Our histories become the history of war as we count our days by the battles of the past.

Babel is the climax of the primeval history, as after scattering humankind over the face of the earth God no longer acts toward humankind as a unity. Rather, he calls Abraham out of his tribe and makes covenant with him to be a great people. In calling Abraham, God creates a rainbow people so that the world might know that in spite of our sinfulness God has not abandoned us. The history of Abraham's people is, of course, one of unfaithfulness as well as faithfulness, yet they remained faithful enough so that they might be truthful about their unfaithfulness.

The faithfulness of Israel is manifest in her unwavering conviction that the main character of the story they tell of the world is not Israel herself but God. As Robert Alter has reminded us, the very narrative art of Israel involves the ability to destabilize any monolithic system of causation in favor of a narrative account of the world. Such an art reflects the profound belief that God, not humanity, is the ultimate determiner of human history. Israel develops the means to be a faithful storyteller just to the extent she resists the temptation to resolve the tension between the divine promise and its failure to be fulfilled and/or the tension between

God's will and human freedom.

Thus the call of Abraham foreshadows God's care for all creation through the existence of a people who can stand as a light to the nations. For again we are reminded that God's salvation is not simply knowledge, even the knowledge captured by a story, but rather salvation is the creation of a people who have the capacity to be timeful. To be timeful means to be capable of rest, of worship, in a world bent on its own destruction.

It is only against the background of Babel, therefore, that we can understand the extraordinary event of Pentecost. The sound that was like the rush of a mighty wind signaled a new creation. The fire of the Holy Spirit burned clean, making possible a new understanding. The Jews of diaspora heard these Galilean followers of Jesus telling of the mighty works of God in their own language. The promised people themselves — who had been scattered among the tribes, learning their languages, were now reunited in common understanding. The wound of Babel began to be healed first among the very people God had called into the world as a pledge of God's presence.

The joy of that healing surely must have made them ecstatic. It is literally a joy not possible except by God's creation. It is a joy that comes from recognizing we have been freed from our endless cycle of injury and revenge. It is the joy of unity that we experience all too briefly in moments of self-forgetfulness. It is no wonder, therefore, that some onlookers simply attributed this strange behavior to the consumption of potent wine.

Peter denies such is the case by pointing out that they can hardly be drunk, since this is only the third hour of the day. Yet what has happened is a matter of time, as this reconstitution of our unity portends the last times. Thus, Peter reminds his hearers that this extraordinary creation is what is to be expected at the end time:

> And in the last days it shall be,
>   God declares,
> that I will pour out my Spirit upon
>   all flesh,
> and your sons and your daughters
>   shall prophesy,
> and your young men shall see
>   visions,
> and your old men shall dream
>   dreams,
> yea, and on my menservants and

my maidservants in those days
I will pour out my Spirit; and they
    shall prophesy.
And I will show wonders in the
    heaven above
and signs on the earth beneath,
blood, and fire, and vapor of
    smoke;
and the sun shall be turned into darkness
and the moon into blood,
before the day of the Lord comes,
the great and manifest day.
And it shall be that whoever calls
    on the name of the Lord shall be saved.

This is strong apocalyptic language, but it is necessary if we are to appreciate the significance of this new creation at Pentecost. Creations are, after all, not everyday affairs. They are dramatic in their power to make and consume time. For this new creation aborning through the power of the Spirit does not make irrelevant all that has gone before nor make indifferent all that comes after. Rather, this apocalyptic time places all history in a new time—the time made possible by the life, death, and resurrection of Jesus of Nazareth.

Some have suggested that the so-called delay of the parousia, that is, the sheer continuation of history after Pentecost, creates an impossible problem for Christians, for it seems that the end did not come. Such a reading, however, fails to remember that the apocalyptic expectations created in the early Christian community draw on the conviction that in Jesus of Nazareth Israel's cosmic desires were being fulfilled. Apocalyptic does not deny the continuation of the history of creation but rather reminds us it is historical exactly because it has an end. That end Peter proclaimed is now present at Pentecost.

That Peter proclaimed the presence of the end time to better his ability to recognize that the fiery Spirit was so timeful was because he knew it as the same Spirit that rested on Jesus of Nazareth. Thus, following Peter's appeal to Joel's prophecy of the last days he said, "Men of Israel, hear these words: Jesus of Nazareth, a man attested to you by God with mighty works and wonders and signs which God did through him in your midst, as you yourselves know—this Jesus, delivered up according to the definite plan and foreknowledge of God, you crucified and killed by the hands of lawless men. But God raised him up, having loosed the pangs of death, because it was not possible for him to be held by it."

The Spirit, to be sure, is a wild and powerful presence creating a new

51

people where there was no people, but it is a spirit that they and we know. For the work it is doing is not different from the work that was done in Jesus of Nazareth. Therefore, in John Jesus tells his disciples that he must go so that the Counselor, the Spirit of truth, might be present to bear witness to him. Moreover, that same witness that the Spirit makes to Jesus transforms the witness of the disciples, as they are now able to see what they have seen from the beginning but not seen at all.

In this transformation of the disciples we see the central theme of the Gospel. To be a disciple of Jesus it is not enough to know the basic "facts" of his life. It is not enough to know his story. Rather, to be a disciple of Jesus means that our lives must literally be taken up into the drama of God's redemption of his creation. That is the work of the Spirit as we are made part of God's new time through the life and work of this man, Jesus of Nazareth.

That is why the Trinity is such a central affirmation to sustain the Christian life. The Trinity is not metaphysical speculation about God's nature in and of itself but rather is our affirmation that God has chosen to include us in his salvific work. Thus, the Spirit proceeds from the Father so that Jesus might continue to be present with us. It is this Spirit that was received at Pentecost that made possible the affirmation that in Jesus of Nazareth we have seen time renewed by the end time having come.

After Pentecost we can better understand how Jesus' life was from the beginning integral to God's life. For creation itself heralds the presence of this Jesus. From the beginning God's being as Trinity, rather than being a denial of time, is an affirmation of God's timefulness. Thus, even at Babel God says "let us go down," prefiguring even then the necessary sacrifice of his Son so that the world might be judged, and if judged, redeemed. For in that sacrifice we are given the grace to know our sin, and judgment is made on the rulers of this world who rule by fraud and fear.

It is no wonder, therefore, that being made part of that judgment by the Spirit at Pentecost we may well be thrown out of synagogues and even killed. Moreover, those who do the killing will think they are serving God, not knowing or acknowledging that we now know that God is the Father because we have beheld his Son. Jesus tells us such hard truths even before we have experienced them because we can only learn such truths well by remembering them in the light of our living faithful to the Spirit's call. Such a faithfulness no doubt will challenge the powers of this world who continue to believe that we lack an alternative to war and violence.   The unity of humankind prefigured at Pentecost is not just any unity but that made possible by the apocalyptic work of Jesus of Nazareth. It is a unity of renewed understanding, but the kind of understanding is not that created by some artificial Esperanto that denies the reality of other languages. Attempts to secure unity through the creation of a single language are attempts to make us forget our histories and differences rather than find the unity made possible by the Spirit through which we understand the other as other. At Pentecost God created a new language, but it was a language that is more than words. It is instead a community whose memory of its Savior creates the miracle of being a people whose very differences contribute to their unity.

We call this new creation, church. It is constituted by word and sacrament as the story we tell, the story we embody, must not only be told but enacted. In the telling we are challenged to be a people capable of hearing God's good news such that we can be a witness to others. In the enactment, in Baptism and Eucharist, we are made part of a common history which requires continuous celebration to be rightly remembered. It is through Baptism and Eucharist that our lives are engrafted onto the life of the one that makes our unity possible. Through this telling and enactment we, like Israel, become peculiarly a people who live by our remembering the history of God's redemption of the world.

The creation of such a people is indeed dangerous, as we know from Babel. For the very strength that comes from our unity has too often led the church to believe that it can build the tower of unity through our own efforts. Not content to wait, in time we try to make God's unity a reality for all people through coercion rather than witness. The church's relation to the Jews is particularly painful to remember in this respect. Such a history of unfaithfulness has led many to downplay the peculiar mission of the church to witness to the world the reconstitution of humankind through the life, death, and resurrection of Jesus of Nazareth.

Pretension and presumptuousness, however, cannot be defeated by false humility. Rather, our task is to be what we were made to be at Pentecost — a people so formed by the Spirit that our humility is but a reflection of our confidence in God's sure work. Without such confidence no doubt the church is constantly tempted to self-righteousness and self-aggrandizement. But we have a sure check against such temptations by the very Savior who has made us what we are. For how can we be prideful when the very God we worship is most fully manifest on a cross?

There is no way, if we are to be faithful to God's gift at Pentecost, that the church can avoid calling attention to itself. To be sure, like Israel, the church has a story to tell in which God is the main character. But the church cannot tell that story without becoming part of the tale. The church as witness to God's work for us in Israel and Jesus of Nazareth means that here the teller and the tale are one. For this is not just another possible story about the way the world is, it is the story of the world as created and redeemed by God. That story, the story of the world, cannot be told rightly unless it includes the story of the church as God's creation to heal our separateness.

After all, as Christians we confess, "We believe in one holy catholic and apostolic Church." That surely seems an odd thing to do, even given the eschatological nature of such a claim, since why do we need to confess belief in something we can to some extent see and experience? That we do so is a recognition that the church, catholic and apostolic, is not our but God's creation. Moreover, it is not a creation that God did at one point in time and does not need to do again. Rather, it is our belief that what God did at Pentecost he continues to do to renew and to sustain the presence of the church so that the world might know there is an alternative to Babel.

So as we celebrate Pentecost, may our joy be so manifest some may even mistake our behavior as that produced by "new wine." For we are a people of God's time, and we rejoice in the knowledge that we are not condemned to repeat the past. That means that we really do have an alternative to Babel, to fear of one another, and finally then to war. Even more happily it means that insofar as we are the church, we do not just have an alternative, we are the alternative. We do not have a story to tell but in the telling we *are* the story being told. So, as we move once again to the feast of the new age, let us praise God for the creation of his church.

2. The "End" of "Narrative Theology"

I would not want questions about the possibilities and limits of narrative for theological reflection to be determined or judged by whether it translates into good sermon practice and even less in terms of my sermon in particular. I am not even sure how good or bad a sermon it may be—it is certainly short on contemporary examples. However, I did try to write the sermon drawing on what I have learned about the narrative character of theological convictions from Professor Frei, as well as others such as David Kelsey, George Lindbeck, Ron Thiemann, James McClendon, and many others.[2] Though the sermon itself does not tell a story, in it I

54

boldly interrelate the birth of the church, the primeval history in Genesis, and the life, death, and resurrection of Jesus in a way that presumes they are narratively interrelated.

Yet why should I have chosen those particular texts? The answer is quite simple—I did not choose them. They were the lectionary texts given me by my church for Pentecost. I was therefore authorized by the church to hold them up authoritatively for the whole church. But why choose the form of a sermon in the first place?[3] Could you not as easily make a case in a Barth-like fashion by doing systematic reflection on scriptural texts? Of course the answer is "yes," except I lack Barth's knowledge of Scripture as well as his genius.[4]

But there is still a more significant reason I have used a sermon, which the sermon itself, I hope, exhibits. Part of the difficulty with the redis-covery of the significance of narrative for theological reflection has been too concentrated attention on texts qua texts. It is no doubt significant to rediscover the literary and narrative character of the texts of the Bible. That is particularly the case if one is interested in redirecting the atten-tion and method of those engaged in the scholarly study of the Bible.[5] But the emphasis on narrative can only result in scholarly narcissism if narrative texts are abstracted from the concrete people who acknowledge the authority of the Bible. Thus, I wrote a sermon in the hopes of reminding us that the emphasis on narrative is unintelligible abstracted from an ecclesial context. Indeed, I suspect the project to develop general hermeneutical theories by some theologians is an attempt to substitute a theory of interpretion for the church.

I do not mean, thereby, to imply that Professor Frei or others who have reminded us of the significance of narrative would approve of this sermon in whole or in any of its parts. Yet I have written a sermon to try to illumine some of the unease Professor Frei has begun to express about the great upsurge of interest in narrative in theology. Having been one of the prime movers behind that development, Professor Frei seems to be ready to declare an end to the story of "narrative theology." Moreover, given the extraordinarily diverse claims made on behalf of the impor-tance of story, one cannot help but be sympathetic with Frei's attempt to distance himself from the groundswell for narrative.

Elie Wiesel's story of the great Israel Baal Shem Tov and his subsequent followers is certainly a good story, but one can be told one too many times that "God made man because he loves stories."[6] After the initial enthusiasm for the rediscovery of the significance of stories, one begins to feel the need for some good, old-fashioned arguments that are scholastic-like in form. Those satisfied with Wiesel's claim would do well to read his later book, *Souls on Fire*, where he tells the same story of how it fell to Israel of Rizhim to avert disaster when all he could do was tell the story of what the Baal Shem had done. Following the story, with its optimistic claim of the sufficiency of stories, Wiesel notes that such stories are no longer sufficient because "the threat has not been averted. Perhaps we are no longer able to tell the story. Could all of us be guilty? Even the survivors? Especially the survivors?"[7] Of course, Wiesel is not thereby retreating from his earlier claim of the significance of stories, but his later gloss is a sobering reminder that when we have said "story" we have just begun, not ended, the project.

Frei has a deeper concern with the enthusiasm for narrative as the key to all theological work than the confusing and contradictory claims made in the name of narrative. Frei rightly fears that the theological construal of Scripture as a narrative of God's work on behalf of his creation might be qualified by claims of the narrative quality of existence and/or the self. When narrative becomes a general category prior to the theological claim, Frei suspects that such a position threatens to become but a masked form of another kind of foundationalism and/or is susceptible to the deconstructionist critique. He makes this point well by observing that the "irony of New Criticism (and it is not the first instance of this kind) is to have taken this specific case and rule and to have turned them instead into a general theory of meaning, literature, and even culture, in their own right. Detached from the original that is the actual, indispensable ground and subject matter of its meaning, the specific rule is turned about instead into its very opposite, a scheme embracing a whole class of general meaning constructs, from a Christian culture (in the religiously imperialistic and more than mildly fantasizing visions of T. S. Eliot's cultural-theological writings) to genres of literature. They are all understood 'incarnationally' or 'sacramentally.' As a result, the original of this process of derivation, the doctrine of the Word of God in the person and destiny of Jesus of Nazareth, has now become an optional member within the general class, in which those who subscribe to the class may or may not wish to believe."[8]

The point Frei is making is very similar to his earlier argument that because a Christ figure must be constituted by universal redemptive scope, an unsubstitutable personal identity in which the scope is enacted, and a pattern enacted by that person's history, any Christ figure's identity is already preempted by the one who is the Christ of Scripture. "In short, there can be no Christ figure because Jesus is the Christ, unless an author depicts the figure in terms of a particular identity and pattern wholly different from that of Jesus' story. But in that case it would not make any sense to talk of a Christ figure at all. To speak of Christ involves an enormous claim—a claim so large that it is made exclusively of whomever it is made. The claim is that in *one unique case* identity and presence are so completely one that to know who he is is to confront his presence. In him and in him alone, so the claim goes on, are also to be found these three elements by which the 'Christ figure' is identified."[9]

This stress on the irreducibility or, if you prefer, unsubstitutability of Jesus is similar to the reason Frei qualifies some of the claims for "realistic narrative" made in the *Eclipse of Biblical Narrative*. Even though his primary thesis concerning the narrative character of the Scripture has been fruitful for recent biblical scholarship,[10] Frei argues that "theories of realistic narrative are not likely to be highly plausible except in tandem with an informal cultural consensus that certain texts have the quasi-sacred and objective literary status of 'classics,' which form the core of a broader 'canon.' The plausibility structure in this case is a literary imitation of a religious community's authority structure; it rests on a tradition, reinforced by communal, usually professional, agencies authorized to articulate the consensus about what is to be included with the canon and what is to be especially exalted within the privileged group as 'classic.'"[11]

Thus, narrative as a category does not precede the content of the Christian witness. Jesus is prior to story, though Jesus' life and resurrection can only be displayed narratively. Yet the "reason why the intratextual universe of this Christian symbol system is a narrative one is that a specific set of texts, which happen to be narrative, has become primary, even within Scripture, and has been assigned a literal reading as their primary or 'plain' sense. They have become the paradigm for the construal not only of what is inside that system but for all that is outside. They provide the interpretive pattern in terms of which all of reality is experienced and read in the religion. Only in a secondary or derivative sense have they become ingredient in a general and literary narrative tradition."[12]

Frei's position in this respect seems quite similar to his interpretation of Barth's theological project as one of conceptual description. He notes that Barth took the classical themes of "communal Christian language molded by the Bible, tradition and constant usage in worship, practice, instruction and controversy, and he restated or redescribed them, rather than involving arguments on their behalf."[13] Therefore, the style of Barth's *Dogmatics* is integral to Barth's theological position. For by his lengthy and leisurely unfolding of Christian language Barth was attempting to "recreate a universe of discourse, and he had to put the reader in the middle of that world, instructing him in the use of that language by showing him how—extensively, and not only by stating the rules or principles of the discourse."[14]

Of course, by associating Frei's basic intent with that of Barth I may only be confirming some of Frei's critics' deepest suspicions. For it would then appear that all the talk about the importance of narrative, particularly in the form of a denial of any foundational starting point, is in fact a cover for a confessional starting point that results in a fideistic theology. Narrative, therefore, becomes but a way for Barthians reinforced by Wittgensteinian "language-game" analysis to avoid dealing with the veridical status of theological claims.

It is not my place to defend Frei (or Barth) from this charge, as he is more than capable of defending himself. But I believe the sermon with which I began, both in its form and content, at least helps throw a different light on Frei's position. By reminding us that narrative works within a timeful community, the alternative that Thiemann notes between narrative as a transcendental quality of experience, on the one hand, or a literary form which demands appropriate interpretative approaches for proper reading, on the other, turns out to be a false choice. According to Thiemann, when the former predominates, narrative is seen as useful for theology primarily by "providing a deep structure which captures the essential temporality of human being and understanding. Narrative provides the key for a revised philosophical understanding of human selfhood which is applicable to specifically Christian tasks. Narrative as a literary category becomes important for theology because 'stories' are the most appropriate form of expression for an essentially temporal self. When the latter conception of narrative predominates, the category is most useful as a tool for the interpretation of *biblical* narrative. While speculation about the transcendental temporality of the self may be interesting and occasionally even helpful, they are not directly or primarily relevant for the task of theology. Theology on this view is the description or redescription of biblical narrative into a coherent language which displays the logic of Christian belief. Narrative highlights both a predominant literary category for interpreting the canon within the Bible and an appropriate theological category for interpreting the canon as a whole. Theology is primarily concerned with the interpretation of text and tradition and only secondarily, if at all, with speculations about the true nature of the self and the deep structures of human understanding."[15] Thiemann rightly thinks Frei's project is the latter alternative, but if I am right about the significance of the sermon, then I think such an interpretation of Frei (an interpretation Frei may himself share) limits the significance of Frei's achievement. Why that is the case I must try to explain.

3. The Significance of Where, How, and Who Tells the Story

As I indicated above, the difficulty with the suggestion that narrative is primarily a proposal about theology's task being largely one of conceptual redescription is that one is unsure how questions of truth can ever be asked. As long as one remains in the "language-game" it may seem intelligible and even significant,[16] but it seems that by the very nature of the "game" one is not permitted to ask questions external to the narrative. So the narrative, particularly the biblical narrative, threatens to create a world that "overcomes our reality."[17] But the very power of the narrative to engulf us makes us doubt its veracity, since we have no means to check its truthfulness. It may be true that the biblical accounts are only "historylike," but does not that history finally have to refer to in a way that makes it liable to standard forms of reference?

Frei's position might be liable to such a critique if he assumed that narrative, and in particular the biblical narrative(s), in and of itself was intelligible. But in fact he has never done that, reminding us that "when Christians speak of the Spirit as the indirect presence now of Jesus Christ and of the God who is one with him, they refer to the church. The church is both the witness to that presence and the public and communal form the indirect presence of Christ now takes, in contrast to his direct presence in his earthly days. In the instance of the church, reference to the Spirit means affirmation of the spatial, temporal basis of Christ's indirect presence in unity with his presence in and to the shape of public events of the world and of human history."[18]

In philosophical terms Frei's appeal to the church as the subject of the narrative as well as the agent of the narrative is a reminder that the narrative does not refer but rather people do. To isolate the biblical narratives in and of themselves would be equivalent to considering the truth and falsity of sentences separate from their context of utterance.[19] Once this is understood, Frei's proposal cannot be seen as an attempt to avoid realist claims but rather as an attempt to situate the context of those claims. It is to remind us, as Janet Soskice has argued, that "the notion of reference is not a useful notion in a theory of meaning, if we mean by reference some freestanding relation supposed to obtain between individual proper names and what they name, complex singular terms and what they denote, and predicates and that of which they are true. When dealing with meaning, we must see that 'Words have no function save as they play a role in sentences . . . '; and so, too, words make no reference beyond that which speakers employ them to make in sentences. It is the fact that it is not strictly words which refer but speakers using words, which makes metaphor possible, and enables us to speak about one thing in terms which are seen as suggestive of another."[20]

As Soskice notes, one of the attractive features of such an account of reference is that it has a significant social aspect, since the notion of membership in a linguistic community is a crucial feature of such a theory of reference—whether that community be one of science or the church. It is not words or narratives which refer, but "speakers using words who refer. So Putnam says, 'The realist explanation, in a nutshell, is not that language mirrors the world but that *speakers* mirror the world; i.e., their environment—in the sense of constructing a symbolic representation of that environment.'"[21]

There is no way such a theory can avoid the importance of experience on which reference is grounded, but each speaker in that community need not have had the particular experience necessarily embodied by different aspects of the language. For good communities depend on "what Putnam has called a 'division of linguistic labour', that is, we rely on authoritative members of our community to ground referring expression. We refer to Columbus when we mention his name, because we have heard the name from others, who heard it from others, etc., going back to Columbus himself."[22] Thus, each speaker of a particular linguistic community is connected through the members of that community, living and dead, to a range of experience exceeding his own.

And so the necessity of the sermon as the communal action whereby Christians are formed to use their language rightly. For it must be remembered that it is not the preacher who makes the sermon efficacious. To think that would be but the form of *ex operator operans* applied to the preached word. Rather, for the preached word to be God's word the Holy Spirit must make us a body of people capable of hearing that word rightly. Put differently, the preached word's power is its capacity to create a people receptive to being formed by that word.

The sermon is a churchly event, even when it is used to witness to those not Christian, as it proclaims the power of God to create a new people by being made part of God's continuing story. Yet Christians confess that any continuation of that story that is valid must take its form from the story of Jesus Christ. As Frei observes, in this respect the "relation between the church and Jesus Christ is somewhat like that between Israel and Jesus. To describe the people of Israel is to narrate its history. And to identify that people with the identity of Jesus Christ is to narrate

60

the history of Jesus in such a way that it is seen as the individual and climactic summing up, incorporation, and identification of the whole people, by which the people receive their identification. The church likewise moves toward an as yet undisclosed historical summing up that must be narrated, though it cannot yet be because the story is unfinished and the new Israel's Kingdom of God not yet climaxed or visible in our midst."[23]

The emphasis on narrative, therefore, is not first a claim about the narrative quality of experience from some unspecified standpoint, but rather is an attempt to draw our attention to where the story is told, namely, in the church; how the story is told, namely, in faithfulness to Scripture; and who tells the story, namely, the whole church through the office of the preacher. For as we see from the sermon above, the story is not self-referential but rather creates a people capable of being the continuation of the narrative by witnessing to the world that all creation is ordered to God's good end. The church is the necessary context of enquiry for the testing of that narrative, as it must always remain open to revision since the subject of its narrative is easily domesticated.

Thus, we do not have to choose between narrative as a transcendental category of experience or a literary form illuminative of Scripture, once we recognize that the church is crucial for the intelligibility of the story that Christians have to tell.[24] For example, it is obviously true that not all of Scripture is narrative in form, but the issue is not which "form" is predominant but how the content of the Scripture is properly displayed. I have suggested that the church is the community that is at once the storyteller as well as a character in the story that is required by Christian affirmation of God's redemption of the world through the people of Israel and the cross and resurrection of Jesus of Nazareth.

Moreover, the church is crucial for sustaining claims of the narratability of the world. Our experience, of the world as well as of ourselves, is open to narrative construal, but experience in and of itself does not entail the form of narrative and/or the kind of story Christians learn to tell about the world and our place in it. The church is, therefore, an ontological necessity if we are to know rightly that our world is capable of narrative construal. Without the church the world would have no history. Such a claim is not just a "confessional" stance but the most determinative realist claim Christians can possibly make.

Which brings us back to Babel. If I have been right, we are in a position to appreciate why the faithfulness of the church is crucial for the destiny of the world. To be sure, God's kingdom is more determinative than the church, yet at Pentecost God storied a people with gifts so that they might be capable of witnessing to the world the renewal of our unity made possible in Jesus of Nazareth. The church's theological witness cannot help, therefore, be anything less than a challenge to the conventional wisdom of the world. For the church is involved in nothing less than offering an alternative to war by providing the world with a history by our willingness as Christians to go making "disciples of all nations, baptizing them in the name of the Father, and of the Son, and of the Holy Spirit, teaching them to observe all that I have commanded you; and lo, I am with you always to the close of the ages" (Matthew 28:19–20).[25]

NOTES

1. Even a book as rich as Robert Alter's *The Art of Biblical Narrative* (New York: Basic Books, 1981) remains formal insofar as he seems to assume that the examination of the form (or art) of narrative will reveal the meaning of the text. It is unfair, however, to accuse Alter of formalism without attending to his claim that the narrative art of the Bible is tied to the monotheistic convictions and the correlative understanding of human nature. See, for example, pages 25, 91, 115, and 126 of *The Art of Biblical Narrative*. That said, it is still the case that Alter owes us a more thorough account of the relation between form and content than he provides in his book. I am grateful to Mr. Michael Cartwright for pointing out the formal nature of Alter's analysis.

In his *Sinai and Zion* (Minneapolis: Winston-Seabury, 1985), Jon Levison provides an extremely interesting discussion of Israel's "monotheism" (pp. 56–70). Levison's analysis provides nuances to Alter's account by noting that it was not "monotheism" in and of itself that provided Israel's historical consciousness but the actual confrontation of Israel with YHWH. As he says, "Israel began to infer and to affirm her identity by telling a story. To be sure, the story has implications that can be stated as propositions. . . But Israel does not begin with the statement that YHWH is faithful; she infers it from a *story*. And unlike the statement, the story is not universal. It is Israel's story, with all the particularities of time, place, and *dramatic personae* one associates with a story and avoids in a statement that aims at universal applicability. In other words, if there is a universal truth of the sort philosophers and even some religions aim to state, Israel seems to have thought such truth will come *through* the medium of history, through the structures of public knowledge, through time, and not in spite of these" (pp. 39–40).

2. For Frei's work see his *The Identity of Jesus Christ* (Philadelphia: Fortress Press, 1975); *The Eclipse of Biblical Narrative* (New Haven: Yale University Press, 1974); and "The 'Literal Reading' of Biblical Narrative in the Christian Tradition: Does It Stretch or Will It Break?" in *The Bible and the Narrative Tradition*, edited by Frank McConnell (New York: Oxford University Press, 1986), pp. 36–77. See also David Kelsey, *The Uses of Scripture in Recent Theology* (Philadelphia: Fortress Press, 1975); Ronald Thiemann, *Revelation and Theology* (Notre Dame: University of Notre Dame Press, 1985); and James McClendon, *Systematic Theology: Ethics* (Nashville: Abingdon Press, 1986). By listing these together I do not mean to imply that they are in agreement or even constitute a common position in general. However, they share enough that they can generate a good argument, for which we should be grateful.

3. I had intended originally to develop a more general thesis concerning the relation of liturgy and ethics as a way to exhibit the centrality of the church for situating claims about the significance of narrative for theological reflection. Such a project turned out to be too unwieldly for one essay. I mention it, however, to remind the reader that the sermon cannot be isolated from the liturgical actions of prayer, praise, and eucharist. The whole

liturgy enacted over the whole Christian year developed over a lifetime is the presumption necessary to enable one sermon to concentrate on a few texts and specifiable topics. The traditional issue of the relation of word and sacrament becomes even more pressing once the narrative character of Christian convictions is acknowledged.

In his *The Identity of Christianity* (Philadelphia: Fortress Press, 1984) Stephen Sykes has rightly directed attention to the centrality of worship not only for the identity of Christianity but for better knowing what it might mean to claim that our convictions are true. He suggests that without distracting from the doctrinal aspect of Christianity, "the phenomenon of Christian worship makes a vital difference to the conditions under which vigorous argument of a radical kind may be regarded as a constructive contribution, not a destructive irrelevance, to the performance of Christian identity in the modern world" (p. 265). Moreover, he notes that three vital conditions are incorporated into worship: "In the first place, the condition for the Christian character of what is done is satisfied by the necessary reference to the achievement of Jesus, which is recalled. *Anamnesis* in worship is of the deeds of Jesus set in the context of God. But secondly, the *anamnesis* is prayer and praise. It is, therefore, a recollection by means of which the intentions of the recollector are inwardly challenged, reoriented and offered up. Finally, the worship is corporate; it is an arrangement so devised as to take place at a time and place known to be convenient for those who desire to assemble" (p. 265). My use of "sermon" is but a shorthand for this sense of worship.

Finally, some may wonder if any church exists where such a sermon could be preached — i.e., it's too "theological," "long," and so on. This is not just an issue of style, for if the argument of the sermon is valid, it means there has to be a people capable of demanding as well as responding to such a sermon. I have no doubt such a people exist, but I am aware some will see the general argument of this essay as but an attempt to avoid the really hard question confronting narrative theology— that is, to tell us we should trust the church as a truthful community is no more helpful than to direct our attention to the narrative character of Scripture. Both are equally arbitrary. This essay is an attempt to show why that is not the case if the church, in fact, provides an alternative to Babel.

4. David Ford's *Barth and God's Story* (Frankfurt am Main: Verlag Peter Lang, 1985) is an extremely enlightening treatment of Barth from this perspective. Ford notes that "Barth's comprehensive alternative world of meaning is an overarching story which is not the traditional one from creation to parousia but is the lifetime of Jesus Christ. A doctrine of time based on an interpretation of the resurrection supports the inclusiveness of that stretch of time, and the Old Testament history and all world history are 'figured' into it" (p. 165). Such "figuring" depends on an account of the church that Barth largely fails to develop.

5. This issue is complex, as it is often not easy to separate claims about the Scripture as canon from the narrative character of Scripture. As Charles Wood suggests, "When one regards the biblical canon as a whole, the centrality to it of a narrative element is difficult to overlook: not only the chronological sweep of the whole, from creation to new creation, including the various events and developments of what has sometimes been called 'salvation history,' but also the way the large narrative portions interweave and provide a context for the remaining materials so that they, too, have a place in the ongoing story, while these other materials—parables, hymns, prayers, summaries, theological expositions—serve in different ways to enable readers to get hold of the story and to live their way into it" (*The Formation of Christian Understanding* [Philadelphia: Westminster Press, 1981], p. 100).

6. Elie Wiesel, *The Gates of the Forest* (New York: Holt, Rinehart, and Winston, 1966), p. XII.

7. Elie Wiesel, *Souls on Fire* (New York: Vintage Books, 1972), p. 168.

8. Frei, "The 'Literal Reading' of Biblical Narrative in Christian Tradition," p. 66. Frei continues, saying, "There may or may not be a class called 'realistic narrative,' but to take it as a general category of which the synoptic Gospel narratives and their partial second-order redescription in the doctrine of the Incarnation are a dependent instance is first to put the cart before the horse and then cut the lines and claim that the vehicle is self-propelled."

9. Frei, *The Identity of Jesus Christ*, p. 65.

10. For example, see R. Alan Culpepper, *Anatomy of the Fourth Gospel* (Philadelphia: Fortress Press, 1983); David Rhoads and Donald Michie, *Mark as Story* (Philadelphia: Fortress Press, 1982); Jack Kingsbury, *Mattthew as Story* (Philadelphia: Fortress Press, 1986); and Dan Via, *The Ethics of Mark's Gospel in the Middle of Time* (Philadelphia: Fortress Press, 1985). I suspect Frei would be less sympathetic with Via's approach, since he tends to assume that a general hermeneutical theory is needed in order to translate the biblical claims into existential truths.

11. Frei, "The 'Literal Reading' of Biblical Narrative in Christian Tradition," p. 68. The general argument by Charles Wood is obviously along these lines. What is frustrating about Frei's (and Wood's) position is the failure to specify the liturgical context through which such consensus is formed. This is not just a genetic point, as without the liturgy the text of Scripture remains just that—text. It is important to remember that before the church had the New Testament it nonetheless worshiped and prayed to God in the name of Jesus of Nazareth. In effect, the worship of the church created Scripture, though once formed Scripture governs the church's worship. For a fascinating account of the development of the Christian interpretation of the Bible, see James Kugel and Rowan Greer, *Early Biblical Interpretation* (Philadelphia: Westminster Press, 1986). In particular, see Greer's discussion of Irenaeus' method that at least in principle requires Scripture to be interpreted in a temporal way (pp. 168–176). Greer notes that Irenaeus tended to qualify this emphasis by using "type" to refer to an earthly representation of a heavenly reality. While I think typological interpretation is unavoidable, the crucial question is what controls the types. Originally, I had written the sermon using first person in relation to the story of Babel— e.g., "So God confused our language." While I certainly think we continue to live out Babel's history, I am equally convinced that we also indicate that is a time theologically in our past. Thus, I tried to relate the texts temporally rather than contemporaneously.

12. Frei, "The 'Literal Reading' of Biblical Narrative in Christian Tradition," p. 72. While Frei is certainly right to emphasize the "plain sense" as primary, I think that he does not sufficiently note that the "plain sense" is that determined through the corporate life of the Christian community.

13. Hans Frei, "An Afterword: Eberhard Busch's Biography of Karl Barth," in *Karl Barth in Re-View*, edited by Martin Romscheidt (Pittsburgh: Pickwick Press, 1981), p. 100.

14. Ibid., p. 111.

15. Thiemann, p. 83.

16. Much silliness has been written for and against the theological use of Wittgenstein's "language-games." For an insightful and careful account of Wittgenstein on this matter, see James Edwards' *Ethics Without Philosophy: Wittgenstein and the Moral Life* (Tampa: University of South Florida Press, 1985), pp. 123–142. Edwards argues that "Language-games can neither be heuristic devices used to illustrate substantive philosophical theses arguable on other grounds, nor can they be the final philosophical standard of sense; both these conceptions fail because they presuppose a 'scientific' model of philosophical reasoning. If language-games are heuristic devices, there must actually be philosophical truths to be argued and illustrated; but the whole tenor of Wittgenstein's later work is to disavow such a 'scientific' (metaphysical) conception of philosophy. And language-games cannot be the final standards of sense, most obviously because language-games can be invented as well as discovered: they can be fantastic as well as realistic" (p. 142). Because Wittgenstein meant his analysis of "language-game" to help us attend to the diversity of ways we use language to help us learn about the way things are, I have always avoided appeal to "language-game" in itself. What is important is not whether this or that is a language-game but what is actually being said.

17. Frei, *Eclipse of Biblical Narrative*, p. 3. How the Gospel "engulfs" the world is not by denying the reality of our diverse narratives but by providing an invitation to be part of a new people. The imperial character of the story which the church embodies requires witness, not coercion. Exactly because the content of the story requires us to recognize our

64

fallibility means we cannot anticipate how God will use our witness in relation to the diverse stories of the world. Indeed, the story we believe entrusted to the church does not displace all other stories, as it does not pretend to tell us all that is worth knowing about our existence—it only tells us what we need to know about God's saving work.

18. Frei, *The Identity of Jesus Christ*, p. 157. John Milbank has put this forcefully in his "An Essay Against Secular Order," (*Journal of Religious Ethics*, 15, 2 [Fall, 1987]), as he says "If we are to say 'salvation is a fact,' 'salvation has appeared on the historical stage,' then we have to enunciate, not just an ecclesiology, but also an ecclesiology which recounts and resumes the church's *actual concrete* intervention in the human social order, where the rules of 'non-interference' have not really applied" (p. 207).

19. Janet Martin Soskice, *Metaphor and Religious Language* (Oxford: Clarendon Press, 1985), p. 86.

20. Ibid., pp. 135–136.

21. Ibid., p. 136.

22. Ibid., p. 145. Such is the reason that questions of authority are unavoidable in any community. In the church it is the responsibility of those we invest with authority to direct our attention to those without whom we could not exist as church—i.e., the saints.

23. Frei, *The Identity of Jesus Christ*, p. 159. Again as John Milbank says, "The church is not primarily a *means* of salvation, but rather a *goal* of salvation insofar as it is nothing other than the community of the reconciled. Our way back to God is through our incorporation into the historical body of the redeemed" (p. 8).

24. As Greg Jones argues, "It is certainly true that there is a narrative quality to human life that is morally significant. But that is not the primary claim Christians are concerned to make. It is rather that the biblical *narrative* seeks to incorporate all people into God's narrative. Thus there is a strong sense in which the narrative of a single human life does not begin with birth and end with death: for by being incorporated into the life of Christ the narrative of a single human life begins at creation and ends with the consummation of the Kingdom. It is by being incorporated into the Church that it is possible to develop the virtues necessary to live truthfully and morally. (Therefore) the narrative of the Christian tradition is a way of displaying two claims: on the one hand it displays the continuing embodiment of the community through the ages (thus showing that the claim is not a utopian fantasy), and on the other hand it displays the claim that each person's salvation is indispensable to the salvation of everyone else, even the dead" ("Alasdair MacIntyre on Narrative, Community, and the Moral Life," *Modern Theology*, 4, 1 [October, 1987]), p. 67.

25. I am indebted to Mr. Michael Cartwright, Mr. Greg Jones, Dr. Richard Lischer, and Dr. Dennis Campbell for their criticisms and suggestions.

RECONCILING THE PRACTICE OF REASON

Casuistry in a Christian Context

1. On Representing Theological Ethics

My assignment is to address the relation between moral theory and concrete moral judgments from the perspective of theological ethics.[1] This would seem to be a straightforward enough task so that I can get down to business rather quickly. But, unfortunately, I must tell you that before I can begin to analyze the "case" I have provided, I need to make clear the status of the perspective from which I am working.

I suspect it is already clear to most of you that in terms of the other approaches represented at this conference—i.e., utilitarianism, Kantianism, contractarianism, and Marxism—theological ethics is different in kind. Each of the others is a theory about morality represented by distinct thinkers and developed through refined discourse and argument. In contrast, theological ethics certainly is not a theory, and it is no easy matter to identify those thinkers who would be considered representative of it as a peculiar genre of moral reflection. To put the matter differently, none of the other approaches, with the possible exception of Marxism, has a body of sacred literature to which the thinker must relate. Christian theologians do not have a theory of moral rationality, since they have something better (or worse, depending on your point of view)—namely a Bible and a church to which they are accountable.

For the theologian, therefore, some of the questions before this conference do not have the same immediacy. For example, we were asked to discuss whether our concrete moral judgments can be derived from our moral theory without reliance on "extra assumptions." To which I can reply only, "What theory?" Or we were asked to consider whether there are better alternatives to this deductive approach when I am even unsure if a religious tradition's way of dealing with moral decisions is deductive. Most religious communities do not start with a theory and then try to determine if x or y is permissible; rather, they began with a sense that assumes x or y is or is not to be done, given the nature of their community. All of which makes it seem that in considering these questions theologians begin with a disadvantage, since we do not begin with a theory of what makes ethics ethics or a theory of moral rationality.

Of course, I am not suggesting that theological thinkers do not represent options that may more or less be characterized in terms of familiar philosophical alternatives. Joseph Fletcher is well known for espousing utilitarianism as the most appropriate form of Christian love. Paul Ramsey is equally well known for arguing that what Christians mean by love is best expressed deontologically. It would be tempting to try to assess the basis of such a difference and how it could be adjudicated for the purpose of this conference, but in the process I would avoid dealing with the question of how theological ethics does or should function.

For I suspect the issue that the inclusion of the theologian amid the philosophers is meant to raise is not how our moral theory makes a difference for moral judgments but how God might make a difference. Therefore, the question is whether belief in God does or can make a difference for moral decisions and their justification. Any constructive response to this question seems doomed, moreover, since most philosophers assume no logical entailment can be demonstrated between belief in God and our moral principles and judgments. Matters are no better, however, if I try to take refuge in theology since many theologians argue it is a theological mistake to try to speak on behalf of God in matters having to do with ethics.

For example, Karl Barth argues when a moralist tries to deduce the good or evil in human conduct as if it were the command of God, he is trying to "set himself on God's throne, to distinguish good and evil and always to judge things as the one or the other, not only in relation to others but also to himself. He makes himself lord, king and judge at the place where only God can be this. He does so by claiming that in a *summa* of ethical statements compiled by him and his like from the Bible, natural law and tradition, he can know the command of God, see through and past it, and thus master and handle it, i.e., apply it to himself and others, so that armed with this instrument he may speak as law".[2] Of course, it is possible to argue, as I would, that Barth is wrong in denying the value of casuistry. But that does not settle the difficulty, for if Barth is wrong he is so because he fails to appreciate how religious communities have always generated informal as well as extremely sophisticated modes of moral reflection which can only be called casuistry. They have done so not in an attempt to preempt God's judgment but in order to be more faithful to God. Indeed, in this respect theological ethics is really much better off than the philosopher, as there exists a rich literature dealing with concrete moral issues for informing the conscience of the faithful.

Yet the matter cannot be solved so easily, for I cannot pretend to speak for all religious traditions. Casuistry among Jews is not the same as casuistry in the Roman Catholic tradition, and they are both different from Protestant traditions. Judaism has a long tradition of reflection derived from the rabbis which is not easily characterized in terms of contemporary philosophical options; Catholicism's casuistical tradition is closely tied to the sacrament of penance and is at least alleged to be based on a version of natural law; Protestants have not developed such an explicit tradition of moral reflection but have generally appealed to Scripture as the ultimate touchstone for their concrete moral judgments. Of course, all of this is made even more complex by the diversity within each of these traditions.

As a result I feel a bit like the Protestant during Brotherhood Week in the local school district who was asked, along with a rabbi and a Catholic priest, to give his religious views on some issue. The rabbi began by developing the history over the centuries of rabbinical reflection on the topic and noted what seemed to be the general consensus; the priest appealed to the Magisterial office of the Church and the best wisdom of the majority of moral theologians; and the Protestant began by saying, "It seems to me." This is a way of saying that what you are going to get from me is not a report about how casuistry is done by theologians in general, but rather an exposition of how I think practical reason should work for Christians. I will do this by directing our attention to the way the Mennonite tradition has handled the question of Christian use of the courts.

2. On Representing Myself

Representing myself, given the subject of this conference, however, is no easy matter. I am one of the persons who has argued that modern ethics has distorted the character of the moral life because of its undue attention on decisions and their justification. Following Iris Murdoch I have argued that decisions are what we do when everything else has been lost. Prior to the question of the kind of choices we must make is the question of the kind of person we should be. Therefore, virtue is prior to decision, character to choice.

Put more accurately, I have argued that situations are not like mud puddles that we cannot avoid, but the fact that you confront a mud puddle depends on the kind of person you are. Casuistry is a necessary activity of any moral position, but its status and way it is done depend on prior communal presuppositions about the kind of people we should be. Elsewhere I have suggested that casuistry is the attempt through analogical comparison to discipline our descriptions of what we do and do not do in the hopes that we can live more truthful lives.[3] So understood, casuistry is not first and foremost an attempt to determine and/or justify our decisions in terms of universally agreed-on rules or principles as it is the way a community explores the implications of its convictions.

From this perspective, as important as the decisions we make are the matters we never bring to decision; or if the matter is brought to decision it is understood to be an exception that requires carefully stated reasons why it is even being considered. Thus, for Roman Catholics the question of whether marriage can be dissolved by divorce is not open to discussion. When you marry, you do so for a lifetime. Annulments can be considered, but they are not a way to "get around" this commitment, though some may use it for that, but rather a way of discovering what such a commitment entails.

My difficulty with "quandary ethics" is not only with its concentration on decisions, but that it too often fails to attend adequately to the question of the description of the "problem." Those who conceive of ethics primarily in terms of resolutions of quandaries tend too readily to accept conventional assumptions about how the "quandary" is to be described. By failing to attend to where we get certain descriptions or how they are to be used, we ignore the significance of a community maintaining the practices that make the description truthful.[4] Indeed, it seems to me that one of the difficulties of theoretical accounts of morality, such as utilitarianism or Kantianism, is their casuistical judgments only make sense because they continue to trade on descriptions that they cannot justify from within their methodological constraints.

When religious traditions attempt to display their casuistry in terms of contemporary philosophical alternatives, they cannot help but leave out an important element of their story. For it appears they must express their moral reflection in terms of adherence to certain fundamental

70

principles by which a range of behavior is approved or disapproved and decisions can be justified. Moreover, certain theological traditions of moral reflection, particularly some Roman Catholic manuals of moral theology, look as if they exemplify this model. However, I would argue that this correspondence is misleading, since the casuistry of religious communities, in particular the Catholic community, only makes sense against the background of a community's practices and convictions.

This is true not only for the Catholic community but for any substantial account of moral rationality. For if, as I have suggested, casuistry is the ongoing attempt of a community to understand itself through analogical comparison, such comparison requires the location of central paradigmatic examples. Such examples are not arbitarily chosen but rather are determined through the experience of a community as developed in a tradition. Some examples become central because they serve to remind that community of what it is about across generations.

As a community develops over time, new and unanticipated problems arise which require reconsideration of those paradigms and their relation to one another, as well as of what was thought to be their implications. The testing of the analogies and disanalogies at once may confirm as well as change assumptions about the meaning of the examples. The crucial point, however, is that the rationality of their process is finally determined by how well the analogical comparisons serve to draw out the implications of those examples for the community.

Even though I cannot pretend to represent more than myself in what follows, at the same time I want to claim that this perspective I develop illumines the casuistical traditions of religious communities. It does so, I think, because it makes clear that moral reflection draws upon and reflects the moral virtues and convictions of those communities. Moreover, by focusing on the community I can show that the dichotomies between reason and revelation, individual autonomy and communal authority, Scripture and rationality are false alternatives when religious convictions are rightly forming practical wisdom.

It is my hope, however, that the constructive account I develop of how casuistry should work in the Christian community will also illumine how moral reason should work for any community. It is my contention that there is not nor can there be any tradition-free account of practical reason. There are certainly different traditions whose material content will make a difference for the kind of questions discussed, but each tradition in its own way will reflect the community that makes the activity of moral reflection intelligible. Indeed, from my perspective the deductive character of much of contemporary moral philosophy is but

71

the mirror image of Protestant fundamentalism. Both assume that moral questions can be decided on the basis of a few principles without any community acting to mediate those principles in terms of the goods of that community.

3. On Representing John Howard Yoder

Before developing these contentions through discussion of my "case," I think it will be useful to attend to John Howard Yoder's recent account of practical reason in the Protestant tradition. In a chapter of his *The Priestly Kingdom*, called "The Hermeneutics of Peoplehood," Yoder notes that there is no reason to think that the designation "Protestant" is a "necessary and sufficient determinant of one distinctive style of practical moral reason."[5] Therefore, he proposes to offer an account of practical reason that is clearly his own, but which he hopes draws out the implicit assumptions about such matters common to the origins of Protestantism.

He begins by noting that the Reformers called the church back to the Catholic principle that all decisions of the church must be determined by an open process. In terms of questions of moral discernment, church order, and of matters of teaching on morality, the Reformers followed the admonition in I Corinthians 14:26 that "at all your meetings, let everyone be ready with a Psalm or a sermon or a revelation." Yoder notes this emphasis was later interpreted, critically by Roman Catholics and com-plimentarily by later Enlightenment figures, as recommending an in-dividualistic interpretation of Scripture and morality. But at least at the beginning the Protestant insistence on both the perspicuity of Scripture along with the priesthood of all believers was an attempt to avoid the alternatives of collectivism and individualism for theological and moral reflection.

Such alternatives could be avoided because it was assumed that the church must be a voluntary community which affirms individual dignity (the uncoerced adherence of the member) without enshrining individ-ualism. "The alternative to arbitrary individualism is not established authority in which the individual participates and to which he or she consents. The alternative to authoritarianism is not anarchy but freedom of confession" (pp. 24–25). Yoder suggests that the struggle in the West between collectivism and individualism is at least partly the result of the failure of the mainstream of the Reformation to challenge the principle of the establishment of the church. As a result the church continued to underwrite those moral judgments that were thought necessary to

72

maintain the wider social order. The moral resources for moral rationality made possible by a voluntary commitment to a community distinct from total society were therefore largely lost.

A further implication of the Protestant Reformation, according to Yoder, is that practical reason as developed in congregational settings should be shaped by the assumption that it must serve the process of reconciliation. Practical moral reasoning is a conversation of a community that can risk judgment because of its willingness to forgive. Moral judgments are not deductive applications of universally valid rules, but the confrontation of one person by another on matters that matter for the whole community. Private wrongs in fact are public matters, since the very nature of the community and its moral discourse depends on calling sin, sin, with the hope of reconciliation. As Yoder notes, most discussions of practical moral reasoning do not concretize decisions about issues in terms of a conversation between people who differ on an issue. Even less do discussions of practical moral reason see that conversation surrounded by a church (i.e., a locally gathered body) which will ratify either the reconciliation or its impossibility. As a result we seem to have no alternatives, both philosophically and theologically, to individualistic intuitionism and complete objective rigidity.

Yoder's characterization of how practical reason should work to inform Christian conscience directs our attention to questions of how our community works, rather than leading us to concentrate on how ideas or principles work. Practical reason is not a disembodied process based on abstract principles but the process of a community in which every member has a role to play. Such a process does not disdain the importance of logical rigor for aiding in their deliberation, but logic cannot be a substitute for the actual process of discernment.

The conversation made possible by such a community draws from people of different gifts and virtues. For example, certain people have the charisma of prophecy, whose primary focus is neither prediction nor moral guidance but stating and reinforcing the vision of the place of the believing community in history in which any moral reasoning gains intelligibility. Equally important are what Yoder calls "agents of memory," those who do not pretend to speak on their own but as servants of communal memory. These "scribes" are practical moral reasoners who do not judge or decide anything but remember "expertly, charismatically, the store of memorable, identity-confirming acts of faithfulness praised and of failure repented" (p. 30). Scripture is crucial for moral reflection, as texts inform the community's memory through the "charismatic aptness of the scribe's selectivity" (p. 31). Such selectivity, however, must be

73

informed as well as critically related to the tradition which is essential to the church's interpretation of Scripture.

The community of practical discourse also depends on what Yoder calls "agents of linguistic self-consciousness." These are those teachers who are charged with the steering of the community with the rudder of language. Such people, realizing at once the power and danger of language, will be attentive to the temptations to use verbal distinctions and/or purely verbal solutions to "solve" substantial problems. Also crucial are "agents of order and due process" who have the task to oversee and lead the community. Their task is to insure that everyone is heard and that conclusions reached are genuinely consensual.

That such agents are required in the Christian community is but a reminder that the existence of such a people is not determined by a series of decisions but rather requires the development of virtues and the wisdom gained from those in the past as well as the present who have attempted to follow Jesus. This entails that practical reason of Christians may be distinctive and particularistic. Yoder, however, does not discount the importance of public comprehensibility or appeal to outside audiences but rather questions whether those who first seek a "natural," "public," or "universal" ground for practical reason can sustain their assumption that such a position can stand alone. From Yoder's perspective such "universal" starting points cannot help but reflect the provincialism of the status quo which the practical moral reasoning of Christians must always be expected at some point to subvert.

So runs Yoder's account of practical reason, to which in the main I subscribe. I hope it is now clear that the alternative I offer is not just a report on how I think Christians should think about concrete moral matters, but also a critique of accounts of practical reason that isolate reasoning from any concrete group of people or tradition. Such accounts of practical reason always end up underwriting our assumption that the way things are are the way they ought or have to be; but our task, through the power of practical reason, is to change the way things are by changing ourselves.

4. On Representing Olin Teague

It is now time to try to make this account of practical reason concrete by considering the case of Olin Teague. Olin's story goes like this:

Olin Teague farms land he inherited from his family that lies midway

74

between Middlebury and Shipshewana, Indiana. He is now in his late fifties. While not wealthy, he makes a modest living raising corn, pigs, and a few milk cows. The latter primarily provides the milk used to make the cheddar cheese his family has made for generations. He has four children, three grown and married, his youngest finishing Goshen College and planning to go to medical school. Olin has promised to help pay her expenses since she is planning to be a medical missionary for the Mennonite Central Committee. Olin is not particularly pious, but he and his family have long been members of the local Mennonite church.

As a way to make extra money to help pay his daughter's medical expenses Olin agreed to let Jim Burkholder, the owner of the Wagon Wheel Cafe in downtown Shipshewana, buy his cheese to sell at his cafe. Because of the large Amish population in the surrounding county, Jim reasoned that tourists would be eager to buy "authentic" farm-made cheese. Olin and Jim agreed on a price for the cheese with the understanding that Jim would pay Olin once a year at the end of the tourist season. At the end of the first year Jim owed Olin $3000. However, Jim told Olin that he could not pay, for even though the cheese had sold well, the cafe had failed to make a profit. He made it clear to Olin that it would be some time before he could pay at all, and perhaps never. Olin was quite upset at this turn of events, but it never crossed his mind to do anything other than talking to Jim about how he might put his finances in order. Olin's daughter, however, had to delay her plans to go to medical school at the University of Indiana.

Most of us, I suspect, have the same response on reading this case— namely, why did it not occur to Olin to sue. After all, these kinds of situations are a dime a dozen in the business world, and such suits are thought to be normal business practice. Indeed, for most of us taking Burkholder to court would not even raise moral issues. In such matters that is simply the way you proceed. Then why did it not occur to Olin to sue?

If you asked Olin himself, the answer you get might prove quite un- satisfactory for illuminating the nature of practical reason. For Olin's most probable answer would be "I am a Mennonite." That is Olin's reason for not suing. From Olin's perspective, to ask him why he does not sue Jim is about as dumb as asking a Texan why he likes Mexican food; they just go together. That does not mean we are prevented from inquiring further into what "being a Mennonite" means to Olin, but our search for further moral rationale should not imply there is something wrong with Olin's reason for not suing Jim.

Of course, "I am a Mennonite" suggests that there is quite a story to tell in order to explain Olin's behavior. The background of the story begins in the history of Israel, where procedures were provided for the total community to share the burden of those who had gotten themselves so deeply into debt that their own and their family's future seemed forever mortgaged. Though there is debate about the extent to which the jubilee legislation requiring the forgiveness of debt (Leviticus 25) was institutionalized in Israel, the very fact Israel preserved such legislation testifies to the concern to limit the destructive debt of those who made up the people of Israel. Those who follow God simply do not condemn one another to live in perpetual economic dependence.

Of equal importance, if not more important, is the extent to which Mennonite life has been shaped by I Corinthians 6:1-11. There Paul admonishes the Corinthians by rhetorically asking,

"When one of you has a grievance against a brother, does he dare go to law before the unrighteous instead of the saints? Do you not know that the saints will judge the world? And if the world is to be judged by you, are you incompetent to try trivial cases? Do you not know that we are to judge angels? How much more, matters pertaining to this life! If then you have such cases, why do you lay them before those who are least esteemed by the church? I say this to your shame. Can it be that there is no man among you wise enough to decide between members of the brotherhood, but brother goes to law against brother, and that before unbelievers? To have lawsuits at all with one another is defeat for you. Why not rather suffer wrong? Why not rather be defrauded? But you yourselves wrong and defraud, and that even your own brethren. Do you not know that the unrighteous will not inherit the kingdom of God? Do not be deceived; neither the immoral, nor idolaters, nor adulterers, nor homosexuals, nor thieves, nor the greedy, nor drunkards, nor revilers, nor robbers will inherit the kingdom of God. And such were some of you. But you were washed, you were sanctified, you were justified in the name of the Lord Jesus Christ and in the Spirit of our God."

For our purposes there is no need to provide extended historical analysis of this passage. No doubt it would be of interest to know what the courts to which Paul refers were like or what kinds of disputes were actually brought before them. But such issues cannot determine the meaning of the text for the moral guidance of the Christian community—at least as far as Mennonites are concerned. For them what is interesting is the kind of community Christians are meant to be in order to hear and live according to this text. For they assume because of the kind of sanctified people Christians have become, these early Christians were right to make the question of appearing in court prismatic for determining the nature of their community.

The admonition not to take one another to court, therefore, is placed against the background of their being a particular kind of people with a distinct set of virtues. Therefore, unlike most Christians who have tried to turn such passages into a legal regulation so one can start to find exceptions to it, Mennonites understand the admonition to be but a logical extension of their commitment to be a people of peace. Their reading of this text and the significance they give it are not because they think every command of the Bible should be followed to the letter, but rather reflects their understanding that the fundamental ministry of Christians in the world is reconciliation.

So their reading of the text and the behavior it prohibits is informed by their understanding of the virtues necessary to be Christian. But it is important to note that they have no "individualistic" conception of virtues; rather, their conception is communal. Reconciliation is a central virtue because it denotes the communal reality that joins Mennonites in a common story and tradition. No doubt at times in their history the prohibition against litigation may have become lawlike for some Mennonites, but even as such it stands as a reminder of the kind of people they are to be.

Because Mennonites read this text as but an extension of their general commitment to peacekeeping, they extend its significance beyond the bare requirements of the text. The text says they are not to take one another to court. Note that is not because they do not make any moral judgments about what is right or wrong. Obviously, Paul is more than willing to make such judgments and in rather harsh terms, at that. This is no easy ethic of tolerance. Indeed, Paul even suggests that Christians are ultimately to judge the world rather than vice versa. So not going to court has little to do with overlooking wrong, but rather has to do with discovering a way that Christians can respond to wrongs that builds up rather than destroys community.

As Guy Hershberger, a contemporary Mennonite theologian suggests, the reason Christians are prohibited from settling their differences in a court of law is that such settlements violate the Christian adherence to love and nonresistance as a basic form of human relatedness. Therefore, he argues, not only should Christians not sue one another, they should not engage in aggressive litigation against any person whether he or she be Christian or non-Christian. "The Christian is commanded to beware of covetousness and to love his neighbor as himself, yes even his enemy if there is such. The Christian must exercise a ministry of reconciliation, bearing witness to the way of the cross in order that the neighbor, even one who may have wronged him, may be won for Christ and brought into the kingdom. Aggressive suits at law are in every sense a violation of this mission, for how can a Christian win a man to Christ when he is suing him at law? It is equally clear that the Christian may not evade his responsibilities so as to be the cause for a just legal action to be brought against him. He who willfully evades the payment of his bills, for example, so as to invite legal action against him is even more in the wrong than the aggressor. According to the teaching of Matthew 18 the one falls under the disciplining of the church as much as the other."[6]

Some in the Christian tradition have argued that the reason Christians should avoid litigation is the abhorrence of publicity as well as the general goal of avoiding the use of coercing power of government. On such grounds they are not as insistent as Hershberger that all coercive litigation is to be avoided. If the only issue is publicity, then it may be possible to go to court without violating Paul's admonition. Hershberger, however, is not concerned with such legalistic readings of the text, since for him the negative prohibition is less important than the positive commitment to find means of reconciliation. Litigation, resting as it does upon ultimate appeal to governmental coercion is (when used in just self-defense) morally the equivalent of the direct appeal to the services of the police. Whether the force is overt or covert is not of deep moral significance as long as the sanctions are coercive in character. The rejection of self-defense by litigation is therefore a part of the general "other-cheek" attitude of the Christian toward evil.[7]

Obviously, this Pauline text is not self-interpreting but depends on further theological construals for its concrete significance to be understood. For example, since Hershberger argues that the basic issue involved in Paul's admonition to avoid the courts is the coercive intent, he does not assume that state machinery is bad in and of itself. On the contrary, it is argued that "since the law exists for the promotion of justice and the protection of human rights, the Christian must stand on the side of law. To be sure lawmakers can go astray, and when they do so the Christian also has the obligation to prophesy against that which is wrong. But he may never stand in the way of the law's pursuit of its rightful purpose. In the payment of taxes and in the honest reporting of business affairs relating thereto; in faithful compliance with laws designed to protect the health, safety, and welfare of the people; and in cheerful cooperation with the state in the furtherance of these ends there should be no question as to the Christian's obligations. This includes laws for the regulation of working conditions, including such matters as wages, length of the working day, and overtime rates. The Christian's business affairs should be in legal order and legal counsel should be freely employed to make sure that they are so. All of this is using the law as a means for the doing of justice to the brother and the neighbor, while evasion of the law would be to deal with him unjustly."[8]

Such is an example of Mennonite casuistry. Moreover, it is not just a position of an individual but it has been confirmed by the Mennonite Church General Assembly in 1981. After a lengthy process they approved a "Summary Statement" called *The Use of the Law* to clarify the Mennonite position on the place of the law.[9] They note such a statement is necessary because of the rapid increase in lawsuits in our society, particularly where liability insurance makes it likely that a high level of monetary compensation may be forthcoming. They suggest that this is a subtle temptation, as such a use of the law might be to satisfy selfish desires rather than to assure justice in human relationships. They note that Mennonites, in spite of their traditional hesitancy to bring suit, have become more involved in legal proceedings, and therefore some guidance is needed.

They begin by affirming the "positive role of law in human society and encouragement for the professional practice of law. It is the role of law to maintain order, to clarify and interpret law and statute, and to determine what justice requires in the light of society's values. The adversarial system, with its rules of evidence, presumption of innocence, and other customs, is designed to find justice on an objective and fair basis. Christians should use the positive provision of the civil law with adequate legal counsel in order to fulfill the intention of law. Carefully drawn contracts and other instruments written according to the provisions of the law, are an obligation of Christian integrity." There is no reason Christians are excluded from using the courts to settle a point of law, secure the interpretation of a contract, establish good zoning laws, etc.

They note in particular that many Mennonites serve poor people who suffer from basic inequities rooted in economic, social, legal, and religious structures which sometimes can be addressed through litigation. While not prohibiting such action they advise that "Church persons engaged in such mission should have their proposals for litigation on behalf of others monitored by a church resource so that reconciliation and peace concerns are not overlooked." By this they mean that no such action should be undertaken without having their views tested by a concrete congregation of people. For they note "the teachings of Jesus and the apostles, the nature of the Scripture, the complexity of our situation, and the conflict between selfishness and altruism within each Christian combine to create a specific need for the involvement of a Christian community or congregation to interpret and apply the Scriptures and discern the will of God in a given situation. While congrega-

79

tional involvement does not guarantee faithfulness in every respect, there is a greater possibility of openness to the renewing Spirit of God than a traditional literalism, individualism, or authoritarian leadership" —in short, moral discernment is the responsibility of the whole community.[10]

When individual Christians face a legal dispute, they must accordingly commit themselves to work with appropriate persons or committees of the congregation. Such counselors should seek to help the believer discern how concerns for justice and suffering love apply, to give support needed to overcome greed or self-justification in order to maintain a reconciliatory stance, and when and if it is necessary for the Christian to accept loss, the church should mutually share losses, if possible. While such counsel does not replace the need for legal advice, Christians should inform their lawyers of their faith and commitment.[11] In particular, Christians should not permit lawyers to make moral choices for them simply on the basis of accepted practices of law. It is the Christian's responsibility to look for alternatives that will avoid the coercive effect of the law in these instances. The report goes into some detail about what such alternatives might involve—e.g., mediation, etc.

Particularly interesting is the commitment of the whole church to absorb some of the loss the refusal to go to court might entail. Usually, moral reason works to show what we have to do given the limits of the situation, but here moral reason expands those "limits," making possible a different alternative. Thus, it has been the practice of Mennonites to aid those who may have been the innocent victims of an accident but who could not receive damages because of their unwillingness to go to court. However, there is no suggestion that if such mutual aid is not forthcoming, they are any less obligated to live in a nonresistant and reconciling way.

However, it is certainly the case that this form of mutual aid has not been as forthcoming as it was in the past. Indeed, it is hard to know which began to occur first—the loss of mutual support or Mennonites more willing to go to court to redress grievances. No doubt *The Use of the Law* is partly an attempt to renew and give rationale to the Mennonite refusal to use courts as Mennonites become subject to the same forces that make most of us so litigious. That such is the case but reinforces the general point that how we reason about concrete cases is determined by the habits and practices of particular communities.

In particular, we see that the casuistry of the Mennonites surrounding the use of law to settle disputes draws on profound assumptions about what constitutes a good community that encourages the flourishing of good people. Their refusal to resort to legal remedies not only among themselves but between themselves and non-Mennonites is not the result of a literalistic application of Scripture. Rather, they take the Scripture seriously for forming their moral reflection about the use of courts because that issue illumines their general sense of what it means to be a reconciled and reconciling people. The virtues of the community make moot the question of whether they should take one another to court. Because that alternative is ruled out does not mean, however, that decisions do not remain to be made. But now they may involve more the necessity of setting up forms of helping the improvident through credit counseling and/or refinancing services.

To take such an approach, moreover, suggests that even though this peculiar "moral problem" is relative to the Mennonites' particular set of commitments, that does not mean they are only interested in their own. For if they are inventive in developing social techniques for themselves, they may also help pioneer social inventions for wider society. Schools, hospitals, factories, and social services were all originally social inventions created by Christian moral commitments that forced us to find reasonable responses. So it may be that the Mennonite commitment to the personal resolution of disputes may help us find means to avoid the depersonalization of our legal system.

I am not suggesting that Olin had thought through all this when he responded to Jim's inability to pay what he owes. He may not even know what I Corinthians 6 says. He may not know how the Mennonite refusal to go to court fits with the pacifistic assumptions of the Mennonites. But that is only important if you assume "know" is to be restricted to "being aware." In a perfectly straightforward sense Olin's habits as a Mennonite made him know what the practical wisdom of the community required of him. He did not have to decide whether he should or should not sue Jim because, given Olin's habits, that simply was not one of the descriptive possibilities. The "decision" he made to talk with Jim about how better to arrange his finances is but correlative to the descriptive possibilities created by the habits and convictions that make Olin Olin.

Before I conclude there are two objections to my presentation of Olin that should be considered, even though I cannot adequately respond to them. First, some may object that I have equated Mennonite with Christian in a manner that cannot be justified. That is certainly descriptively true, as most Christians do not share the Mennonite hesitancy to go to court. Normatively, however, I think they should, and insofar as all Christians assume the centrality of God's reconciling work in Jesus as central to their faith, Mennonites at least have the basis to carry on the

81

argument. Such an argument would need to attend to historical developments as well as more strictly theological considerations about the nature
of the church. For even among those Christian traditions that have
abandoned the admonition for Christians not to go to court there remain
institutions that at least suggest that such a concern is not unimportant—e.g., the continuing presence of ecclesiastical courts. So to observe
that many Christians do not conform to the practice of the Mennonites
is not the end of the matter but just the beginning.

The second objection is that my presentation of Olin as a representative of Mennonite practice is all well and good but irrelevant to the "real
world." Most people do not share Olin's community, and therefore quite
a different way of resolving disputes must be sought. Fairness, not
reconciliation, must be the hallmark of all relations as well as practical
reason. Again, I have no stake in denying the descriptive power of this
objection, but see no reason why I should let it determine the presentation of how I think Christians should reason practically.

Instead, I think much might be made of how the alternative I have
presented might make a difference for how some of our current moral
practices could be changed. For example, the current difficulty of the
physician-patient relation might appear quite differently if there were
some alternative to the adversarial manner of resolving error in medicine. I am not suggesting that patients should forgive and forget physician error but that too often patient and physician alike are caught in an
adversarial position ruled by the ethos of fairness that distorts the complexity of medical care. Such issues are obviously too involved to pursue
here, but I hope that I have said enough to hint that the perspective taken
here is not hopelessly irrelevant to the secular context.

5. On Representing God

I began by disavowing my ability to represent adequately theological
ethics, particularly if that designation is meant to represent all ethics
associated with religious traditions. Different religious traditions will
generate different conceptions of practical reason. Instead, I have tried
to present an account of how practical reason should work within a
Christian community. In particular, I have stressed that rationality is a
communal process which involves Scripture and virtues, as well as
judgments about particular practices and their implications for other
aspects of our lives. Rationality in a Christian context, therefore, both
shapes and is shaped by the fundamental commitment of that com-

munity to be a community of the reconciled as well as reconciling. The "case" I chose to analyze, while clearly not a significant moral issue from some perspectives, has helped, I hope, to illumine these general contentions.

I am aware that this presentation must appear exceedingly strange to philosophers. Formal considerations of the nature of rationality qua rationality have been ignored. No attempt has been made to characterize the prohibition against litigation in the Mennonite community in terms of deontological or teleological alternatives. That does not mean, however, that the process of reasoning about litigation among Mennonites is devoid of logical features. Rather, the logic serves their material commitments rather than vice versa. Thus, questions of when litigation can be used are carefully considered in terms of the reason for prohibiting litigation between Christians in the first place. If the reconciling intent is not abrogated by the process itself, they reason analogically that certain kinds of litigation may be permitted.

Even though such a procedure may strike philosophers as unphilosophical, I should think it is not without philosophical interest. For example, in *Ethics and the Limits of Philosophy* Bernard Williams makes the interesting observation that though virtue affects how one deliberates, it often is not clear in what way the virtues actually affect deliberation. Someone who has a particular virtue commits actions because they fall under certain descriptions, but Williams contends it "is rarely the case that the description that applies to the agent and to the action is the same as that in terms of which the agent chooses the action. A courageous person does not typically choose acts as being courageous, and it is a notorious truth that a modest person does not act under the title of modesty."[12] It should, therefore, be of considerable interest how Mennonites understand, as well as the early Christians seem to have understood, the relation of the virtue of reconciliation to litigious activity. In particular, it strikes me that the role of community for understanding such a relation is one aspect often overlooked in philosophical accounts of practical reason.[13]

Yet it is not my place to tell philosophers what they may or may not find of philosophical interest in what I have done. However, I cannot pretend that matters between theologians and philosophers can be left so independent and peaceful. Obviously involved in the very manner I have presented my case is a philosophical point, or perhaps better, a critique of the contemporary philosophical passion to reduce practical rationality to a single pattern. It seems to me that Williams is right to see this drive toward a "rationalistic conception of rationality" not as a requirement of philosophical discourse in itself but rather coming "from the social features of the modern world, which impose on personal deliberation and on the idea of practical reason itself a model drawn from a particular understanding of public rationality. This understanding requires in principle every decision to be based on grounds that can be discursively explained. This requirement is not in fact met, and it probably does little for the aim that authority should be genuinely answerable. But it is an influential ideal and by a reversal of the order of causes, it can look as if it were the result of applying to the public world an independent ideal of rationality."[14]

I hope it is clear from my presentation that there is nothing about the community-specific account of rationality I have provided that denies the importance of giving reasons for our actions. The issue is not whether it is important to give reasons; what is crucial is the kind of reasons we need to give and to what purpose they are to serve. Mennonites are no less committed than Kantians to work toward a society in which moral conflict can be resolved short of violence. The difference is that Mennonites do not think such resolutions occur by trying to take a shortcut around the necessity of the process of reconciliation through the positing of a disembodied "rationality."

Philosophers have a terrible hunger for the universal. That they do so is admirable, since that hunger is often charged by the moral commitment of a peaceful community. Yet their search for the universal too often looks to the development of general theories of rationality devoid as much as possible of distinctive content. In contrast, I am arguing that the way forward is through the appreciation of particular communities which are committed to finding as much shared understanding as possible on particular issues.[15] If such communities do not in fact exist, then no amount of philosophical reflection on practical reason will be of much use.

But, finally, what does all this have to do with God? One might well agree with all or at least some of what I have done and still think God is largely irrelevant. Reconciliation is a good idea for most communities. The fact that the Christians have a set of peculiar views about Scripture is their problem. Moreover, as I noted, most Christians do not believe that appeals to Scripture are sufficient to settle moral issues. So there is nothing about my account that would entail the necessary belief either in God or in the proposition that God shapes morality through particular commandments.

I shall not try to respond to these kinds of observations directly. Instead, I will tell you a story. It is a true story, unlike the one I made up about Olin and Jim. A few years ago, an Amish family was taking a ride in their buggy between Middlebury and Shipshewana. A group of high school boys from LaGrange, Indiana, were out in the country, driving fast and generally raising hell. Passing this family's buggy they threw a stone into it, unintentionally killing a young child. They were subsequently apprehended, but the county prosecutor could not try them for the actual crime because the Amish family would not testify at the trial. As a result, they were convicted of a much less severe crime. During their time in prison, the Amish family sought them out in order to effect a reconciliation.

I do not tell this story because I think it proves that God exists. Rather, I tell it because I think the behavior of this Amish family, and of the community that supports them, would be unintelligible without their belief in a God who refused to let our sin determine his relation to us. Even more strongly I believe that the behavior of the Amish in this case can easily be construed as decidedly immoral if such a God neither exists or, more importantly, lacks the characteristics they attribute to him. Only when the question of God's existence is raised in terms such as these do I suspect it is even a question worth considering.

NOTES

1. This paper was prepared for a conference at Rice University to have philosophers who represented the positions I list explore the difference their position makes for thinking about a particular case. The organizers of the conference were good enough to include a theologian, but I felt it necessary to suggest why that is not another philosophical option.

2. Karl Barth, *Church Dogmatics*, 3/4, translated by A. T. Mackay, et. al. (Edinburgh: T. and T. Clark, 1961), p. 10.

3. In particular, see "Casuistry as a Narrative Art" (Chapter Seven) of my *The Peaceable Kingdom: A Primer in Christian Ethics* (Notre Dame: University of Notre Dame, 1983), pp. 116–134. Even though analogy is at the heart of the practice of practical reason, it would be a mistake to conclude thereby that what is needed is a "theory of analogy." Rather, as David Burrell maintains, what is needed is a series of reminders about the way we can and do negotiate analogous expressions. "We must not look for a theory, but are rather invited to look to our own usage and sharpen our consciousness of its actual conditions. Rather than demand criteria *tout court*, we are reminded that many such criteria are already operative in our reasoning, and asked to scrutinize the ways we *use* the ones we do rely upon" ("Arguments in Theology: Analogy and Narrative," in *New Dimensions in Philosophical Theology*, edited by Carl Raschke [Chico, California: Scholars Press, 1982], p. 44). See also J. F. Ross, *Portraying Analogy* (Cambridge: Cambridge University Press, 1981).

4. One of the reasons that the issue of description has been so overlooked in contemporary moral philosophy may be the assumption that the distinction between fact and value is written into the very nature of moral language. In contrast, Bernard Williams argues that the fact/value distinction has largely been brought to our language rather than being found there. When we actually look at moral language, according to Williams, we find that moral notions are "thicker," since they presume a union of fact and value—e.g., treachery, promise, brutality, and courage. Williams goes on to suggest "the way these

notions are applied is determined by what the world is like (for instance, by how someone has behaved), and yet, at the same time, their application usually involves a certain valuation of the situation, of persons or actions. Moreover, they usually (though not necessarily directly) provide reasons for action" (*Ethics and the Limits of Philosophy* [Cambridge, Massachusetts: Harvard University Press, 1985], pp. 129–130). Julius Kovesi's *Moral Notions* (London: Routledge and Kegan Paul, 1967) continues to be unfairly ignored for consideration of these questions.

5. John Howard Yoder, *The Priestly Kingdom: Social Ethics as Gospel* (Notre Dame: University of Notre Dame, 1984), p. 21. Further references to this chapter will appear in the text.

6. Guy Franklin Hershberger, *The Way of the Cross in Human Relations* (Scottdale, Pennsylvania: Herald Press, 1958), p. 318.

7. I owe this way of putting the matter to John Howard Yoder's informal paper "Possible New Procedures For Use in Areas Where Existing Legal Procedures are Not Compatible With Scriptural Principles." This was prepared for use in helping reformulate the Mennonite stance toward litigation. I am indebted to Yoder for directing me to the background documents of this debate among Mennonites.

8. Hershberger, p. 317.

9. *The Use of the Law: A Summary Statement* (Scottdale, Pennsylvania, 1982). This is the printed statement that was adopted by the Mennonite Church General Assembly in Bowling Green, Ohio, August 11–16, 1981. The document is introduced by Ivan Kauffmann who notes that the issue of the Christian use of the law has been an issue since the early 1950s. Many Mennonites feeling alone as they worked to be faithful to Christ in the midst of business looked for direction. In response, the Mennonite Auto Aid sponsored a study of litigation from 1959 to 1965. That study, along with a conference on the issue, drew no conclusions. In 1976, a task force was appointed by the general board, which resulted in the 1981 statement. I have purposely drawn on a church-related document rather than the reflection of a single individual since too often we associate rationality with the work of individuals. The traditional anonymity of Catholic moral theologians is a morally significant sign that their task was fundamentally communally determined.

The Use of the Law is not paginated, but since it is only twelve pages long I think no one will have trouble finding my references.

10. For an interesting contrast see James Gustafson's *Ethics from a Theocentric Perspective* (Chicago: University of Chicago Press, 1981), pp. 333ff. Many of Gustafson's analyses of the elements of discernment, such as evaluative description of circumstance, the significance of space and time, and intuition, are compatible with the process the Mennonites use. What is missing, however, is any sense of the importance of actual exchange of views within a concrete congregation.

11. *The Use of the Law* notes "when members are part of large or corporate entities involved in litigation, the local congregation might not be an adequate source for counsel. In such instances the individual member and the congregation may well seek help from the conference to identify counsel and help in the situation, which would usually include business and professional peers in the church. Managers or business enterprises generally have not had the benefit of direct church support. Effort should be made in the various areas of the church to see that adequate counsel is available to all who desire such counsel."

12. Williams, *Ethics and the Limits of Philosophy*, p. 10.

13. I suspect one of the reasons for this is the philosopher's concern to avoid relativism. For example, Williams notes "the trouble with casuistry, if it is seen as the basic process of ethical thought, is not so much its misuse as the obvious fact that the repertory of substantive ethical concepts differs between cultures, changes over time, and is open to criticism. If casuistry, applied to a given local set of concepts, is to be the central process of ethical thought, it needs more explanation. It has to claim that there are preferred ethical categories that are not purely local. They may be said to come from a theory of human nature; they may be said to be given by divine command or revelation; in this form, if it

is not combined with the grounding in human nature, the explanation will not lead us anywhere except into what Spinoza called 'the asylum of ignorance.' An exponent of the casuistical method could perhaps fall back simply on the idea that the categories we prefer are the ones we have inherited. This has the merit of facing an important truth, but it will not be able to face it in truth unless more is said about ways in which those categories might be criticized" (pp. 96–97). I hope the analysis I have provided of a community committed to reconciliation necessarily generates such criticism.

14. Williams, *Ethics and the Limits of Philosophy*, p. 18. Elsewhere Williams rightly suggests "the dispositions help to form the character of an agent who has them, and they will do the job the theory has given them only if the agent does not see his character purely instrumentally, but sees the world from the point of view of that character. Moreover, the dispositions require the agent to see other things in a noninstrumental way. They are dispositions not simply of action, but of feeling and judgment, and they are expressed precisely in ascribing intrinsic and not instrumental value to such things as truthtelling, loyalty, and so on" (p. 108).

15. For a similar claim, see Williams, *Ethics and the Limits of Philosophy*, p. 117.

PEACEMAKING

The Virtue of the Church

If your brother sins against you, go and tell him his fault, between you and him alone. If he listens to you, you have gained a brother. But if he does not listen, take one or two others along with you, that every word may be confirmed by the evidence of two or three witnesses. If he refuses to listen to them, tell it to the church; and if he refuses to listen even to the church, let him be to you as a Gentile and a tax collector. Truly, I say to you whatever you bind on earth shall be bound in heaven, and whatever you loose on earth shall be loosed in heaven. Again I say to you, if two of you agree on earth about anything they ask, it will be done for them by my Father in heaven. For where two or three are gathered in my name, there am I in the midst of them. Then Peter came up and said to him, "Lord, how often shall my brother sin against me, and I forgive him? As many as seven times?" Jesus said to him, "I do not say to you seven times, but seventy times seven."

Matthew 18:15–22

This is surely a strange text to begin an article on peacemaking as a virtue. The text does not seem to be about peacemaking but about conflict making. It does not say if you have a grievance you might think about confronting the one you believe has wronged you. The text is much stronger than that. It says if you have a grievance you must, you are obligated to, confront the one you believe has sinned against you. You cannot overlook a fault on the presumption that it is better not to disturb the peace. Rather, you must risk stirring the waters, causing disorder, rather than overlook the sin.

But on what possible grounds could Christians, people supposedly of peace, be urged actively to confront one another? It seems out of character for Jesus to urge us to do so, and out of character for the Christian

89

community to follow such an admonition. Yet I want to suggest that we will understand peacemaking as a virtue only when we see that such confrontation is at the heart of what it means to be a peacemaker. Even more important, however, I think that by attending to this passage we will be able to see how peacemaking, as well as any virtue, is correlative to a community's practices.

This is a crucial issue if we are to appreciate peacemaking as a virtue. It is interesting to note how seldom peacemaking is treated as a virtue. Courage, temperance, and even humility are usually acknowledged as virtues much more readily than is peacemaking. For many, peacemaking may sound like a "good thing," but they would be hesitant to call it a virtue. Peacemaking is usually seen more as a matter of political strategy than a disposition forming the self. Some people may even be peaceful, but that hardly seems a virtue.

Why do we seem reticent to think of peacemaking as a virtue? I suspect it is because we think of virtues as personal characteristics that everyone should possess irrespective of their membership in any specific community. But, as I hope to show, such an understanding of virtue is far too limited, if not an outright mistake. For as Aristotle argues, some virtues, such as justice and friendship, are correlative to certain kinds of relations and cannot exist without those relations being valued by a community.[1] Peacemaking is that sort of virtue insofar as the church believes that peace (and a very particular kind of peace at that) is an essential characteristic of its nature.

As important as understanding why we rightly consider peacemaking a virtue is how we understand what kind of activity it is. It is in this context that the passage from Matthew is so important for helping us understand peacemaking as a virtue. Normally we tend to think of peacemaking as the resolution of conflict rather than the encouragement of conflict. That such is the case, I suspect, is also one of the reasons that peacemaking, even if it is understood as a virtue, is not really all that appealing. Have you ever known anyone, yourself included, who would rush out to see a movie or play about peace?

We say we want peace, but in fact we know we love conflict and even war. Indeed, I suspect that one of the deepest challenges for those of us who call ourselves pacifists is that on the whole peace just does not seem very interesting to most people. We may all say that we want peace, but I suspect that most of us would be deeply upset if we got it. We want to work for peace, we like the struggle for peace, but the idea that peace might actually be achieved would actually scare us to death. For we associate peace with rest, but we fear that rest without conflict is but

90

another name for death. We thus pray like Augustine to give us peace — but not yet.

We simply have to admit that for most of us peace is boring. Of course, in the midst of terrible turmoil we may well think we could stand a bit of boredom, but it is interesting how often people look back on past "troubles" nostalgically. Life needs movement, which most of us believe, rightly or wrongly, entails conflict. Therefore, peacemaking for most of us appears a bit like Bernard Shaw's views of heaven — namely that on reflection he thought he preferred hell, since at least hell promised to contain some interesting people.

But this text from Matthew puts the issue of peacemaking in quite a different light. As I noted above, Jesus does not suggest that if you have a grievance against someone in the community it might be a good idea for you to "try to work it out." Rather, he says that you must go and speak to the one whom you believe has sinned against you. Such a speaking, of course, may well involve nothing less than confrontation. You must do it first alone, but if reconciliation does not take place then you must "go public," taking witnesses with you. If that still is not sufficient, you must take the matter before the whole church.

Our first reaction to this text is to think that surely this procedure is far too extreme for most of our petty conflicts. I may get angry at someone, but if I wait I discover that I will get over it. Moreover, who wants to appear like someone who is too easily offended? No one likes people who tend to make mountains out of molehills, especially when they claim to be doing so only because of the "principle involved." Even more important, most of us learn that time heals all wounds, and thus we are better off waiting for some conflicts to die through the passage of time.

Yet Jesus seems to have been working with a completely different set of presuppositions about what is necessary to be a community of peace and peacemaking. It seems that peace is not the name of the absence of conflict, but rather peacemaking is that quality of life and practices engendered by a community that knows it lives as a forgiven people. Such a community cannot afford to "overlook" one another's sins because they have learned that such sins are a threat to being a community of peace.

The essential presupposition of peacemaking as an activity among Christians is our common belief that we have been made part of a community in which people no longer regard their lives as their own. We are not permitted to harbor our grievances as "ours." When we think our brother or sister has sinned against us, such an affront is not just against us but against the whole community. A community established as peaceful cannot afford to let us relish our sense of being wronged without exposing that wrong in the hopes of reconciliation. We must learn to see wrongs as "personal," because we are part of a community where the "personal" is crucial to the common good.

It is an unpleasant fact, however, that most of our lives are governed more by our hates and dislikes than by our loves. I seldom know what I really want, but I know what or whom I deeply dislike and even hate. It may be painful to be wronged, but at least such wrongs give me a history of resentments that, in fact, constitute who I am. How would I know who I am if I did not have my enemies?

It seems our enemies are exactly who Jesus is forcing us to confront. For he tells us that we cannot cherish our wrongs. Rather, we are commanded to engage in the difficult task of confronting those whom we believe have sinned against us. Such confrontation is indeed hard because it makes us as vulnerable as the one we confront. The process of confrontation means that we may well discover that we have been mistaken about our being wronged. Still more troubling, it means that even if we have been wronged, by confronting our brother or sister we will have to envision the possibility that, like Jonah, he or she may repent and we will therefore have to be reconciled. We will be forced to lose the subject of our hatred.

From this perspective peacemaking is anything but boring. Rather, it is the most demanding of tasks. One of the interesting aspects of this passage in Matthew is it assumes that the Christian community will involve conflict and wrongs. The question is not whether such conflict can be eliminated but rather how we are to deal with the conflict. Conflict is not to be ignored or denied, but rather conflict, which may involve sins, is to be forced into the open. That we are to do so must surely be because the peace that Jesus brings is not a peace of rest but rather a peace of truth. Just as love without truth cannot help but be accursed, so peace without truthfulness cannot help but be deadly. In short, peace keeping is that virtue of the Christian community that is required if the church is to be a community of people at peace with one another in truth.

The truth seems to be about the last thing we want to know about ourselves. We may say that the truth saves, but in fact we know that any truth worth knowing is as disturbing as it is fulfilling. Surely that is why Jesus is so insistent that those who would follow him cannot simply let sins go unchallenged. For when we fail to challenge sinners, we in fact abandon them to their sin. We show we care little for them by our unwillingness to engage in the hard work of establishing a truthful peace.

That the church is such a community of truthful peace depends on it being a community of the forgiven. As the text from Matthew notes, Peter realized that Jesus' command that we confront the sinner is not an easy one. For such confrontation is based on the presupposition that forgiveness is also to be offered. But how often, Peter asks, can forgiveness be offered—seven times? We cannot help but be sympathetic with Peter's question, for it just seems to be against good sense to be ready to offer forgiveness. What kind of community would ever be sustained on the presupposition that forgiveness is always available?

Yet there seems to be no limit to forgiveness, as Jesus elaborates his response to Peter by telling the story of the servant who, having been forgiven his debt, refuses to forgive a fellow servant his debt. The lord of the unforgiving servant, on being told of his servant's behavior, threw him in jail until he paid his debt. And so, we are told, our "heavenly Father will do to every one of you, if you do not forgive your brother from your heart." (Matthew 18:35) What it seems we must remember, if we are to be peacemakers capable of confronting one another with our sins, is that we are forgiven and we are part of a community of the forgiven. Our ability to be truthful peacemakers depends on our learning that we owe our lives to God's unrelenting forgiveness.

The forgiveness that makes peacemaking possible, moreover, does not mean that judgment is withheld. The question is not whether we should hold one another accountable but what is the basis for doing so and how is it to be done. To be sinned against or to know we have sinned requires that we have a language and correlative habit that makes it possible to know what it is to be a sinner. Only on such a basis do we have the capacity to avoid arbitrariness of judgment as we learn to see our relations with one another as part of a continuing tradition of discourse which helps us serve a common good. That good, at least among Christians, is to be a community of the forgiven empowered to witness to God's kingdom of peace wrought through Jesus of Nazareth.

We, therefore, do not confront one another from a position of self-righteousness; we must come to the other as one who has been forgiven. Such a perspective, I think, throws quite a different light on this passage from that which is often given it. Too often it is assumed that this text legitimates our confrontation with the brother or sister on the assumption that we have power over the brother because we have been wronged and thus can decide to forgive. Forgiveness from such a position is but another form of power, since it assumes that one is in a superior position. But the whole point of this text is that we confront one another not as forgivers, not as those who use forgiveness as power, but first and

93

foremost as people who have learned the truth about ourselves—namely, that we are all people who need to be and have been forgiven.

That is why we must and can confront one another as sinners, because we understand ourselves to share with the other our having been forgiven. We thus share a common history of forgiveness and repentance which makes our willingness to confront one another a process of peace rather than simply another way to continue conflict. That is why those who refuse to listen must be treated as a Gentile or tax collector, for they are acting like those who have not learned that they have been forgiven. To act like one not needing forgiveness is to act against the very basis of this community as a community of peacemaking. That is why they must be excluded: they must learn that they are not peacemakers insofar as they refuse to live as the forgiven. From such a perspective there is no more violent act than the unwillingness to accept reconciliation freely and honestly offered. But the truth is that few of us are willing to be so reconciled.

From this perspective, we should not be surprised if peacemakers and peacemaking appear anything but peaceful. Moreover, if the church is to be a community of peace in a world at war, it cannot help but be a community that confronts the world in uncompromising manner. The task of peacemaking cannot ignore real wrongs, past or present. The peace that the world knows too often is but order built on forgetfulness, but that is not the peace of the church, which is built on forgiveness. No genuine peace can come from simply forgetting past wrongs, but rather must come by encompassing those wrongs in a history of forgiveness. Those peacemakers, however, who insist on reminding us of our past sins cannot help but often appear as troublemakers.

This is particularly true when so often the wrongs that we must remember are those that no amount of effort or goodwill can make right. No matter how hard Christians work against anti-Semitism, there is finally nothing that can be done to make "right" the terror of the Holocaust. If there is to be a reconciliation between Christians and Jews, it cannot come through forgetting such a terrible wrong but by learning to face that history as a forgiven people.

This is but to remind us that peacemaking as a virtue has a peculiar stake in the temporal. Peace, as well as forgiveness, must take place in time. Disembodied beings cannot know peace; only beings who know themselves as timeful are capable of being at peace. As we are told in Ephesians, the relation between Israel and the Gentiles has not been resolved by some temporal decree, but rather "now in Christ Jesus you who once were far off have been brought near in the blood of Christ. For he is our peace, who has made us both one, and has broken down the dividing wall of hostility, by abolishing in his flesh the law of commandments and ordinances, that he might create in himself one new man in the place of the two, so making peace, and might reconcile us both to God in one body through the cross, thereby bringing the hostility to an end. And he came and preached peace to you who were far off and peace to those who were near; for through him we both have access in one Spirit to the Father" (Ephesians 2:13–18).

Peacemaking among Christians, therefore, is not simply one activity among others but rather is the very form of the church insofar as the church is the form of the one who "is our peace." Peacemaking is the form of our relations in the church as we seek to be in unity with one another, which at least means that we begin to share a common history. Such unity is not that built on shallow optimism that we can get along if we respect one another's differences. Rather, it is a unity that profoundly acknowledges our differences because we have learned that those differences are not accidental to our being a truthful people—even when they require us to confront one another as those who have wronged us.

If peacemaking as a virtue is intrinsic to the nature of the church, what are we to say about those without the church? First, I think we must say that it is the task of the church to confront and challenge the false peace of the world which is too often built more on power than truth. To challenge the world's sense of peace may well be dangerous, because often when sham peace is exposed it threatens to become violent. The church, however, cannot be less truthful with the world than it is expected to be with itself. If we are less truthful we have no peace to offer to the world.

Secondly, Christians are prohibited from ever despairing of the peace possible in the world. We know that as God's creatures we are not naturally violent nor are our institutions unavoidably violent. As God's people we have been created for peace. Rather, what we must do is to help the world find the habits of peace whose absence so often makes violence seem like the only alternative. Peacemaking as a virtue is an act of imagination built on long habits of the resolution of differences. The great problem in the world is that our imagination has been stilled, since it has not made a practice of confronting wrongs so that violence might be avoided. In truth, we must say that the church has too often failed the world by its failure to witness in our own life the kind of conflict necessary to be a community of peace. Without an example of a peacemaking community, the world has no alternative but to use violence as the means to settle disputes.

I have tried to show how peacekeeping as a virtue is community specific—that is, how it is an activity intrinsic to the nature of the church. Yet the fact that peacekeeping is community specific does not mean it ought to be community restrictive.[2] The "brother" referred to in Matthew is no doubt a member of the Christian community, but the Matthean community is also one that understood it was to go among the nations to witness to God's peace. Therefore, the habits of peacekeeping acquired in the church are no less relevant when the church confronts those not part of our community and who may even threaten or wrong our community. For it is our belief that God is no less present in our enemy calling us to find the means of reconciliation.

If the tack I have taken is close to being right, then I think it puts pacifism into a different perspective from normal.[3] For pacifism is often associated with being passive in the face of wrong. As a result some even suggest that pacifism is immoral insofar as the pacifist suffers wrong and as a result fails to fulfill the obligation to the brother by resisting his injustice. But peacemaking is not a passive response; rather, it is an active way to resist injustice by confronting the wrongdoer with the offer of reconciliation. Such reconciliation is not cheap, however, since no reconciliation is possible unless the wrong is confronted and acknowledged.

Contrary to usual stereotypes, this means that peacekeepers, rather than withdraw from politics, must be the most political of animals. Peacekeeping requires the development of the processes and institutions that make possible confrontation and resolution of differences so that violence can be avoided. The problem with politics, at least as politics is currently understood, is not that it involves compromises but that it so little believes in truth. As a result, it becomes but a form of coercion without due acknowledgment that it is so. In such a situation the church can be a peacemaker by being the most political of institutions.

No doubt peacemaking, as I have tried to depict it, is a demanding business. I think it is impossible to sustain it if it is thought to be a virtue of heroic individuals. Rather, peacemaking must be a virtue of a whole community, so that the kind of support and care necessary to sustain peacemaking as an ongoing task will be forthcoming. As Christians, however, we cannot help but rejoice that God has called us to be peacemakers, for what could possibly be a more joyful and exciting task than to be a part of God's peace.

Peacemaking

NOTES

1. Aristotle, in truth, is a bit unsure if friendship is a virtue. He says it either is a virtue or at least "involves virtue." The reason he is hesitant is that he has no conceptual means to say how a virtue can be a quality of a relation. This remains a difficult issue worth considerable reflection, but I have refrained from pursuing it in this essay.

2. I am indebted to Mr. Greg Jones for this helpful way of putting the matter. I also owe Dr. Harmon Smith much for his painful but truthful critique of an earlier draft of this essay.

3. For a further development of this point see my "Pacifism: Some Philosophical Considerations," *Faith and Philosophy*, 2, 2 (April, 1985), pp. 99–104.

II
THE MINISTRY OF THE CHURCH

THE GESTURE OF A TRUTHFUL STORY

1. On "Religious Education"

I worry about the idea that religious education is some special activity separated from the total life of the church. When that happens, it makes it appear that what the church does in its worship is something different from what it does in its education. I would contend that everything the church is and does is "religious education."[1] Put more strongly, the church does not "do" religious education at all. Rather, the church is a form of education that is religious. Moreover, if that is the case, then I think there is a very close relation between Christian education and social ethics – at least if how I understand social ethics is close to being right. Such an assertion is by no means clear, nor are its implications immediately apparent. I will try to unravel that claim by analyzing first a similar contention about Christian social ethics – namely, that the church does not *have* a social ethic but rather *is* a social ethic.[2]

2. The Church Is a Social Ethic

The claim that the church is a social ethic is an attempt to remind us that the church is the place where the story of God is enacted, told, and heard. Christian social ethics is not first of all principles or policies for social action but rather the story of God's calling of Israel and of the life of Jesus. That story requires the formation of a corresponding community which has learned to live in a way that makes it possible for them to hear that story. The church does not have a social ethic but is a social ethic, then, insofar as it is a community that can clearly be distinguished from the world. The world is not a community and has no such story, since it is based on the assumption that human beings, not God, rule history.

101

Therefore, the first social task of the church is to help the world know that it is the world. The distinction between world and the church is not a distinction between nature and grace. It is, instead, a distinction that denotes "the basic personal postures of men, some of whom confess and others of whom do not confess that Jesus Christ is Lord. The distinction between church and the world is not something that God has imposed upon the world by prior metaphysical definition, nor is it only something which timid or pharisaical Christians have built up around themselves. It is all of that in creation that has taken the freedom not yet to believe."[3]

The fact that the church is separated from the world is not meant to underwrite an ethic of self-righteousness on the part of the church. Both church and world remain under the judgment of the Kingdom of God. Indeed, we must remember that the church is but the earnest of the Kingdom. Those of us who attempt to live faithful to that Kingdom are acutely aware how deeply our lives remain held to and by the world. But this cannot be an excuse for acting as if there were no difference between us and the world. For if we use our sin to deny our peculiar task as Christians and as members of the church, we are unfaithful both to the Kingdom and to ourselves—and most importantly to the world itself.

Moreover, when we deny the distinctive task of the church, we implicitly deny the particularity of the narrative that makes us what we are in the first place. As Christians, we are not, after all, called to be morally good but rather to be faithful to the story that we claim is truthful to the very character of reality—which is that we are creatures of a gracious God who asks nothing less of us than faithful service to God's Kingdom. In short, we are people who know who is in control. What it means to be Christian, therefore, is that we are a people who affirm that we have come to find our true destiny only by locating our lives within the story of God. The church is the lively argument, extended over centuries and occasioned by the stories of God's calling of Israel and of the life and death of Jesus Christ, to which we are invited to contribute by learning to live faithful to those stories. It is the astounding claim of Christians that through this particular man's story, we discover our true selves and thus are made part of God's very life. We become part of God's story by finding our lives within that story.

For the church to be, rather than to have, a social ethic means that it must be a community where the truth is lived and spoken. The story that forms the church is, as I have suggested, a reality-making claim that tells us the truth about the world and ourselves. Such truth is indeed hard. It means that we cannot know the truth until we have been transformed by the story. We cannot know Jesus without becoming his disciples.

102

There is, therefore, an unavoidably self-involving character to Christian convictions. They require that our very selves be transformed if we are to face the truth that we are sinners, yet saved.

A community of such people cannot help but be a social ethic, since it must stand in sharp contrast to the world which would have us build our relations on distortions and denials. The world is where the truth is not spoken for fear such truth might destroy what fragile order and justice we have been able to achieve. But the church, which claims to be constituted by a people who have no fear of the truth, must be a polity where the truth is spoken, even if such truth risks pain and threatens disorder. The church is thus a polity that takes as its constitution a story whose truth creates a people who love honestly because they have the confidence that such love binds their lives to God's very character.

Such a community cannot help but stand in sharp contrast to the world. A people formed in the likeness of God cannot be anything less than a community of character. That is, it is a community which takes as its task the initiation of people into the story in a manner that forms and shapes their lives in a decisive and distinctive way. Put bluntly, the church is in the world to mark us. The church, therefore, aims not at autonomy but at faithfulness. We believe that it is only as we learn to be faithful that we have the ability to be free. Freedom, contrary to much contemporary thought, consists not in having no story but rather comes only through being trained and acquiring the skills of a truthful story.

That is why the church, in contrast to many communities, knows that the only way to learn to be faithful is through initiation by a master. Most of contemporary morality, in both its philosophical and popular expressions, assumes that the moral life is an achievement which is open to anyone. On such a view of the moral life, what is required is not a master but simply the ability to make well-reasoned decisions. In contrast, the church knows that the life of faithfulness is not easily acquired but involves those skills that can be learned only through apprenticeship to a master. Living morally is not simply holding the right principles; it involves nothing less than learning to desire the right things rightly. Such desiring is not so much a matter of choice as it is the slow training of our vision through learning to pay attention to the insignificant. Such attention is gained only as we have the story mediated to us by masters who have learned what the story says by learning how difficult it is to hear it. In short, the church is the group of people capable of engendering and recognizing saints.

To be able to do that is no small feat. Saints cannot exist without a community, as they require, like all of us, nurturance by a people who, while often unfaithful, preserve the habits necessary to learn the story of God. Moreover, such a community must have the skills of discernment that make its members capable of recognizing the saints in their midst. Recognizing the saints, especially while they are still alive, is no easy task either, for by their very nature saints remind us how unfaithful we have been to the story that has formed us.

3. The Church as a Community of Virtue

To be a community capable of engendering as well as of recognizing the saints requires that we be a people formed by the virtues of hope and patience. These are the virtues, the habits, crucial to learning well the story of God. To learn that story means we must desire nothing less than the accomplishment of God's rule, the Kingdom, over all nations and peoples. That rule is nothing less than the establishment of peace between ourselves and God, from which we learn how to be peaceful in ourselves and with one another. Because we have tasted this peace, because we have found how marvelous it is to have violence routed out of our souls, is why we so desperately desire it for all. We know that God's peace is not easily made one's own. But we have confidence that if we are faithful to God's Kingdom, God will use our faithfulness to realize this Kingdom for all.

Just to the extent that we have been taught to hope, we must also be patient. God does not will that the Kingdom be accomplished through coercion or violence. In the cross, we see how the Kingdom will come into the world, and we are charged to be nothing less than a cruciform people. We must, then, learn to wait as we seek to manifest to the world God's peace which comes into our lives by no other means than the power of that truth itself. Such waiting is painful indeed in a world as unjust and violent as ours. But we believe it justified, since we have been promised that God will use our waiting for the complete triumph of the Kingdom. Moreover, patience is required because at least part of what it means for the church to be, rather than to have, a social ethic involves a rethinking about what is meant by social ethics. Too often, in an effort to appear socially relevant, the church has accepted the world's agenda about what "real" politics involves. Thus, calls for us to serve the world responsibly have too often resulted in the church simply saying to the world what the world already knows. We thereby end up trying to secure a "justice" that is only the continuation of some people's domination over others.

In contrast, I am suggesting we must be a patient people, as well as a courageous people, who have the skills to think through the current illusions about social justice and peace. We must be the kind of community that can draw on the character of convictions that expose the sentimentalities of the world—not the least of which is the assumption that nation-states have the right to qualify our loyalty as members of the church. It takes a patient as well as courageous people to manifest that the unity of God's eschatological meal is the only true internationalism.

> [Such a meal] posits and proclaims a unification of mankind whose basis is not some as yet unachieved restructuring of political sovereignties but an already achieved transformation of vision and community. That all mankind is one cannot be demonstrated empirically nor can it be brought about by political engineering. That all mankind is one must first be affirmed as a theological proclamation. Only then is the engineering and structuring which are needed to reflect it even conceivable. It could just as well be said that Christian internationalism is the true unity which the servant church must let be restored.[4]

Nor must we forget that the most embarrassing divisions in the church are not between Catholic and Protestant, U.C.C. and Methodist, Presbyterian and Church of Christ, liberal and conservative, but among social and economic classes and between races and nationalities. Such divisions give lie to the fact that we are one people rooted in the God who has called us into the Kingdom inaugurated by Jesus' life and death. Thus, the first concern of any Christian social ethic must be with the fellowship of the church. We must be a community with the patience, amid the division and hatreds of this world, to take the time to nurture friendships, to serve the neighbor, and to give and receive the thousand small acts of care which ultimately are the heart blood of the Kingdom. That we must take the time to help the neighbor in need, no matter how insignificant that neighbor or his or her need is from the perspective of the world, is but a sign that we recognize that we are called not to make history come out right but to be faithful to the kind of care we have seen revealed in God's Kingdom.

In this respect, the church as a social ethic must take its lead from those like Mother Teresa. From a perspective that would associate the church's social task with effectiveness, Mother Teresa is a deeply immoral woman. She takes the time to hold the hand of a dying leprosy victim when she could be raising money in Europe and America for the starving in India. Yet, she sits holding the hand of a dying person—doing that while surrounded by unbelievable suffering and injustice—because she knows that by exactly such care God will have the Kingdom come. And she knows she can do so because she does not seek to be like the powerful to help the poor and dying. She has learned instead that power derives from being faithful to God's Kingdom of the poor.

4. Politics as Gesture

This, surely, is not the word we want to hear today. We want a word that puts the church on the right side for a change—the side for political change and justice. This news I bring, therefore, seems more bad than good. If being Christian does not put us where the action is, if being Christian does not put us on the side of the progressive forces in this or any other society, then I suspect many of us would be a good deal less happy about being Christian. The claim that the church is, rather than has, a social ethic cannot help but appear to many as a dangerous withdrawal of the church back into a self-righteous pietism which ignores the social agony of the world. At best, such a Christian social ethic is but a gesture; at worst, it is a failure of Christians to face responsibly the complexity of the social problems confronting us in these troubled times.

I am ready to concede that the church and Christian social ethics as I have tried to depict it are but gestures, but I do not think that to be a damaging admission. Nothing in life is more important than gestures, as gestures embody as well as sustain the valuable and significant. Through gestures we create and form our worlds. Through gestures we make contact with one another and share common tasks. Through gestures we communicate and learn from each other the limits of our world.

In this sense, the church is but God's gesture on behalf of the world to create a space and time in which we might have a foretaste of the Kingdom. It is through gestures that we learn the nature of the story that is the very content and constitution of that Kingdom. The way we learn a story, after all, is not just by hearing it. Important and significant stories must be acted out. We must be taught the gestures that help position our bodies and our souls to be able to hear rightly and then retell the story. For example, while we may be able to pray without being prostrate, I think prayer as an institution of the church could no longer be sustained without a people who have first learned to kneel. If one wants to learn to pray, one had better know how to bend the body. Learning the gesture and posture of prayer is inseparable from *learning* to pray. Indeed, the gestures are prayer.

Of course, some of our most important gestures are words. But we can easily overestimate their significance if we assume that words can be separated from the context of their enactment. For example, the Apostles' Creed is not simply a statement of faith which can stand independent of the context in which we affirm it. We must learn to say it in the context of worship if we are to understand how it works to rule our belief and school our faith. The Creed is not some deposit or sum of the story; rather, it is a series of reminders about how best to tell the story that we find enacted through the entire liturgy.

In the same way, baptism and the eucharist stand as crucial gestures which are meant to shape us rightly to hear as well as enact the story. Through baptism and eucharist we are initiated into God's life by our becoming part of Jesus' life, death, and resurrection. These are essential gestures of the church; we cannot be the church without them. They are, in effect, essential reminders for the constitution of God's people in the world. Without them, we are constantly tempted to turn God into an ideology to supply our wants and needs rather than have our needs and wants transformed by God's capturing of our attention through the mundane life of Jesus of Nazareth.

Thus, liturgy is not a motive for social action, it is not a cause to effect. Liturgy is social action. Through liturgy we are shaped to live rightly the story of God, to become part of that story, and are thus able to recognize and respond to the saints in our midst. Once we recognize that the church is a social ethic—an ethic that is, to be sure, but a gesture—then we can appreciate how every activity of the church is a means and an opportunity for faithful service to and for the world. We believe that the gesture that is the church is nothing less than the sign of God's salvation of the world.

5. Christian Education for the Mentally Handicapped

But what does all this have to do with Christian education—and, in particular, the claim that the church does not do religious education but is a form of education that is religious? First of all, it reminds us that religious education has as its first task the initiation of a people into a story. Its task is not to teach us the meaning of that story but to teach us the story. There is no point that can be known separate from the story. There is no experience that we want people to have apart from the story. There are no "moral lessons" that we wish to inculcate other than the story. The story is the point, the story is the experience, and the story is the moral.

The task of religious education, therefore, involves the development of skills to help us make the story ours. Or, perhaps better, the task of religious education is to help remind us of those skills present in the church that are essential for helping us make the story ours. Such reminders may well involve psychological insights into how such skills work, but the former cannot be a substitute for the latter. The content of the story must control where and how the story is to be made our own.

Put simply, religious education is the training in those gestures through which we learn the story of God and God's will for our lives. Religious education is not, therefore, something that is done to make us Christians or something done after we have become Christian. Rather, it is ongoing training in the skills we need to live faithful to the Kingdom that has been initiated in Jesus. That Kingdom is constituted by a story which one never possesses, but rather one which constantly challenges us to be what we are but have not yet become.

The primary task of being educated religiously—or better, Christianly—is not the achievement of better understanding but of faithfulness. Indeed, we can only come to understand through faithfulness, as the story and the corresponding community which form our life ask nothing less from us than our life. The story requires that we learn to live as a people who have been forgiven and thus can be at peace with ourselves as well as with others. We do not learn to be forgiven by intellectually admitting that we often have failed to live up to our own moral ideal, but rather by learning to depend on God as the source of life and the sustainer of our community. What we are asked to be is first and foremost a people who embody and manifest the habits of peace characteristic of a forgiven people—not just those who provide worldviews through which to make sense of the world.

We become faithful just to the extent that we learn to participate in the activities of the people of God we call the church. Therefore, it becomes our duty to be a people who submit to the discipline of the liturgy, as it is there that we are trained with the skills rightly to know the story. We are required to care for one another and to accept the care of others, for it is by learning to be cared for that we learn to care. Such duties may be no more than gestures, but they are the essential gestures that initiate us into the narrative of God's dealing with people.

Yet all this may still sound far too abstract. Therefore, let me try to provide a concrete case which I hope will draw out the implications of the position I have tried to develop. One of the tasks people concerned with religious education have taken for themselves has been the attempt to find ways to help people better understand what it means to be a Christian. This most often has taken the form of encouraging greater study of Scripture and theology, the assumption being that we will be better Christians if we simply know more. While I have nothing against the study of Scripture and theology, I think our emphasis in that respect has tended to make us forget that the way we learn the story is by learning gestures as simple as how to kneel. More troubling, such an emphasis excludes in a decisive manner a whole group of people from participation in God's Kingdom, for what does one do with the mentally handicapped?

The mentally handicapped are a reminder, a test case, for helping us understand how any account of religious education involves assumptions about the nature of Christian convictions and the church. It is certainly true that the mentally handicapped may not be able to read the story; nor are they always able to "understand" the "meaning" of the story; nor do they know what social implications the story may entail. But what they do know is how the story is embodied through the essential gestures of the church. They know the story through the care they receive, and they help the church understand the story that forms such care. Moreover, they learn the story through its enactment as they feel and are formed by the liturgy that places us as characters in God's grand project of the creation and redemption of the world. They know that they, too, have a role in God's people as they faithfully serve God through being formed by a community that is nothing less than the enactment of that story.

It is important that we guard against a possible misunderstanding which may be occasioned by interjecting a discussion of the place of the mentally handicapped in religious education. I am not suggesting that they represent some bottom line or minimum criterion which must be met for religious education. On the contrary, I am suggesting that they offer a clue about the center of the task of Christian education and why it is that the church as such is Christian education. If faithfulness is our task, if it is through faithfulness that we rightly learn to hear, tell, and embody the story, then the mentally handicapped are a crucial and ever-present reminder that such is the case.

Nor am I suggesting that the mentally handicapped are somehow naturally ready to be formed by the story. They are no less sinful than are any of the rest of us. Their desires require training no less than do our desires. Faithfulness is not a natural task for the mentally handicapped or for us. We equally must be trained to face the world, as it is not as we would like it to be. In like measure, we all must learn to accept and give forgiveness, as we also must learn to be people of peace and justice.

However, there is another connection between the argument I have tried to make about the church as a social ethic and the implications of that for religious education and the mentally handicapped. At least part of what it means for the church to be a social ethic is that it has the time to care in an unjust world for those who do not promise to make the world better or more just, or to direct the course of history. The church as God's gesture in and for the world must be the people who manifest our conviction that we do not live on the world's time but in God's time. I suspect we do that best when we show ourselves to be a people who have the time to care for one another even when some of us happen to be mentally handicapped.

It may seem extremely odd to end an essay on Christian education by calling attention to the mentally handicapped. To end this way seems to suggest that our intellectual skills are not as important as we would like to think. I must admit, moreover, that I am not entirely unhappy with such a conclusion—even though it is clearly exaggerated. After all, I am among those who have engaged in that most ambiguous enterprise that we identify as theology. And I believe that the church is less if it does not engender and sponsor the critical activity we call theology.

Yet in an interesting way that activity, and the educational institution necessary to sustain it, draw on the same presuppositions and virtues that sustain the church's commitment to having the mentally handicapped among us. The activity of theology can only be sustained by a community that has learned to wait patiently in a world of suffering and injustice. Theology and theologians do little to make the world better. Rather, our craft involves the slow and painful steps of trying to understand better what it means to be a people formed by the story of God. Let us not forget, then, that as theologians we, no less than the mentally retarded, depend on and serve a church which provides us with the gestures necessary for being the people of God.

NOTES

1. The phrase "religious education" seems to me to be misleading, if for no other reason than that the content of "religious" is vague at best and at worst may involve reductionistic assumptions about positive Christian convictions. Moreover, it is by no means clear how "religious" or "Christian" can qualify "education," since it is not clear whether "education" is coherent enough an activity or idea for us to be able to know what difference any qualifier would make.

2. For a fuller analysis of this claim than I can offer here, see my *A Community of Character: Toward a Constructive Christian Social Ethic* (Notre Dame: University Notre Dame Press, 1981) and *The Peaceable Kingdom: A Primer in Christian Ethics* (Notre Dame: University of Notre Dame Press, 1983).

3. John Howard Yoder, *The Original Revolution* (Scottdale, Pennsylvania: Herald Press, 1971), p. 116.

4. Ibid., p. 130.

110

THE MINISTRY OF A CONGREGATION

Rethinking Christian Ethics for a Church-Centered Seminary

1. The "Church" and Christian Ethics

When Protestants say they do not believe in God, they mean that there is no point to life. This is all there is. When Jews declare unbelief, they mean that God has proved to be an unjust tyrant and in protest they refuse to worship such a God. When Catholics say they no longer believe, they mean that they are angry at the Church. Gross generalizations, to be sure, but like most generalizations they all contain a grain of truth. More important for the subject of this essay, however, is that these generalizations remind us that often those who use the same terms— e.g., unbelief—are in fact talking about quite different matters.

I think such a reminder is important for any attempt to rethink, and perhaps even reform, seminary education in relation to congregational life or, as Dr. Hopewell's letter asked me to do, "to explore how your field of study illuminates the actual culture of a local church and how, in turn, the life of that congregation might condition the manner in which you would teach in an M.Div. program."[1] The problem with such a charge is that on hearing it almost everyone might agree that it is an extremely good idea—indeed, it seems to be an "idea whose time has come." The difficulty, however, is that words like "church" and "congregation" are so vague that our agreement might well mask deeper disagreements if we explore further what we mean by those terms.

For example, it took me some time to understand that when I said "church" around Roman Catholics they understood something quite different from what I intended. Thus, my oft-stated claim, "The church does not have a social ethic; the church is a social ethic," was and is sometimes resisted by Roman Catholics for reasons I at first did not

111

understand. I only began to understand such resistance when I realized that for Roman Catholics "church" suggests a complex hierarchial structure which climaxes in Rome. Therefore, my claim that the church is rather than has social ethic can sound like a form of Papal supremacy to Roman Catholic ears. That I did not understand such was the case is partly because my understanding of "church" is determined by the small, white frame building on the corner of Pleasant Mound Drive and Buckner Boulevard in Pleasant Grove, Texas, where my family went to hear Brother Russell preach and where sometimes after service we had picnics in the graveyard behind the church. That is a long way from Rome.

Of course, theologians are supposed to know better than to let such "pictures" of the church determine their theology. "Church," after all, is not a descriptive term but a theological claim about God's creation of a new people. It is, of course, a theological issue how the doctrine of the church is to be correlated with the empirical church, but such an issue rarely seems to require the theologian to discuss what goes on in any actual community. Dr. Hopewell's letter and this project, however, are clearly meant to counter this kind of abstractness insofar as we are to suggest how our field of study might illumine the life of "a local church," but I am unsure with which local church I should begin.

In the face of this kind of difficulty there is a temptation to use this forum as an opportunity to develop further my argument that the integrity of Christian ethics as a theological discipline requires a recovery of the significance of the church—thereby continuing to use "church" in a vague and unspecified way. If challenged that no one knows of an empirical church that looks like the one for which I am calling, I can give the ultimate theological "out"—namely, my task as a theologian is not to say what the church is but what the church ought to be. Yet I cannot be happy with that response, as it seems finally to entail a distinction between the visible and invisible church which I think is theologically untenable.

In hopes of avoiding the temptation to speak only about an ideal church and in an effort to meet some of Dr. Hopewell's expectations, I am going to tell a story of an event in a congregation's life. I want to be candid, however, about the status of this narrative. I am sure it neither deserves to be regarded as nor do I intend it to be "a case study."[2] I have not tried to do the sociological or historical work required for that kind of enterprise. More important, however, is that my perspective is not sociological or anthropological but normative. The selection of the event as well as the way I have chosen to relate it are meant to serve not just as an example but as an argument for how Christian ethics should be done, as well as for how seminary curriculums should be restructured if the congregation is to be taken seriously. The account I provide is meant to be an example of the kind of church that seminaries should seek to serve, enrich, and, if necessary, help create.

Moreover, the way I tell the story of this church is obviously informed by, as well as being an attempt to test, my constructive theological and ethical interests. For example, one of the criticisms often leveled against my emphasis on the centrality of the church for Christian ethics is that it lacks the realism schooled by the empirical character of the contemporary church, that the kind of church for which I call does not exist and probably cannot exist, given the political and economic realities of our world. I hope to counter such criticisms by the account of the church I provide. The church I describe is real and has acted and is acting very much like what I think the church should be. Another criticism is that my sense of the church is "sectarian," since my "ethic" would finally make it impossible for Christians to participate in the life of our society. While I do not think that "participation" is a good in and of itself, I hope my narrative of how one church acted will help illumine why I think the alternatives of church/sect, withdrawal/participation, are false. So in effect I am going to use this example to try to counter criticism of some of the emphases I have developed in Christian ethics.

While the study I provide certainly reflects as well as develops themes in my own theological agenda, I think the issues I want my example to address are not limited to or peculiar to my own work. For example, twenty years ago Langdon Gilkey noted that the great problem of American denominations is that they are a sect-type "in Christendom, in culture. The separated community has become the community church, related inherently and intentionally to the world. This new form creates the present possibility of the transformation of the world of which it is now fully a part. Unhappily, it is also the source of most of our serious problems. As we have noted, this new form preserves no essential area separate or removed from cultural domination. Unlike the church-type, it has no sacred hierarchy, no holy sacraments, no holy dogmas; and yet, unlike the sects it possesses no separated communal, moral, and intellectual life. Having no separate areas which might be able to preserve the holy *from* the world, and thus be enabled to mediate the holy *to* the world, this church is in fact in imminent danger of being engulfed by the world."[3]

In short, the church in America is dying of its own success. As a "sect" it created a culture which in principle is built upon freedom of religion, but to preserve that "freedom" the church now finds it necessary to underwrite rather than criticize the society which allegedly allows it to be free. Please do not misunderstand me. I am not suggesting that religious freedom is a complete sham. Rather, I am suggesting that the church that is "free" is so because it presents our society with so little threat. This condition, moreover, grips Christians of both the left and the right, as both tend to speak back to our society baptized idealizations first learned from society itself.

As a result, for many working in the field of Christian ethics the church is more of a problem than a resource for constructive theological reflection. Though teachers of seminary ethics are more likely to affirm, at least in principle, a relationship between Christian ethics and participation in the church's ministry, as Dieter Hessel has observed in fact "ethics as taught in seminary still tends to view the ministering congregation as an *addendum* to the 'real subject matter' of biblical and theological ethics, philosophical and political theory, or social policy evaluation. Ethics as a discipline of biblical and systematic theology remains separated from exploration of ministry as a practical theological concern."[4] Thus we have created a situation where the most pressing issue in seminary is how courses in theology and ethics can be made "relevant" to the actual work of the ministry.

Tom Ogletree notes in his 1984 presidential address to the Society of Christian Ethics that most Christian ethicists do not see their task as providing moral guidance for Christian communities and congregations. As a result "of powerful forces, such communities have come to have significance chiefly in the private sector, in relation to families and residential neighborhoods. Given this confinement, they have had little direct access to the great social questions of the day. In many instances they have become places of escape from disturbing realities in modern society, encouraging nostalgic attachments to former ways of life and viewpoints, furnishing moral and religious justifications for advantaged classes, and abandoning the victims of social dislocation in rapidly changing urban environments. To put the point baldly, most of the Christian congregations we know first hand are not disposed to share the passion for social justice which many of us profess. They appear most interested in maintaining secure spaces which can sustain them in their attempts to cope with the daily problems of living."[5]

Yet Ogletree argues that any constructive thinking in Christian ethics in the future will require an ecclesial context. "If we are to be interpreters of Christian ethics in our time, we will have to give fresh attention to the church as a community capable of sustaining a distinctive moral vision of the world."[6] Yet the very community capable of sustaining that vision seems to be exactly what is missing. As a result, Christian ethics increasingly is done as a form of philosophical analysis rather than as a service in and for a concrete people who bear the name "church." That, I think, is the "problem" confronting Christian ethics and why so many who are trained in Christian ethics have difficulty taking the church seriously.

Yet, like Ogletree, I believe we have no choice. We have to take the church seriously if Christian ethics is to have something interesting to say vis-a-vis our society. For, ironically, just to the extent Christian ethicists have abandoned the church because of its "suburban captivity" we have been unable to maintain our theological integrity.[7] My example is meant to address just these issues, for I hope to show that church is much more than a formal abstraction for Christian theological and ethical reflection.

2. An Event in the Life of a Congregation

The event I relate occurred in the most unlikely of settings—namely, an administrative board meeting of a local United Methodist church. No doubt that is one of the last places one might expect anything significant to happen. Moreover, most of the people at the board that night probably thought it was a fairly routine meeting, but as a member of the board I was struck by what happened. Before describing the meeting, however, I need to give some background about the church.

Broadway United Methodist Church is on the south side of South Bend, Indiana, and three blocks off the town's main street, Michigan Avenue. It is one of those sections of town with which we have become all too familiar—namely, a neighborhood that began to "go down" about twenty years ago but has not quite reached bottom. Originally it was an area of town where many of the workers at the Studebaker plant lived. Though the houses were not impressive, they were nice, two-story, comfortable homes. In the early sixties, however, a "city-planning" decision was made in the name of urban renewal, to put a highway through a mainly black area of the city. Having little choice, poor, mostly black people began to rent in the area around Broadway. This process only increased with the closing of Studebaker and the subsequent loss of the neighborhood's economic base. The neighborhood, however, is integrated, with many young couples moving back into the area since it provides reasonably priced housing. There is even a fairly active neighborhood association which has fought the nearby porno-stores as well as the prostitution trade centered on the corner of Broadway and Michigan—three blocks from the church.

Broadway United Methodist Church, taking its name from the street that it fronts, is a fairly large building which witnesses to its once large and lively congregation. It has a long history in South Bend, being first an Evangelical church constituted by German pietists and housed in the center of the city. It became an Evangelical United Brethren Church, moving to the south side of town where the congregation was primarily located.[8] The church building, like its congregation, was solid with no frills, many of the members being craftsmen who worked at Studebaker.

2.1. Acknowledging Where We Are

The congregation now numbers about a hundred with the average Sunday attendance ranging between forty and sixty. The loss of its congregation can be attributed to several factors. The closing of Studebaker certainly resulted in a reduction in the congregation, but many in the church remained extraordinarily loyal. Even if they moved, some continued to drive a good distance to return to the church for worship. However, the integration of the church in the early sixties, coupled with a series of disastrous pastors, came close to sealing the church's doom. No doubt the church was seen as having a very questionable future by denominational executives as, given the surrounding neighborhood, there seemed to be little chance of a recovery.

However, in the early seventies a pastor was appointed to the church who simply refused to believe the church was doomed. He got the appointment because he was coming back into the North Indiana conference from California and was thus given a "problem" church. What was a "problem" for others, however, he saw as an exciting possibility. By visiting the sick, organizing the church, helping develop an urban ministry, the pastor helped the members of the congregation gain a new sense of confidence in their value to one another and, in particular, to the neighborhood. When I joined the church in the late seventies, I found a congregation that was extremely heterogeneous, as there was a broad range in race, ages, economic backgrounds, and education. They were an extraordinary group of committed people determined to do much more than just survive[9]—they were determined to be present as the church on the Southeast side battling any person or institution that hinted they should give up.

The board meeting I will describe took place around 1983. The first item on the agenda involved the question of the leaky roof on our education building. This addition to the church was the last great project of the church before its decline. Since we no longer had enough members to have a full Sunday school, the building was now used primarily by the Head Start program for which the church was the primary administrator. Therefore, we were having to consider repairs on that part of the building that housed a program many churches would have not considered integral to the life of the church.

We had gotten estimates, and it turned out that the repairs would be quite extensive if the job was to be done right. It was going to cost us at least five thousand dollars, a huge sum for our church. The board had a lengthy discussion of the various bids, considering such matters as which company had the best reputation and what kind of roof seemed to promise the most lasting potential. After much discussion the board voted to accept the most expensive bid because it would install the kind of roof that promised to serve the church best over the long run.

To my mind what was remarkable about this discussion and decision was what was not discussed. No one raised the question of whether we ought to rethink making this kind of investment, given our situation in the neighborhood. No one suggested that we might think about saving this money for possible relocation in the suburbs. Rather, it was simply assumed that all the important moral commitments had been made and they were no longer subject to decision. As a result the decision to reroof was made in a businesslike way, with no one noticing that the church was going on record that it would rather be present in this neighborhood than be a success elsewhere.

But the neighborhood noticed. The machinery that pulled up to the church to do the necessary reroofing signaled to the people of the neighborhood that they were not going to be abandoned, at least not by this church. Of course, some might have suggested that we ought not to spend the money on the building but instead buy more food for our food pantry through which we gave food to anyone who asked for it. But that for us was not a real choice, as we first had to maintain the building if we were to show that we were committed to being present as God's people on the Southeast side of South Bend, Indiana.

This point was made quite clear to us a little later. We had been providing a place for "Faith Center," a predominantly black pentecostal church, to worship during the week and on Sunday. We had hoped this might lead to a long-term arrangement, but the pastor of Faith Center was clear that such an arrangement would not be satisfactory. As he pointed out, though we had black members, we were still perceived as a white church and that created problems for them. Secondly, he said that our building was just too shabby for them, noting that how we cared for the building was an indication of how we cared for the church and one another, as well as the neighborhood. Though we thought his judgment a bit harsh about our physical "plant," we knew we could not claim that our church building was without blemish.

2.2. Acknowledging Who We Are

The next agenda item in this board meeting seemed to have more significant ecclesiological implications for those more attuned to straight theological issues. The worship committee had submitted a report which suggested we ought to move to celebrating eucharist every Sunday. This report was the culmination of a long process in the church. Since the church had originally been Evangelical in its background, eucharistic practices had not been frequent. The new pastor, however, was liturgically conscious and had slowly increased the celebration of the eucharist to once a month, then to most feast days, until finally the church was celebrating the eucharist almost thirty times a year. Indeed, one of the things that attracted me to the church was the frequency of the eucharist.

The worship committee had drafted a paper on eucharistic practice in the church and in particular dealt with John Wesley's views about the importance of constant communion. The paper was distributed to the congregation, and a time was set for us to discuss it after service on Sunday. The discussion was very positive about both the paper and our increasing the celebration of eucharist. Issues such as whether too frequent eucharistic practice might destroy its "special nature" were seen as false problems. As was pointed out, the more the eucharist was served the more special it became.

It should be said that the sense of the congregation had been developing over many years through the patient work of the pastor. He was always candid about his hope that the congregation would want to move to every Sunday eucharist, but he never tried to force his will on the congregation. Rather, through his preaching, by taking the eucharist to our many members in nursing homes and those too ill to come to church, and in countless other ways, he helped us see how the eucharist made our care for one another and our communal life intelligible. I am sure that some people put up with the pastor's "high church views" because they had learned to love and respect him as a person who cared, but they also were learning that how he cared had much to do with the importance of the church's common work as determined by the eucharist. It should be noted that they were more than ready to oppose him on matters where they thought he was wrong—thus, in spite of his appeals to tradition there was enough opposition that he was unable to have the front doors of the church painted red. As one member put it, "Oak grain ought to show."

The worship committee's report and suggestion that we ought to move to every Sunday eucharist was thus not an unexpected development. The board discussed the worship committee's report generally in quite favorable terms. Anxious that the church move to every Sunday eucharist and feeling the time was ripe for action, I suggested that the next step should be a vote to accept the report and in the process to move the church to every Sunday eucharist. There was general agreement that this would be appropriate, and we prepared to vote.

We were, therefore, shocked when our pastor, who tended to say little at our meetings, announced in a rather loud voice, "You should not vote on this issue." My immediate reaction, and I suspect it was shared by others, was to think, "Who the hell was he to tell us not to vote?" After all, this was the duly constituted body of the church for governance, and we had every right to vote on this matter. Secondly, I thought the pastor had lost all political sense. Here was a matter, for which he had worked for years, coming to a vote in which he would have clearly won, and he would not let us vote.

He explained, however, that it is the norm of the church that the eucharist be celebrated every Sunday. For numerous reasons we had not been in accordance with the norm, which from his perspective was unfortunate, but that did not give us the right to decide whether or not we would serve the eucharist by vote. As he put it, we no more had the right to decide how often the eucharist would be celebrated than we did to decide whether we would say the Lord's Prayer every Sunday. Both were obligations that as a community we were invited to obey or, rather, they were privileges in which we ought to rejoice.

He then suggested a way he would handle the matter, with the board's approval. He would announce to the church that there was strong sentiment in the church to move to every Sunday eucharist. Recognizing that there might be some who strongly dissented from this policy, he would announce a time for them to come to express their disagreement. If many felt strongly that such a move would make it impossible for them to continue to worship with us then, he said, we might have to wait a little longer. Not to wait, he suggested, would belie the very unity we find in the eucharist. The board agreed to his suggestion. The meeting was called and the issue discussed, with the result that we began having every Sunday eucharist.

2.3. *Acknowledging Whose We Are*

The board meeting ended soon after this decision, and the effects of that discussion as well as the subsequent eucharistic practice resulted in developments which we had not foreseen. It is generally assumed that Protestant churches that "go in for high-church stuff" are often rather well off and more aesthetic than socially aware. That such was not the case at Broadway I have already tried to suggest by noting how the decision to reroof the education building occurred at the same time as the discussion about the eucharist. A further confirmation of the close connection between the congregation's eucharistic practice and its understanding of social mission was exemplified soon after.

About three months after the board meeting the Outreach Committee came to the church with a proposal. I need to make clear that the people on this committee were not "special" in the sense that they had prior theological training. Like most people in the church they were just "folk." The chairman of the committee was an extraordinary lay person who had originally come to the church as a Methodist volunteer to do community service and stayed on, buying a house in the neighborhood. The committee's proposal was not just something he wanted to do; rather, it reflected a consensus the committee had reached by drawing on their common experience.

The Outreach Committee began with our concern about being a church in an area of high unemployment within a city of high unemployment. The planned unemployment the Reagan administration had used to bring down inflation had hit South Bend particularly hard. Soup kitchens had sprung up to feed the poor and unemployed, but somehow the committee felt a soup kitchen, as much good as one might do, was not what we were about. So the committee suggested to the board that as we had slowly learned the significance of sharing a meal together, perhaps we could share a meal with the neighborhood. Such a meal would not be the same as the meal we share when Christ is the host, but at least it expressed the kind of community that that meal has made possible. So they suggested that every Sunday after worship the church have a lunch and invite anyone who would want to come. We, therefore, would not so much feed the hungry as share a meal with them.

The board accepted the Outreach Committee's proposal. The church was divided up into five teams, each taking responsibility to prepare the meal for one Sunday. At first the attendance was rather low, but as word got around we would often have between forty and sixty people at the Sunday lunch. A few who shared our meal might sometimes come to church before the lunch, but we gained no new members from the effort.

Yet that meal has become central to the church's life, as it made clear that we were not simply another social agency that does a little good, but a people called out to witness to God's presence in the world. That presence which comes in the meal we share sustained that church's ability to be present in that neighborhood as a symbol that all was not lost.

3. Christian Ethics and Seminary Education

So ends my story, though there is obviously much I have left out and I have had to resist telling the subsequent history of Broadway.[10] However, telling more of the story would not help me meet the unease no doubt felt by many about what implications such a story might have. Some may find the story interesting enough and at least it seems to have a happy ending, but may wonder what finally is the point of telling such a story. What, if anything, can be made of this one incident in the life of this one rather obscure congregation?

First, I think it makes clear that the disdain many theologians and ethicists have for the "middle-class" church is unjustified. The story I have related is not a fiction. Though I have not described in detail individual members of the congregation or the board, they are real people who work at the phone company, teach school, have babies, care for sick parents, and take the time to come to church and attend meetings. Moreover, neither they nor Broadway are unique or special. What was done there is done in every church, so I believe churches which do not face the immediate challenge of survival can use their strength wisely. The crucial issue is whether the church is willing to trust that God is really present among us, making us his church.

Second, this story challenges some of our most cherished distinctions that have shaped our reflection in Christian ethics. Is the account I have given an example of a church- or sect-type ethic? Or is this an example of the "denomination," so acutely described by Gilkey, trying to recover some sense of its theological integrity? What such a story does, I think, is to remind us what we know but often forget—namely that church, sect, and denomination are not descriptive but ideal types. They are not alternatives with which we are stuck but rather are meant to be heuristic devices which can help us understand better empirical reality. In other words, they are the means to try to help us tell the story of a congregation like Broadway well rather than being alternatives that necessarily determine our only options.

Yet too often I think we let such categories get in the way of how we

121

tell the story. For example, I think it would be a distortion of what was happening at Broadway to say they were acting like sectarians. It is true that they were not trying to develop an ethic sufficient to sustain a civilization, but neither did they understand themselves as "withdrawing" from their social order. Indeed, many in the church understood themselves to be politically "conservative" and would be shocked at any suggestion that they were social radicals. It is also true that they understood that their first task as a church is to be faithful rather than effective. Yet that required them to be concerned about the neighborhood, and that concern meant that they had to care about what was happening in the politics of the city, and so on.[11]

Particularly important in this respect is the extraordinary range of activities in which the members of the church were involved. For example, some gave a great deal of their time to publishing and distributing *The Neighborhood News*. This small paper dealt with the good and bad news of the neighborhood and did much to help everyone have a sense of common purpose. Some spent much time organizing for the church fund-raising events such as bazaars and competitive runs for the local runners. Such activities were not only meant to make money but to attract people to the area who otherwise would have been afraid to venture into that part of the city. Some took the time to attend city council meetings and became involved more deeply in local and state politics. And the list can be extended. What is remarkable, however, is how people in the church appreciated the contribution each was making, realizing that the diversity of activities contributed to what we were as a common people. If the church was "sectarian," it was strangely so.

The sense of how the activities of the members enriched the life of all, however, should not be limited to their social and political involvement. For, as our pastor often reminded us, the church entailed a constant willingness on the part of each of us to share with one another our particular stories. That does not mean that the church required everyone to "spill their guts," but rather the church became the occasion where our individual lives were enriched as we learned to share a history through our common worship. Such a history made it possible for us to appreciate the many and varied paths that brought each of us to be part of Broadway and thus one another. In the process we learned to value our differences as much as we rejoiced in what we had in common.[12]

Yet it may be objected that though all this may be true, these "points" still do not seem to add up to anything substantive for how we understand Christian ethics and/or seminary education. What difference does or should this story make for the role of the theologian? At the very least

I think that it reminds us that one of the essential tasks the theologian-ethicist performs is to help congregations like Broadway appreciate the significance of their common acts. The way I have told the story of the board meeting is not the way most who were at the meeting would have told it. They might not have seen the significance of reroofing the education building in the way I did; they would have not reported and interpreted the pastor's "no" to voting in the way I did. Even though my telling of the story is clearly dependent on my theological training I know that the congregation would find my account helpful. For example, I told the story as we went through the process of securing a new pastor. The story helped remind us who we were as well as helped our new pastor understand who we were.[13]

I am not suggesting that every church needs to have a theologian to help it discover the theological and ethical significance of its everyday activities. Indeed, given the convictions of many contemporary theologians I cannot help but think that that might be disastrous for the church.[14] I suspect it would not be long before churches, like some Indian tribes in America who threw anthropologists out of their communities because the Indians felt that the anthropologists' interpretative frameworks distorted their experience, would, or at least should, throw theologians out for the very much the same reason. Rather, I am suggesting that it is the task of those committed to the theological enterprise to develop the linguistic skills that can help congregations understand better the common but no less theologically significant activities which constitute their lives.

For example, the pastor at Broadway would sometimes tell us that every Sunday, as he looked out at the congregation—which was often quite skimpy—he felt he was looking at a miracle. At first I thought that such language was exaggerated, but the more I thought about it as well as experienced life there Sunday after Sunday, I became convinced that such language was appropriate. For there was no good reason that he or we should expect that anyone would be there, and yet we were there—diverse people who in many ways were essentially strangers yet joined by our determination to worship, convinced that through our presence to one another we were in the presence of God.

As a result I am convinced that no theology or ethic is truthful that does not help people, such as those at Broadway, appreciate the significance of their worship. Indeed, I suspect much of the difficulty of current church life and our corresponding theology is that we have not paid serious attention to how difficult it is rightly to understand the common things we do as Christians—e.g., pray, baptize, eat meals, rejoice at the birth of a child, grieve at illness and death, reroof church buildings, and so on. In the absence of our ability to describe theologically the significance of these activities, we find we misdescribe and distort what we do by the necessity to resort to descriptions and explanations all too readily provided by our culture. Any explanation is to be preferred to no explanation.

This process occurs both at crude and sophisticated levels. For example, when asked why they go to church many say that there they meet the kind of people they really like (people like themselves) or that that is the way the children learn morals. No doubt such explanations are part of the truth, but they may also be formulas for self-deception and lead us to miss the "miracle" that we are there to worship God. At a more sophisticated level we have learned to use sociological and psychological explanations to "understand" the nature of the church. As a result those trained to be ministers in the church are often more adept at sociological accounts of church life than they are at helping their congregations appreciate the fact that it is God who makes their life possible.[15]

I believe that one of the most promising ways to reclaim the integrity of theological language as a working language for a congregation's life is for seminaries to make liturgy the focus of their life. I do not mean simply that seminaries should have more worship services, though if done well that might be helpful. Rather, I mean that the curriculum of the seminary should be determined by and reflect the liturgical life of the church. For example, why should seminaries continue to teach courses in "Old Testament" and "New Testament" as if those were intelligible theological subjects? Liturgically the Scripture functions not as text but canon. Yet in our classes we treat the Scripture primarily as text, and then as those responsible for the training of ministers we are puzzled why Scripture plays so little part in the life of most Protestant congregations. Is it not the case that we must admit, in the classical words of Pogo, that "We have met the enemy and he is us"?

But at least if we recognize such is the case perhaps we can begin to respond creatively to the current malaise in seminary education. It is not as if those who specialize in Scripture are more or less guilty than those of us who work in theology and ethics. For example, I suspect that the very distinction between theology and ethics reflects a failure to take seriously the liturgical life of congregations as central to our educative task. It is perhaps a sign of hope that many are attempting to recover liturgy as central to our theological work or that ethicists are discussing the liturgical shaping of the moral life.[16] But I think we cannot be satisfied with these developments, as too often discussion about the relation of theology and liturgy threatens to be but an attempt by intellectuals to relieve the boredom of the current scholarly paradigms that determine their discipline. As a result I fear it may become but another "interest" of some intellectuals which will have the usual short run at the box office.

That is why my "example" of Broadway is so important. There I saw a congregation formed and disciplined by the liturgy that made possible an extraordinary social witness. That congregation's life belies distinctions between theology and liturgy, ethics and liturgy. The meal they prepare every Sunday for the neighborhood is not the way they express their social ethical commitments in distinction from their liturgical life.[17] Rather, the meal they prepare and liturgical life are for them parts of a single story. The theological task is first and foremost to help us and them understand why that is the case.

Put as directly as I can, the emphasis on "the congregation" or "a congregation" for rethinking seminary education, if it is to be productive, requires that seminary faculties recognize that their legitimacy depends on how well they help Bishops perform their office.[18] The task of the seminary is to train seminarians by telling the many stories of the congregations, past and present, that constitute the church of Jesus Christ—and that is part of the Bishop's task, as the Bishop is the agent of the Church's unity insofar as that office makes it possible for individual congregations to recognize the life they share is also shared by other congregations. I suspect that is why, in spite of appearances to the contrary, New Testament and Church History often provide the most positive long-term help for people in the ministry, for it is there they really learn the many stories of individual congregations through which we learn to be the church.[19] As a result they know there are alternatives to the current stories of the church.

The task of Christian ethics, therefore, is simply the task of theology itself—namely to help the churches share their stories truthfully. Just as the people at Broadway learned that they could and must share their separate stories through their participation in the eucharist, so those of us charged to be theologians continue that task among the many churches. That does not mean that we are "just storytellers," but it does mean that without stories such as that of Broadway all of our scholarship and intellectual skills make little sense.[20]

Appendix

After writing this I thought I should share it with some of the people at Broadway. As a result I received the following letter from a lay member of the church, which is so much better than my essay it is embarrassing, but it at least makes the essay worthwhile. I asked my friend's permission to attach it to the article and he kindly consented. No other comment needs to be made, as it speaks for itself.

Dear Stanley,

Thank you for your letter. As I read it I recall with great fondness your endearing voice and presence. We miss you and we speak of you and Adam whenever good times are recalled.

I'm sorry you haven't found the church to join—sorry mainly for the church that lacks your influence. Don't look for another BCP (Broadway Christian Parish); it is impossible to replace a loved one and I can tell by reading your paper that you do love us. In the years you were with us you helped greatly in making BCP into what it is. Now, if you want a church like Broadway where you are, you will have to help build one as you did here. Please join a church and, for joy or sorrow, take it seriously, my dear Christian ethicist.

Today in South Bend the sun was blinding on 8 inches of new snow and the cold was sharp. There were about 20 of us for worship and at lunch we were joined by about 20 neighborhood people. For the first time that I remember or know about we had a brief fight with more name calling than blows. I often wondered what our reaction would be but beginning with Karen we simply put ourselves between the adversaries and it all soon quieted down and people left. Can you imagine little Karen leading us like that into a situation of real risk? Our minister doesn't eat lunch with us, he was home with his family.

I'm not as good a story teller as you are but the purpose of my story is to tell you that the "minister as leader" model leaves me wanting something else. I would be much happier with the "minister as teacher and example" model. Please don't get my message wrong, I'm not blaming George[21] for not being superman. I can, however, imagine a church where the people themselves adhere more closely to Christian discipline and show greater faithfulness to their narrative than does the minister *and that situation is OK with the people*. In other words the minister-teacher would expect that his people would be the primary leaders in the local church. So, I'm praying that it was very right that we, the people, manage crisis, that we do it in a way consistent with the story, and *normally* without the leadership of a minister. Furthermore, when the minister is present in crisis he would assume an equal role with the people and the people would not necessarily look to *his/her* wisdom to bail *them* out of a hard place. None of this makes any sense administratively, I am suggesting the virtual removal of what constitutes the cornerstone of many a congregation's structure. I want ministers to quit playing superman and quit taking full responsibility for the church as a captain takes responsibility for his ship. The people must minister to the people and learn the skills from the minister. Too often the outward character of the congregation is determined by the minister, a powerful leader, administrator and worker who tries to fill a void left by a vegetating congregation. The divinity school must start training congregations through its graduates. *The school must see its graduates as extensions of the school.* It seems to me that there would be a need for a professional journal published by the school and as free from denominational influence as is humanly possible. The teaching of ministers should not end with graduation.

I have no idea why you would ask me for comment on the subject you are addressing but, as you can see, I can be presumptuous enough to talk about any subject and give lots of advice to anyone without due regard for the disparity of our academic achievements. But, I shall exploit with glee the opportunity. I will trust you to forgive me for wrongly interpreting your ideas and for completely missing the mark for you.

I've taken the liberty to write my comments directly on the copy you sent as I thought that would make them correlate better to your work. I hope you can understand my writing. As you will see, I have but 3 primary areas of concern:

1. I'm worried that ministers will be transformed before congregations. I think you believe ministers can have profound influence on a congregation. But you do state somewhere that you see transformation happening first at the local church level. We are in agreement there. We need ministers who can tolerate congregations as they find them, just as we need lay persons with the same toleration. But the first order of business for both ministers and lay persons would be to have the congregation become active participants in salvation history and encourage others to follow.

2. There is not one activity of the church (BCP) that is crucial to our life together unless it be the Lord's Supper. Of course the soup lunch is different than most of the other ministries because it is done by the people and not by employees. I hope as time goes by the congregation will leave the endless chain of committee meetings and use their time in more activities like the soup lunch. We need leaders like Conrad[22] to make things like that happen. [Isn't he the kind of leader we need? If he were the minister he would be very much *less* effective (I really mean faithful) because he would be engulfed in irrelevant busy work. The thought occurs to me that we might be better off to have our minister work away from the church most of the week.]

3. Please spare me the "good, loving patient leadership" stuff. We need a person who knows what's going on (the story) and, by whatever style, draws us deeper into it. I was amused by your tale of the Parish Board when John would not let us vote on weekly communion. I think the really astonishing thing about the incident was that our good, loving, patient leader threw the Book of Discipline right through the oak grain doors and said "NO YOU DON'T." *And we didn't.* But we, with his leadership, did act more consistent with our story. Let the styles fall where they may; give us people who know what needs to be done and the courage to do it. Can you give us ministers who can lead us away from dependence on their leadership?

I've said enough. I cautiously hope that is some small benefit to you here. I wish you joy in your work wherever it takes you and whatever tasks you are called on to do.

Lovingly,
Dave

NOTES

1. Elsewhere Dr. Hopewell expands on this by suggesting a seminary's need for a "fundamentally revised curriculum, different both in form and focus, that shifts theological education from a clerical to a congregational paradigm. The primary object of the program would be the development of the congregation, not the student. The proposal is not necessarily a plea for more contextual or field education in the curriculum, nor one that advocates a greater proportion of pastoral theology courses. Such measures by themselves do not change a program's fix upon the individual. Instead the proposal seeks an accomplishment deeper than a physical or political association. It aims to join seminary and congregation in a quest for the redemptive community. It lays upon each partner the responsibility, now consigned to the church in general, to pursue the means by which a particular group of human beings gathered in the name and power of Christ in fact work together to fulfill the Christian promise" ("A Congregational Paradigm for Theological Education," *Theological Education*, XXI, 1 [Autumn, 1984], pp. 63–64). This essay was written as part of the Lilly project, begun by Dr. Hopewell before his untimely death, to reform seminary education by making the congregation the subject of seminary curriculum.

2. I have in mind the crossdisciplinary approach found in *Building Effective Ministry: Theory and Practice in the Local Church* (San Francisco: Harper & Row, 1983) edited by Carl S. Dudley. However, I also do not want to be too modest about my use of an example for the position I develop. I suspect one of the reasons that the life of the congregation has been ignored by theologians and in seminary education is a correlate of the prejudice since the Enlightenment against examples for intellectual work. From such a perspective, examples at best are considered anecdotal and cannot have the status of evidence or knowledge. As a result the nature and status of practical knowledge has been ignored, particularly in modern philosophy and theology. To make the congregation a central concern in seminary education, therefore, cannot be but a new pedagogical strategy which requires that we challenge the assumption that theology is from beginning and end a form of practical knowledge.

3. Langdon Gilkey, *How the Church Can Minister to the World Without Losing Itself* (New York: Harper & Row, 1964), pp. 19–20. Gilkey argues that this analysis is true for most American religious groupings, as the various denominations in America have, in spite of different histories, theologies, and governments, come increasingly to resemble one another. Though notable exceptions could be named, I think he is generally right that the ethos of the white American Protestant congregation, irrespective of its formal allegiance, conforms to the denominational type. That is, perhaps, why the attempt to study the place of "a congregation" for seminary education without reference to denominational identity makes descriptive sense—whether it can be justified normatively is quite another matter.

4. Dieter T. Hessel, "Christian Ethics and the Congregation's Social Ministry," *The Annual of the Society of Christian Ethics, 1984*, edited by Larry Rasmussen (Waterloo, Ontario: Council on the Study of Religion, 1984), p. 45. In his article Hessel suggests that though I reassert that the church is a distinct society with an alternative social vision, I am led to "some problematic social policy prescriptions which undergird a particular (conventional?) view of virtue and character." But the whole point of my argument has been that it is quite unconventional for the church to be the kind of society that can encourage the growth of virtue and character.

128

In his "The Revival of Practical Theology?" (*Christian Century*, 101, 4 [February 1–8, 1984]) Don Browning makes a similar charge. Noting that some may be tempted to construe Ed Farley's call in *Theologia* for theology again to become *habitus* and *paideia* in terms of the renewed interest in virtue and character, Browning suggests this would be a mistake. For the emphasis on virtue, according to Browning, lacks the character necessary to sustain the public ministry of the church. He suggests we must "abstract from the Christian story a more identifiable set of principles and procedures which could be used in public debates over the country" (p. 136). Without arguing the point, I think this way of putting the matter cannot help but underwrite the divorce of seminary education, particularly in terms of ethics, from the life of the congregation.

5. Thomas Ogletree, "The Ecclesial Context of Christian Ethics," *The Annual of the Society of Christian Ethics, 1984*, p. 4. There is no question of the descriptive power of Ogletree's observation, but the problem is not simply that congregations have become bastions of middle-class respectability. At least part of the problem is the presumption of the ethicists that we know what are "the great social questions of the day" or that our passion for "social justice" is any less accommodationist than is the middle-class church. At least part of the case for attending to the life of congregations for the development of Christian ethics requires that we attend to the possibility that "attempts to cope with the daily problems of living" is a resource for a recovery of a more radical social stance of the church.

6. Ibid., p. 10.

7. For an account of Christian ethics which develops this point, see my "On Keeping Theological Ethics Theological," *Revisions: Changing Perspectives in Moral Philosophy*, edited by Stanley Hauerwas and Alasdair MacIntyre (Notre Dame: University of Notre Dame Press, 1983), pp. 16–42.

8. However, the church has always had a history of many of the members living a good distance from the church.

9. How I became a member at Broadway is a tale in itself, but I was at least initially attracted by being challenged by the pastor. After I had given a talk at a continuing education seminar for United Methodist clergy of the conference, he had the nerve to ask me (in the bathroom at that) where I went to church. After I reported that I tended to bounce around, he suggested that I certainly did not live out the theological claims I professed. I figured anyone who would challenge me that way could not be all bad. After attending the church for some time and deciding to join, I was, moreover, a bit taken aback when he would not allow me to join the church unless I went through weekly membership classes for six months—from his perspective, I may know a lot about theology but that did not mean I knew enough about what it meant to be member of this church. I learned much.

The way I tell the story may give the impression that the pastor is the central figure in the story of Broadway. That is certainly not the case, as he would be the first to say. In fact, after reading the first draft of this paper, he insisted that I say that he in many ways followed the congregation's lead. For example, the decision to stick it out in the neighborhood was made before his arrival. Indeed, it is not so much that they "made a decision" but rather they were just not the kind of people that give up easily. I regret I lack the space and the skill to depict the character of all the people in the church for each, in their own way, was as important as the pastor.

10. For a fuller account of how narrative might prove illuminating for understanding as well as developing congregational life, see James Hopewell, "The Jovial Church: Narrative in Local Church Life," in *Building Effective Ministry*, pp. 68–83.

11. It may be that my story only confirms Ogletree's observation that Christian ethicists ignore the church because the church, given its relegation to the private sector, no longer has "direct access to the great social questions of the day." Thus, most Christian ethicists tend to relate more to denomination-wide committees or commissions for social justice than to individual churches. Yet it is my contention that there is no greater "social question" for our day than the attempt to create the kind of viable community to which the people at Broadway were committed.

129

12. On a personal level I was pleased that while members of the church took pride in knowing that a theologian from Notre Dame was a member, they nevertheless expected me to wash dishes after the lunch. (Since I could not cook, I had to do something.)

13. One of the issues that I think this stress on the congregation raises is the relation of the congregation to wider church structures. I think it is fair to say that the United Methodist hierarchy of the Northern Indiana conference was not sure how to take Broadway—what does one do with a United Methodist church that serves the eucharist every Sunday? If the focus on the congregation at least envisages some renewal of the congregation, then I think issues of the governmental structure of the wider church in which that congregation exists cannot be avoided. Personally, I have little confidence in church renewal from the top down. The best we can ask, I think, and it is quite a lot, is for denominational hierarchies not to hurt or impede developments at the local level.

14. I think it is an indication of some of the deepest problems of modern theology that theologians tend to be more shaped by their graduate-school training than their ecclesial identification, if they have any. Thus, school designation, that is, whether one is a process thinker or a Barthian, is more determinative of how one works than whether one is Lutheran or Methodist. As a result theologians tend to train ministers to make congregations fit the image of their particular theological allegiances rather than help them respond to the past and present theological resources of the congregation.

15. None of the above is meant to deny the value of sociological, psychological, and general social-scientific accounts of the life of congregations. James Gustafson's *Treasures in Earthen Vessels: The Church as a Human Community* (New York: Harper Brothers, 1961) is still as relevant today as it was when it was written. The issue is the uncritical use of social-scientific paradigms which often, if applied rigorously and consistently, methodologically preclude the theological claims necessary for the church's intelligibility. For two essays that make contributions helpful for recapturing the theological account necessary to understand a congregation's life, see the essays by Joseph Hough and David Pacini in *Building Effective Ministry*. For example, Pacini suggests that behind many social-scientific accounts lies an implicit assumption that life is essentially mechanistic such that life processes take place according to mechanical sequences that admit of predictability. Fascinated with the power for control such a model gives us, we become fascinated with how social mechanisms function and direct our attention away from values, beliefs, and intentions. Moreover, we tend to think such a perspective is inclusive and all-embracing, thus failing to notice the extent to which it is a reflection of our own notion of inclusivity. The use of such mechanistic metaphors in our secular culture, combined with claims of universality, "reflects nothing other than the world view of the middle class, ordered by its penchant for management and its conviction that life processes are to be managed according to standards of predictability and lawlike generalization" ("Professionalism, Breakdown, and Revelation," pp. 146–147). The issue is, therefore, not simply descriptive but normative.

16. Geoffrey Wainwright's *Doxology* (New York: Oxford University Press, 1980) is the most outstanding example of a theologian working in this manner. However, equally significant is Robert Jenson's *Visible Words: The Interpretation and Practice of Christian Sacraments* (Philadelphia: Fortress Press, 1970). Jenson's emphasis on the necessity of God having a body is the heart of the matter.

17. I must now write in the third person since I no longer live in Indiana and can no longer attend at Broadway.

18. Some may think that my reference to Bishops in this context is too ecclesially specific. I debated whether to put the point in more "neutral" language, but I decided against it since I think in fact the point I am making rightly notes one of the crucial bases for the office of Bishop. Of course, I would not deny that a church without bishops may find persons and institutions who do not carry that name but in fact perform the task.

19. Though often presented as an attempt to provide an alternative to a "theological" approach to Scripture, from this perspective the recent development of the "social world" methodology in the study of early Christian literature may in fact be the most interesting

theological development we have had for some time. See, for example, Wayne Meeks' *The First Urban Christians: The Social World of the Apostle Paul* (New Haven: Yale University Press, 1983) and Rowan Greer's *Broken Lights and Mended Lives* (University Park, Pennsylvania: Pennsylvania State University Press, 1986).

20. I am indebted to John Westerhoff, Harmon Smith, Dennis Campbell, Michael Cartwright, Greg Jones, John Smith, and David Koehler for reading an earlier draft of this essay. I wish I would have been able to respond to all their good criticism and suggestions.

21. George was the new minister who stayed for two years. The church now has a minister who is a woman.

22. The Chairman of the Outreach Committee I mentioned in the paper.

CLERICAL CHARACTER

1. The Oddity of "Ministerial Morality"

We live in a time in which we are forced to reconsider matters most of us would like to think have long been settled. Thus, we are now asked to develop an ethic explicitly for the clergy. Such a request surely seems odd, since being a minister and being moral have been thought to go together like horse and carriage. Of course, the morality required of ministers has been assumed to be that required of anyone, it is just "more so" for the ministry. For example, we all know that adultery is wrong, but if a minister is caught in adultery somehow it seems more serious. Or we think that we generally should be kind, but given the competitive world in which we must make a living, we know we cannot always be such, but the minister should always be kind because they have been given permission to opt out of our economic system. Of course, as a result it is alleged they often fail to understand the "real" world.

This traditional view of the morality expected of the clergy is open to serious objection. To expect ministers to be moral, only more so, seems to imply that the validity of the ministry depends on the holiness of the person performing the office. Donatism dies hard, as like most heresies its mutations seem endless. Indeed, the expectations of Protestant congregations about the kind of life their ministers should have is now the natural home of Donatism. It seems the less Protestants appreciate the sacerdotal functions of the ministry it seems the more they expect their clergy to conform to an uncompromising moral ideal. Having little sense that ordination involves any intrinsic character and set of responsibilities, Protestants, it almost seems, find it necessary to find some special role that justifies identifying some as ministers. That role too often turns out to be that clergy are expected to live up to an ideal morality which the laity commends but does not intend to live, or at least finds it cannot live. The minister, and also his family, should live up to the ideal since, after all, someone has to set an example.

This understanding of the morality required of the clergy often becomes a terrible double-bind for those in the ministry. For the clergy are expected to be different—altruistic, infinitely understanding, self-effacing—yet their success often depends on their having a winning personality which suggests that in spite of their being a minister they are really, underneath, just like us. For example in its crude form this double-bind entails that ministers should not use "rough" language, but it is a point in their favor, at least for some members of their congregation, if the minister at times is led to say, "damn." After all, such behavior shows that even the minister is human and thus legitimates our own behavior.

It may be that the concern to develop a ministerial morality is due to the displeasure of some toward the increasing refusal of many clergy to conform to this set of expectations. Many in the ministry find the hypocrisy and, worse, self-deception such a morality engenders is too hard to live for a life time. Better for the clergy and the laity to say what we have known all along—namely, there is no difference between the clergy and anyone else. Some ministers' marriages will fail, some will be ambitious, some will be less than forgiving, some will even be less than honest, especially when their self-interest is involved, but that does not mean they are disqualified from the ministry. Just as one can still be a good lawyer or doctor while being less than morally admirable in other aspects of their life, so one can be a minister in the same manner. What matters is not the kind of persons they are, but whether they can responsibly deliver their professional service.

That we seem caught in such unattractive alternatives is an indication that a discussion of ministerial morality is long overdue. However, I think we will make little headway in understanding the nature of the kind of morality necessary to the ministry if we let the agenda be set by the kind of issues I have discussed above. By responding to the call to develop an ethic for the clergy we can too easily accept a far too limited sense of "ethics." The temptation is to think the task to be the development of a code, similar to that of the medical and legal professions, to guide the training and/or behavior of ministers. I have no wish to deny the usefulness of such codes or to deny such a code might be of some use for the ministry. However, I think such a "legalistic" response would be insufficient for helping us develop a sense of the kind of morality appropriate to the ministry. For the ministry, as well as the law and medicine, in-

134

volves more than questions of what is permissible and impermissible but raises the question of the kind of person that one should be to be a minister. It is not enough, in other words, that those called to the ministry refrain from or do certain things; it is necessary that they be the kind of persons, that they have the character, to sustain them in the ministry.

Such a suggestion, I suspect, will appear to many to be so obvious it is hardly worth mentioning. Yet as is so often the case when we fail properly to appreciate the obvious, we distort our own best insights. For example, I suspect many laity care more about the kind of person their minister is than whether the minister perfectly corresponds to some moral ideal. The problem is not that the laity fail to care about the kind of person the minister is, but too often the kind of person they want their minister to be is not shaped by any appreciation for the office to which the minister is called. For one of the most profound moral challenges that the clergy face in our day is the disparity between the theological definition and the sociological reality of the ministry.

2. The Character of the Ministry and Ministerial Character

These are extremely complex issues which involve questions of the nature of the ministry, the sacraments, and morality. In short I am suggesting that the character of those serving in the ministry should be determined by the character of the office to which they have been ordained. In other words, there is a connection between the sacramental character of the ministry and the moral character of those who serve in the ministry. Part of our current difficulty is the failure of laity and minister alike to appreciate that those who have been called to the ministry are or at least should be made different by that calling.[1] Put simply, ordination bestows on the ministers a power that not all in the church possess—e.g., they alone can preside at the eucharist.[2] To possess such power requires them to have the character sufficient for that task as well as to protect them and the church from abuse of that power.

I am aware that such language may sound far too "Catholic" for Protestant ears, but I think it is not only theologically justified but also more nearly does justice to the empirical realities of the ministry. If the particular character of the ministry is not acknowledged, the character of the office as well as those occupying it becomes far too subject to the cultural sentimentalities that currently sustain the assumption that "religion

135

is a good thing." Moreover, it is important that the question of ministerial office and character be put in terms of power, for it is not any specifiable knowledge or skill that makes the ministry—though certainly knowledge and skill will, I hope, be present—but rather the power the minister has been given to perform the rites of the church for the church. For as most ordination rites make clear, "all the baptized share the gifts of the Spirit, the command to evangelize, witness, heal and serve."[3] The ministry, therefore, requires no skills or gifts that are not generally available to anyone in the church. Rather, ordination is but the way "some Christians are designated for the task of equipping the saints, caring for the church, building up the community, representing the church as a whole. In ordination the church puts some of its folk under orders; it makes them official 'community people.' "[4] In short, it gives them power.

The ministry is thus set apart and identified with specific persons not because it involves matters reserved to the minister or priest, but because those activities that characterize the ministry are properly activities of the whole church. The clergy do what they do because what they do are activities that all Christians share in common. That is, the things that make the ministry what it is are those things that make the church the church. The ministry is determined by the mission that is the church to witness to God's presence in the world through the proclamation of the word, baptism and eucharist, and the upbuilding of the holy.[5] These activities determine the character of the ministry, so even if someone lacks a full range of "social skills" he or she may nonetheless occupy the office of the ministry.

Such an account of the ministry will no doubt strike many as being out of touch with reality. In short, it may be good theology but it is terrible sociology. For to be a minister today requires one to be part social worker, part counselor, good with young people, an engaging speaker, fair administrator, moral exemplar without being judgmental, and a host of other functions and characteristics. The problem, in other words, is that the loss of any center to the office of the ministry has meant that the ministry has become a hodgepodge of tasks which threatens to destroy anyone who tries to fulfill these often incompatible demands. The question of the moral character of the clergy is, therefore, inseparable from a recovery of the character of the ministry itself.[6] We cannot know what kind of people we should want to have in the ministry until we know better what we want the ministry to be.

But that, it seems, is exactly what we are unsure about. In 1934, Mark May observed, "What is the function of the minister in the modern community? The answer is that it is undefined. There is no agreement

among denominational authorities, local officials, seminaries, professors, prominent laymen, ministers or educators as to what it is or
should be. The work of the lawyer, the physician, the teacher, the artist,
the writer and the engineer, is clear-cut and rather sharply defined (at
least in the mind of the average man), so that when a young man
chooses one of these professions he has some idea of what he is getting
into. But not so with the ministry. Entering the ministry is more like
entering the army, where one never knows where he will land or live or
what specific work he will be called upon to perform."[7] There seems
little reason to think our situation has changed since the publication of
May's book.

3. The Ministry as a Profession

Given the ambiguity of the ministerial role it is not surprising that one
of the dominant trends in recent times has been to model the ministry
and, correlatively, ministerial ethics after the professions of law and
medicine. Thus, a letter I received, inviting me to write for a journal an
essay on ethics for the ministry, suggested that I should "address conceptual and theoretical issues in professional ethics for practicing ministers."
That sounds harmless enough, but the clear presumption is that min-
sterial ethics is but another form of a more general area called "professional ethics." It is certainly not my intention to deny all connections
among issues in law, medicine, and the ministry—questions of confiden-
tiality, relations among peers, and other such issues—but yet I think it
would be a mistake to model how we think of the moral formation for
the ministry on the other professions; or, put more accurately, I think it
would be a mistake because of contemporary assumptions about what
kind of ethic should characterize those professions and how new members should be formed by that ethic.

I suspect at least part of the temptation to model the ministry after law
and medicine derives from the sense on the part of many that the
ministry lacks the prestige or competence of law and medicine. In *The
Gentlemen Theologians* E. Brooks Holifield notes that with the rise of
urban parishes the clergy suddenly found themselves compared with
lawyers and physicians in a manner that at once enhanced as well as
threatened their self-perception. He quotes George Howe, professor of
biblical literature at Columbia Seminary as warning, "All the professions
are advancing. We must at least advance with them, and if possible keep
before them, or be despised."[8]

Howe's advice has been heeded by most Protestant denominations for, as Dennis Campbell has observed, over the past thirty years there has been a trend to make the ministry more professional.[9] He notes this development has been due less to a concern with tradition than an assumption that professionalization will improve the quality of practice of the ministry. Yet as Campbell suggests, though the adoption of the secular professional model has been done with the best of intentions, it has lacked rigorous theological rationale. Theological schools have adopted the professional model in hopes of raising the standards of the ministry, so that now the tendency is to make "learning take precedence over call" in judging the adequacy of an individual for the ministry.[10]

I suspect another indication of the dominance of the professional model is the prominence of CPE in ministerial education. "Clinical" seems to promise the objective standards necessary to supply the pastor with the skills needed to claim to be part of a profession—namely, the ability to distinguish between one's professional role and one's own feelings and convictions. Thus ministers are taught that they must not confuse their function as counselor with their ministerial role, even though they may perform the former in the name of the latter, since the latter may entail moral judgments that might not be therapeutic.[11] Exactly to the extent ministers are able to distance themselves from their ministerial office they "act like a professional" and thus receive esteem from the other professionals they are so desperate to emulate. Such professionalization seems better than being lost amid the chaos of the ministerial role.

In fact, the professionalization of the ministry does contain an ethic which trains people in a very determinative way. So it is not as if we need to consider what ethic we should teach for the ministry but what ethic is already being taught through our attempt to professionalize the ministry. Alasdair MacIntyre has pointed out that the ethic that dominates most professional life is seldom noticed or acknowledged because it does not appear to be an ethic. Yet, he suggests, the "expert"—namely, one who promises to have the skills and knowledge to fulfill the consumer's desires—has become the standard and morality of professional practice.[12] To the expert the world is constantly open to manipulation as living itself becomes but an exercise in "problem solving." We should not be surprised if the ministry follows this development so that we assume the ministry requires those who have acquired the skills to be effective "communicators" or know how to "people manage."

This sense of expertise goes hand in hand with the current concern in law and medicine to develop more accurate codes of ethics. The more a profession thinks of itself as being defined by its members' "expertise," the more it becomes important to protect the profession from being held accountable to those who are not "experts." Though codes can well indicate the basic requirements for the practice of a profession as well as serve a useful educative function, they can also be used to safeguard the profession from the very people it is its task to serve. When this happens, the very nature of a profession and its moral practice is rendered unintelligible. For even though the skills and knowledge that characterize a professional may be highly specialized and acquired through rigorous training and much experience, the professionals are justified only because they serve a good affirmed as essential to a community's common good. Thus, law and medicine became "professions" because they professed dedication to certain goods of a community sufficient to justify their being set apart for no other task than that activity.

It is often overlooked that those who go into the professions, including teaching, are allowed to live lives that would otherwise be described as irresponsible. Members of a profession are allowed, for example, to spend most of their time in study—an activity that does little to add to the material wealth of a civilization. The justification for such a privilege can only be that the community thinks that setting aside some individuals for such study serves the goods that make that community what it is. Thus, the lawyer is allowed to spend most of his or her life "practicing law" because the law embodies the community's commitment to order its relations in a just and peaceful manner. The physician is allowed to spend years in study and to spend infinite time caring (ideally) even for the dying because of our commitment not to abandon the ill. In like manner the church sets aside some of its own to do nothing but study Scripture, lead worship, and make the church present to the ill, because the church is a community which believes such tasks are at the heart of what makes the church the church.

The development of codes to regulate the behavior of lawyers and physicians, moreover, depends on the assumption that the skills of these professions are of service to a designated client whose interests are overriding. Thus, physicians are required to care for their patients whether they like them or not. Moreover, they are required to care for those patients in a manner that their care cannot be qualified in the interest of another patient or even for the good of humanity. Lawyers are required to seek judgments in the best interest of their client no matter what they may think of their client's general mode of life. The commitment to the individual client thus gives a moral purposiveness to medicine and the law that can make the attempt to articulate a "code of ethics" a positive development. The code is meant to express the profound moral commitment to serve the person in need even when the utilitarian ethos of our society wishes to qualify such service.

The ministry, however, is not fundamentally determined by an over-riding commitment to an individual client. So the very idea of a "code of ethics" for the ministry is not intelligible, as the ministry lacks the necessary moral presumption for such a code. Of course, there is a sense that the ministry does have a "client" whose good overrides all other considerations. Without loyalty to that client, moreover, there is no way to maintain the integrity of the ministry as it threatens to be dissipated in the whirlwind of service to the unlimited needs of a people who are unsure of what makes them a community in the first place. The ministry, in short, is about service to God by serving a people who require no other service than to have their lives constantly directed to the living God. The minister is no generalist skilled in the latest counseling tech-nique but rather is the one singled out to direct all the needs of the community in the service of God. Morally, what sustains those in such service is not to be found in a code, but in character.

That such is the case, moreover, can be illustrated in relation to medi-cine and law. For those professions "ethics" can no more be captured through a code than it can for the ministry. Those who wrote the first codes of ethics for law and medicine assumed such codes made sense only if those who adhered to the codes were people of character or were, as it was put in the nineteenth century, gentlemen.[13] For it was the mark of a gentleman, a person of character, that they were not different from the way they appeared.[14] Persons of character are self-assured, so they are not easily detracted from their duty even though their duty may well mean they must act against their own interests or the interests of those they most care about. Yet they hold to their duty, to their character, because they are convinced no one owes anything to one's family, friends, or society more important than to be a person of character. It is our most important public duty. To be anything else means society has no way of guarding itself against the lie. Without such protection, more-over, we are abandoned to a world of manipulation and ultimately, violence.

It is one of the ironies of our time that codes are increasingly "revised" in order to avoid character judgments about those who are in and would enter the professions. After all, it is said, what persons do with their private lives is their own business. It is not important that persons be good, but that they be "competent," "know their business," and be tech-nologically proficient—in short, be an expert. To the extent such strategy is successful, and there is no question that within its own presuppositions it is successful, we lose the sense that law and medicine are or were fundamentally moral arts.

4. Why Character is Required

But why do the law and medicine (and the ministry) require practitioners of character? First and foremost they deal with matters that matter – birth, sex, marriage, death, and salvation. But such matters are not clear cut; they involve questions that can only be resolved through wise counsel and judgment. Put differently, the professions deal in contingent matters which require wisdom if we are more nearly to approximate the good.[15] For well-trained and experienced practitioners many judgments may well begin to look "routine"; however, skillful professionals know they can never routinize their work, for to do so would result in a failure to serve each person's particular needs.

But why does the particularity of judgments intrinsic to professional practice require those who practice the profession be people of character? Quite simply, judgment requires wisdom, which is a peculiar combination of skillful mastery of one's craft, experience, insight, and most important of all, self-knowledge. Aristotle was fond of using the example of the experienced physician to elicit the sense of wisdom he thought necessary for knowing how to live well. Aristotle suggested that physicians often know the right thing to do even though they do not know – at least "know" in the sense of being able to give a general principle – why they do what they do. That is why the professions can never be learned abstractly but require apprenticeship, for only by being initiated by a master do we gain some idea of the kind of people we need to be to be capable of judgments.

Of course, those who are called to a profession must still be schooled. Part of what it means to become a professional is to learn the wisdom of the past – a wisdom that defies complete articulation into principle or technique – so that the next generation does not have to repeat the many mistakes of the past. Those who submit to such an education must be willing to be disciplined and formed to be worthy to represent and practice their profession. Therefore, training to be a professional must be a moral training which at least puts one on the road to having a character sufficient to sustain the promised service to others.

From this perspective there is more continuity among the ministry, law, and medicine than first appeared; for they are all activities in which learning to do them well requires the development of character sufficient

141

to sustain the goods intrinsic to their practice.[16] If we are to think about "ministerial ethics," therefore, we must think about the kind of persons who are capable of sustaining the practice of the ministry for a lifetime. Questions of talent and intelligence are not unimportant, but only when talent and intelligence are shaped or embodied in character can we have the confidence that a person is ready to meet the demands of service to God through being an official of God's church.

To interject the idea of character into a discussion of "professional ethics" will strike many as an unwelcome development. For how does one ever know if a person has character; how does one train someone to have character? In the legal profession, questions of character almost appear to have been reduced to whether a person has ever committed a felony; in medicine, character is determined by one's willingness to persevere in the face of the often close to inhumane treatment one receives in medical school;[17] for the ministry the question is whether one is a practicing homosexual. It seems that questions of character in our pluralistic culture simply cannot be adjudicated, and thus we best turn back to a legalistic model for determining the ethics of the law, medicine, and even the ministry.

But if we do so, we must recognize we have changed the fundamental character of the professions as moral practices. I think, however, no profession can avoid questions of character no matter how hard they may try, and that is particularly true of the ministry. It is not enough that the clergy do not lie, cheat, or behave promiscuously, but ministers must have a character capable of sustaining their peculiar responsibility of performing the official acts of the Christian community. Ministers are not "better" than any other Christian, but they have made themselves open to a call from others that may well make them different. Thus, when the pastor visits a family whom death has touched, the pastor is rightly reminded he or she is there not just as another friend but as the pastor— that is, the one who represents the church and thus must be God's presence no matter how inadequate he or she may feel to that task.[18]

Such a perspective does not mean that God has and will continue, no doubt, to use people of questionable "morality" to be officials of the church. A call for the importance of character is not an attempt to sneak the Donatist point of view in through the back door. But what must be said is that while God's grace can be found through the most unlikely servants, it is nonetheless the case that the ministry is sustained by those who have learned that the very ability to be faithful ministers of God's church requires character. Yet it is also the case that some acquire character by living up to the expectations of God's people and by doing so, become more than they knew they were. I suspect every minister has at one time or another in their ministry found such to be the case. Indeed, it may well be that the first characteristic necessary to be a minister is the recognition that we must depend on others to be able to sustain the task.

5. Constancy in Ministry

I have argued that no attempt to develop an ethic for the clergy can be adequate that does not attend to questions of character. Much more needs to be said about the kind of character necessary for the ministry, and the space I have left allows me to make only a few suggestions in that respect. At the very least, however, an emphasis on character means the church will have to be concerned with a wide range of issues for the calling and training of people for the ministry. It is not enough that a person is not "immoral"; neither should they be vain, proud, intemperate, cowardly, ingratiating, and unloving. Moreover, it must be asked whether a person exhibits the patience and hope so necessary to the ministry. For without patience and hope there is little chance a person will have the constancy to sustain him or her through the disappointments and betrayals so often involved in the ministry.[19]

I can think of no virtue more necessary to the ministry today than constancy.[20] Without steadfastness to self and to one's task ministry cannot be sustained. Without constancy the minister is tempted to abandon the church to the ever-present temptation to unbelief and unbelief's most powerful ally, sentimentality.[21] A minister must live and act believing God is present in the church creating, through word and sacrament, a new people capable of witnessing to God's Kingdom. The minister must be filled with hope that God will act through word and sacrament to renew the church, but he or she must be patient, knowing that how God works is God's business. From the crucible of patience and hope comes the fidelity to task that makes the ministry not a burden but a joy. So finally we must ask of those in ministry whether they are capable of joy; if they are not they lack a character sufficient to their calling. For a person incapable of joy will lack the humor necessary for the self-knowledge that that character requires.

Constancy, moreover, suggests the kind of character required by the nature of the ministerial office. Just as ordination is a sign of God's faithfulness to the church, so the ministers are required in all that they are and do to be constant.[22] Ministers may well have "winning personalities," but such a trait is no substitute for the church's judgment that this

143

person will be faithful to their calling even if such faithfulness risks popularity. That such is the case is but a reminder that questions of ministerial morality are not only about the persons who enter the ministry; they are also about the Church, for the church must be composed of people who require their minister to do the unpopular thing. A ministry of character is only possible if we are a people of character.

It may be objected that it is not enough for ministers to be constant but they must also be competent. That, of course, is true, but then neither are constancy and competency unrelated. The crucial question is what makes a minister competent. The power bestowed by the church on the minister, that which gives the minister authority in the church, certainly requires the development of definite skills. But too often such skills are associated with knowing how to get along with people, rather than constant study of Scripture, liturgical leadership, and discernment of challenges currently facing his or her congregation. Given the undefined nature of the ministerial task today, only a person of character will be able to sustain the discipline necessary for the development of such skills, for ministers are often rewarded more for being personally accommodating than for preaching in an exegetically responsible way.[23]

I am aware that this perspective may well strike many as so ideal as to be unrealistic. Do I really expect twenty-five-year-old individuals to display such character? If they do not it is hardly a fault, as they have not as yet lived long enough to gain the experience to be persons of character. That is why it is so important that those whom the church calls to be our officials be carefully examined and tested, for we must know them capable of becoming people of character even if such character is only beginning to be developed as they enter the ministry. We ordain them, believing the ministry itself is a call to develop the character necessary to be of service to the church. Seminaries do not, after all, "make" ministers but rather prepare some to be made ministers as God acts through the needs and expectations of a concrete people who have been formed to want and need the right things rightly.

Seminaries cannot, therefore, assume they have the right to preempt the church's prerogative to determine fitness for ministry. But that does not mean seminaries are, therefore, given a license to be unconcerned about the shaping of the character of their students. It is not enough to train people in Scripture, church history, theology, and ethics, but that training must serve to make their lives, and their professors' lives, available to God's shaping as officials of the church. As Aristotle maintained and as we constantly rediscover, we become persons of character by being in the presence of persons of character—both the living and the

144

dead. If, therefore, we are to begin to think about the ethics of the ministry we can do nothing better—and our seminaries have no more important function—than to direct those preparing for and in the ministry to reflect on those lives that have honored their calling as ministers.[24]

NOTES

1. Many in the ministry have difficulty accepting the fact that by becoming a minister they have, in effect, been set apart. Sometimes the refusal so to understand their role is an attempt to avoid the kind of moral expectations described above—that is, one should represent a moral ideal that makes one innocent if not childlike. There are certainly good reasons for anyone to want to avoid that set of moral assumptions, but to deny the special character of the ministerial calling is ultimately a formula for irresponsibility and self-deception. Ministers are invited to enter into the lives of others with a kind of intimacy that few others are permitted. They are asked to exercise certain responsibilities for a community which cannot help but make them different. It is a false humility that would encourage them to refuse to accept the fact that they will be and are made morally different by being a minister.

2. It is interesting how seldom the power exercised by ministers is properly appreciated. The failure to do so, moreover, creates an unhealthy situation, for when power is not acknowledged then it cannot help but be manipulative. One of the deepest self-deceptions among Christians is the assumption that the church is maintained free from any appeal to power. What must be recognized is that power is rightly part and parcel of any community and particularly the church. The question is not power or no power, but the kind of power and how it is distributed. For a very useful discussion of power in the church see Stephen Sykes, *The Identity of Christianity* (Philadelphia: Fortress Press, 1984), pp. 51–80.

3. William Willimon, "The Spiritual Formation of the Pastor: Call and Community," *Quarterly Review*, 3, 2 (Summer, 1983), p. 33.

4. Ibid., p. 33.

5. I cannot attempt here any adequate defense of these claims but for a fuller account along the lines suggested, see Thomas Oden's *Pastoral Theology: Essentials of Ministry* (San Francisco: Harper & Row, 1983), pp. 49–60. The claim that one of the "marks" of the church is the "upbuilding of the holy" is particularly important for the subject of ministerial ethics. It is, however, one of the most overlooked and underdeveloped areas of ecclesiology. For if the church as a whole has no sense of what it means for members to aid one another in learning to live more nearly exemplary lives, then an emphasis on the character of the minister cannot help but reinforce the idea of a two-stage ethic—one for the ministry and one for the laity. It is interesting to note that many Protestants who criticize Catholics for maintaining a two-stage ethic continue to assume that the minister should be held to a higher standard of behavior than should the laity. Of course, the problem is in the metaphors "higher and lower," as they give the impression of superiority which distorts the nature of the different gifts and responsibilities that are necessary to sustain the church.

6. There is still no better description of this problem than that of H. Richard Niebuhr in *The Purpose of the Church and Its Ministry* (New York: Harper & Row, 1956). Moreover, Niebuhr rightly saw the problem as perennial. Thus he says "Temptations to abandon the proper work of the ministry because of ambition or the desire to please are encountered—and succumbed to—at all times. Temptations to continue a traditional course by virtue of sheer inertia are also familiarly human. But what critics who point to these reasons for the loss of certainty seem too often to forget is that the Church is never only a function of a culture nor ever only a supercultural community; that the problem of its ministers is always how to remain faithful servants of the Church in the midst of cultural change and yet to change culturally so as to be true to the Church's purpose in new situations. Those who

suggest that the ministry should provide for its continuation by turning itself into a kind of social or counseling service ignore the nature of the ministry and really provide for its discontinuation. So do those who seek a remedy for present ills by insisting on unchanging adherence to a form of the ministry developed in some earlier cultural period" (pp. 56–57). By calling for a recovery of the character of the ministry I do not mean to suggest that ministers should no longer be involved in counseling, even though counseling may not be integral to the ministerial task, but rather that the question is how they learn to counsel as ministers of the church of Jesus Christ. The difficulty occurs when counseling determines the character of ministry rather than vice versa.

7. Quoted by Niebuhr in *The Purpose of the Church and Its Ministry*, p. 51.

8. E. Brooks Holifield, *The Gentlemen Theologians* (Durham: Duke University Press, 1978), p. 34.

9. Dennis Campbell, "The Ordained Ministry as a Profession: Theological Reflections on Identity," *Quarterly Review*, 3, 2 (Summer, 1983), p. 24. For Campbell's more extensive reflections, see his *Doctors, Lawyers, Ministers: Christian Ethics in Professional Practice* (Nashville: Abingdon Press, 1982). In his *A History of Pastoral Care in America* (Nashville: Abingdon Press, 1983), E. Brooks Holifield notes that reform movements in medicine and law in the nineteenth century made ministers suspicious that they were not "professionals." As a result ministers took up the complaint that popular regard for the clergy had declined, especially among the educated (p. 173).

10. Campbell, "The Ordained Ministry as a Profession," p. 25. Of course, it is not just a matter of making learning take precedence over call but the kind of learning that is involved. That is why the issues Edward Farley raises in his *Theologies: The Fragmentation and Unity of Theological Education* (Philadelphia: Fortress Press, 1983) are so important. If seminary education should be, as he argues, a *therapeia* then the close connection between call and learning may appear to be quite different. The current interest in "spirituality" in so many Protestant seminaries, I think, reflects more the disease from which we suffer than its cure. For spirituality so understood still stands in too much discontinuity with what is done in the classroom. Courses in spirituality will be of little help if we continue to assume study of the New Testament or theology to be simply a means to make students more capable of service in the ministry. All education is an exercise in moral formation even if the course is said to be "strictly academic." For some extremely apt reflections on how theology is a *habitus* as well as the shape of theological education in general, see Charles Wood's *Vision and Discernment* (Atlanta: Scholars Press, 1985). In particular, see pp. 26–35.

11. Alasdair MacIntyre, *After Virtue* (Notre Dame: University of Notre Dame Press, 1981), p. 72. MacIntyre suggests that with the ethos of expertise comes a corresponding set of presuppositions—namely, the aspiration to value neutrality in (as far as possible) all disciplines and the claim of manipulative power in the service of efficiency.

12. For a fuller analysis of medicine as a moral art rather than a guild based on expertise, see my *Suffering Presence: Theological Reflection on Medicine, the Church, and the Mentally Handicapped* (Notre Dame: University of Notre Dame Press, 1986).

13. For this point, particularly in the legal context, I am indebted to Tom Shaffer's many articles on the subject of legal education. See, for example, his "Moral Theology in Legal Ethics," *Capital University Law Review*, 12, 2 (Winter, 1982), pp. 179–183, and "Christian Lawyer Stories and American Legal Ethics," *Mercer Law Review*, 33 (1982), pp. 877–901. Shaffer's case is both historical and normative so, he argues, the first development of codes for ethics of the lawyer presupposed the ethics of the gentleman, but it is also the case that no account of legal ethics can be sufficient that ignores the importance of the character of the lawyer. Thus Shaffer is fond of quoting Atticus Finch in *To Kill a Mockingbird*, who justifies his willingness to defend an unpopular client, "I can't be one man in town and another man at home."

The development of codes of ethics for physicians no less emphasized that physicians should be people of high moral character. Indeed, most licensure procedures still require that the person being given a license to practice medicine be of "good moral character." See, for example, Paul Camenisch, "On the Matter of Good Moral Character," *Linacre Quarterly*, 45, 3 (August, 1978), pp. 273–283.

14. In his *The Gentlemen Theologians* Holifield notes that the ministry found itself in a particular tension for the minister was at once required to be sensitive to society's judgments of propriety, but they were also warned never to appear to be what they were not. Thus he quotes Thornwell to the effect that "The most serious form of hypocrisy is that in which a man pretends to be a character to which he is really a stranger," and notes William McKendree, a much admired minister of the day, was commended as "one of that kind of men who do not care what others think of them" p. 37.

15. Charles Wood rightly challenges the oft-made dichotomy in theology between theory and practice, noting that each theological discipline is at once theoretical and practical. Instead, he notes that the important distinction is between vision and discernment. The former is the necessity of theology to develop a synoptic overview of the Christian witness; the latter is insight into particular things in their particularity. Theology requires both, as there is no "vision without discernment, and no discernment without vision" (pp. 75–76). Genuine theological education is thus the cultivation of theological judgment: "activities such as the imaginative grasp of the Christian witness in its unity, the assessment of one's own distinctive situation as a context for witness, and the testing of actual or potential efforts to convey the gospel. Vision and discernment are not merely routine performances. They require intelligence, sensitivity, imagination, and a readiness to deal with the unforeseen. It is precisely this *habitus* which is the primary and indispensable qualification for church leadership, if church leadership itself means anything more than the routine performance of established functions" (*Vision and Discernment*, pp. 93–94).

16. MacIntyre describes a practice as "any coherent and complex form of socially established cooperative human activity through which goods internal to that form of activity are realized in the course of trying to achieve those standards of excellence which are appropriate to, and partially definitive of, that form of activity, with the result that human powers to achieve excellence, and human conceptions of the ends and goods involved are systematically extended" (*After Virtue*, p. 175).

17. However, moral training does occur in medical schools, though it is seldom acknowledged as such. For example, see Charles Bosk's extraordinary account of the training of surgeons in his *Forgive and Remember* (Chicago: University of Chicago Press, 1981).

18. Dennis Campbell nicely makes the point in his "The Ordained Ministry as a Profession," p. 28.

19. For a treatment of the centrality of patience and hope as virtues necessary to locate the self within God's story, see my *The Peaceable Kingdom: A Primer in Christian Ethics* (Notre Dame: University of Notre Dame, 1983).

20. For an account of the nature and significance of constancy as a virtue, see Alasdair MacIntyre's *After Virtue*, pp. 222–226, as well as my "Constancy and Forgiveness: The Novel as a School for Virtue," *Notre Dame English Journal*, 15, 3 (Summer, 1983), pp. 23–54. This essay is an extended treatment of these themes in Trollope.

21. Indeed, I think the greatest immorality of the contemporary ministry is its willingness to substitute socialization for belief in God. Too often either an implicit atheism is accepted or ministers do not believe their congregation can be held together by belief in God. Pastors fail to challenge the congregation to trust that God creates and sustains the church. As a result the church becomes the means of underwriting the dominant ethos of our culture, the social status of the members, rather than being a people who think nothing is more important than the worship of God.

22. Oden notes that Chrysostom, drawing on Scripture, noted four primary qualifications for the office of elder: (1) unimpeachable character, (2) sexual fidelity in marriage, (3) being a good parent, and (4) "under no imputation of loose living" (*Pastoral Theology* p. 68). While it would be a mistake to overrationalize this list, I think it at least denotes that a sense of constancy is crucial to all that the minister does. That is why there is no easy distinction between office and person in relation to the ministry.

147

23. Or again, without denying the need for the ministry to develop good counseling skills, I think that surely something has gone wrong when such skills are thought more important than knowledge of Scripture or theology.

24. In this respect I think it particularly important that in training people for the ministry we attend more to the kind of people under whom they serve. We might well encourage, moreover, more attention in seminaries to biographies and autobiographies of ministers, for character is finally determined by example.

I would like to thank Tony Stonebruner, Charles Hoffacker, John Hougen, Jim McDonald, and Mel Keiser for criticizing this essay during our common participation in the Colledge Colloquium. I only regret I was not able to incorporate all of their valuable suggestions. I also benefited much from Karen Lebacqz' critique of the first draft of this essay.

THE PASTOR AS PROPHET

Ethical Reflections on an Improbable Mission

1. The Difficulty of the Prophetic Role

Being a pastor and being a prophet are roles most assume cannot be easily reconciled. Indeed, many claim one cannot be both. Some pastors, such as Martin Luther King, Jr., may be prophetic, but most pastors have to carry on the day-to-day tasks of ministry which are anything but prophetic. The sick must be visited, the couple seeking divorce must be counseled, and the Staff/Parish Relations Committee meeting must be attended. The problem, moreover, is not that such activities leave little time for being prophetic, but if one tries to be prophetic, the caring function of the pastoral tasks proves impossible. For the moral outrage that fuels the fires of a prophetic calling seems incompatible with the kind of openness necessary to being a caring pastor.

For example, consider Amos' message to the rich matrons of Samaria, in Amos 4:1–2:

> Hear this word, you cows of Bashan,
> who are in the mountains of Samaria,
> who oppress the poor, who crush the needy,
> who say to their husbands, "Bring, that we may drink!"
>
> The Lord God has sworn by his holiness
> that, behold, the days are coming upon you,
> when they shall take you away with hooks.

Generally, it is not the best pastoral practice to approach the women of one's congregation with the appellation "cows of Bashan." Moreover, Amos' depiction of these well-to-do women who have turned their husbands into servants is unrelenting. It is so because he draws a direct

149

connection between their lives of luxury and the injustice perpetrated on the poor. He does not even try to help them see that there might be other possibilities which could make their lives more fulfilling, but instead delivers an uncompromising message of destruction. This kind of prophetic role simply does not seem compatible with the best insights of clinical pastoral education. After all, Amos should have realized that these "cows" are also people in pain who deserve the same kind of care that he thinks should be directed toward the poor. If we are to minister to the "cows of Bashan," it seems that Amos' rhetoric, as well as his practice, will have to change.

The problem of being a prophetic pastor is particularly compounded by the cultural situation of the church. The church must find a way to sustain itself in a buyer's market. The church no longer represents a community of authority through which the minister exercises leadership by calling the community to live in accordance with its own best convictions. Rather, the church has become a voluntary institution in which membership is determined by the consent of the individual believer. As Joseph Hough has observed, in such a situation the authority of the religious leader is increasingly based "not on his or her ability to interpret a body of authoritative teaching, but on the ability to persuade religiously inclined persons of at least the importance of, if not the superiority of, his/her own teaching."[1]

Indeed, that way of putting the matter is almost too optimistic, as membership in a church and loyalty to a pastor are seldom determined by a sense of the importance of the pastor's teaching. More important is whether the pastor has a winning personality. Such a situation is not conducive to encouraging pastors to take up a prophetic role. The congregation may put up with the pastor being concerned with social issues, such as U.S. nuclear policy, but they will hardly put up with the pastor turning the same kind of critical scrutiny toward his or her own congregation. We are all like the old woman who "Amened" her pastor when he preached against drinking, cursing, and philandering but when he criticized the use of snuff, said, "Preacher, you've done stopped preaching and started to meddle."

Yet I think it is a mistake to assume that the inability of clergy to be prophetic is due solely to the necessity to please their constituency. As Reinhold Niebuhr suggested in his *Leaves from the Notebook of a Tamed Cynic*, the situation is much more complex. He says:

> I am not surprised that most prophets are itinerants. Critics of the church think we preachers are afraid to tell the truth because we are economically depen-

dent upon the people of our church. There is something in that, but it does not quite get to the root of the matter. I certainly could easily enough get more money than I am securing now, and yet I catch myself weighing my words and gauging their possible effect upon this and that person. I think the real clue to the tameness of a preacher is the difficulty one finds in telling unpleasant truths to people whom one has learned to love. To speak the truth in love is a difficult, and sometimes an almost impossible, achievement. If you speak the truth unqualifiedly, that is usually because your ire has been aroused or because you have no personal attachment to the object of your strictures. Once personal contact is established you are very prone to temper your wind to the shorn sheep. It is certainly difficult to be human and honest at the same time. I'm not surprised that most budding prophets are tamed in time to become harmless parish priests.[2]

Thus, Niebuhr observes that clergy cannot rush into a congregation that has been fed from its infancy on the individualistic ethic of Protestantism and that is immersed in a civilization in which individualism runs riot and expect to develop a social conscience among the people in two weeks. Nor do they have the right to insinuate that the church is full of hypocrites because the members do not see what they see.

Of course it is not easy to speak the truth in love without losing a part of the truth, and therefore one ought not to be too critical of those who put their emphasis on the truth rather than on love. But if a man is not willing to try, at least, to be pedagogical, and if in addition he suffers from a martyr complex, he has no place in the ministry. Undoubtedly there are more ministers who violate their conscience than such as suffer for conscience sake. But that is no reason why those who have a robust conscience should not try to master the pedagogical art.[3]

As Niebuhr observes, "if the Christian adventure is made a mutual search for the truth in which the preacher is merely a leader among many searchers and is conscious of the same difficulties in his own experience which he notes in others, I do not see why he cannot be a prophet without being forced into itinerancy."[4] But one must observe that Niebuhr himself did not remain in the parish ministry.

It seems, therefore, that the improbability of the pastor as a prophet— or at least the same person being at once a prophet and pastor—manifests the classic tension between love and justice. Just to the extent we seek justice we often seem to have to do the unloving or at least the harsh thing. The tension is, of course, an old one, although it has taken many different forms over the years. It is sometimes depicted as that between the priest and the prophet; at other times it seems to be the tension

151

between realist and idealist. The kind of love and care that is necessary for the upbuilding of the community finally seems to be in tension with the demand that we be a people in critical judgment on our society. No easy resolution seems possible.

Yet I am not completely happy with this account of our situation. Indeed, I regard the current tension between those who would emphasize more the nurturing aspect of ministry and those who would stress the prophetic as disastrous both for the training of ministers as well as for the practice of the ministry.[5] What we need is a recovery of how the pastoral tasks are fundamentally prophetic when they are appreciated as necessary for the upbuilding of a prophetic community. Because we lack the conceptual and sociological terms necessary to move such a claim beyond mere assertion, the attempt to make such a claim is by no means easy. However, I hope at least to begin that process by developing an account of prophecy that will illumine the nature of ministry.

Before trying to develop my constructive suggestions, I think that it is important to challenge a certain picture of the ethical significance of the prophets. Ethicists have tended to underscore the tension I have tried to depict by downplaying the pastoral side of the ministry in favor of the prophetic. That they have done so is not surprising, as Christian ethics as a distinguishable discipline began in America among Protestants with a rediscovery of the ethical significance of the prophets. No one exemplifies this better than Walter Rauschenbusch, whose account of the prophets is well worth our attention. Rauschenbusch's depiction of the prophets, particularly when assessing their ethical significance, continues to be widely shared even though his account in many ways distorts the nature of prophecy. These distortions help to explain why we continue to suffer from the assumption that when a minister becomes a prophet he or she becomes less a pastor.

2. Rauschenbusch on the Prophets

Rauschenbusch begins *Christianity and the Social Crisis* with an extended discussion of the prophets.[6] That he does so is not simply because he was trying for historical completeness, but because the prophets stood for everything he thought was right about Christianity. Indeed, for Rauschenbusch, it is not Jesus who completes the prophets, but rather Jesus is but the prophetic spirit rising from the dead. The rest of the Old Testament, therefore, can safely be ignored because the prophets "are the beating heart of the Old Testament. Modern study has shown that they were the real makers of the unique religious life of Israel. If all that proceeded from them, directly or indirectly, were eliminated from the Old Testament, there would be little left to appeal to the moral and religious judgment of the modern world."[7]

Rauschenbusch does not attempt to describe the work of the prophets in historical sequence. Rather, he tries to lay bare the large and permanent characteristics which are common to all prophets and which he assumes have lasting relevance. The first and most important of those characteristics is the prophetic insistence that right life is as important as true worship. "The prophets were the heralds of the fundamental truth that religion and ethics are inseparable, and that ethical conduct is the supreme and sufficient religious act."[8] They therefore challenged the "primitive religious" conviction that God is a tribal God concerned primarily with worship and controlling nature. Brushing aside sacrificial ritual, Hosea spoke for all the prophets by proclaiming that God desires "steadfast love and and not sacrifice" (Hos. 6:6).[9]

But it is equally important to note that the morality that the prophets insist is central to our relation with God is not

merely the private morality of the home, but the public morality on which national life is founded. They said less about the pure heart for the individual than of just institutions for the nation. The twin evils against which the prophet launched the condemnation of Jehovah were injustice and oppression. The religious ideal of Israel was the theocracy. But the theocracy meant the complete penetration of the national life by religious morality. It meant politics in the name of God. That line by which we have tacitly separated the domain of public affairs and the domain of Christian life was unknown to them.[10]

The prophets were public men and their primary concerns were with public affairs. They were not religious individualists, but they thought of Israel and Judah as organic totalities. They thus anticipated our modern scientific comprehension of social development which rightly contends that society is more than a collection of individuals. Just as individuals can sin, so can whole societies, and it was with the latter that the prophets were uniquely concerned.

Moreover, the prophets' social concern, even for the most aristocratic among them, was entirely on the side of the poorer classes.

The edge of their invectives was turned against the land-hungry of the landed aristocracy who "joined house to house and laid field to field," till a country of sturdy peasants was turned into a series of great estates; against the capitalistic ruthlessness that "sold the righteous for silver and the needy for a pair of shoes," thrusting the poor free-man into slavery to collect a trifling debt; against the venality of the judges who took bribes and had a double standard of law for the rich and the poor. This dominant trait of their moral feeling reacted on their theology, so that it became one of the fundamental attributes of their God that he was the husband of the widow, the father of the orphan, and the protector of the strangers.[11]

According to Rauschenbusch, there were good historical reasons for the prophets to side with the poor. For

when the nomad tribes of Israel settled in Canaan and gradually became an agricultural people, they set out on their development toward civilization with ancient customs and rooted ideas that long protected primitive democracy and equality. It was the decay of the primitive democracy and the growth of luxury, tyranny, extortion, of court life and a feudal nobility, which Samuel wisely feared when the people demanded a king.[12]

Thus, early Israel was much like the period in America's development when there was no social caste and a fair distribution of the means of production prevailed.

In fact, the rise of the prophets corresponded to the increase and unequal distribution of wealth in Israel. "The old democratic instinct of the people angrily resented this upstart tyranny."[13] Thus, Amos was the first of the great social prophets who not only uttered the message of God, but also expressed the feelings of the agrarian class. "The championship of the poor by the prophets was not due to the inflow of novel social ideals, but to the survival of nobler conceptions to which they clung in the face of distorted social conditions created by the new commercialism. They were the voice of an untainted popular conscience, made bold by religious faith."[14]

The prophets, however, were not only social reformers; they also called the nation to be true to itself. Consequently, the same national crisis that created the kingship also began the higher career of the prophets. Until that moment they had been mainly soothsayers whose predictions had not been based on any fundamental moral convictions. But now their patriotism was the emancipating power that allowed them to save the faith of the people amid the ruins of their national past.

They asserted that Jehovah is fundamentally a god of righteousness, and a god of Israel only in so far as Israel was a nation of righteousness. God moves on the plane of universal and impartial ethical law. Assyria belongs to him as well as Israel. He would live and be just even if Israel was broken. Israel was not a pet child that would escape the rod. Its prerogative was the revelation of God's will and not any immunity from the penalities of the moral law. The relation of the nation to Jehovah was not a natural right and privilege, but rested on moral conditions.[15]

Owing to the breadth and inclusiveness of their religious sympathy, the prophets were able to discover the significance of individual piety. Thus, Jeremiah, amid the breakup of the nation, heard the

insistent inner voice of God, and the consciousness of this personal communion with Jehovah was his stay and comfort. This was a wonderful triumph of religion, an evidence of the indestructibility of the religious impulse. It was fraught with far-reaching importance for the future of religion and of humanity in general. The subtlest springs of human personality were liberated when the individual realized that he personally was dear to God and could work out his salvation not as a member of his nation, but as a man by virtue of his humanity.[16]

This discovery of personal religion was never an end in itself, but rather a means to an end that was always social. Now the prophets sought to build up a society that honored the dignity of the individual.

The gain that came with the discovery of personal religion brought with it a loss. The social vision became bleak in the exile, so rather than condemn the sins of human beings against other humans, as the older prophets had done, Ezekiel dwelt on the sins of human beings against God. Not justice but holiness became fundamental, and the latter was understood primarily in terms of ceremonial correctness. Despite the prophetic character of Ezekiel's life, it is impossible, suggests Rauschenbusch, not to sense the beginning of religious decadence in Ezekiel's vision. "Religion had grown narrower and feebler when it was forced from the great national and human interests into an ecclesiastical attitude of mind."[17]

So runs Rauschenbusch's account of the ethical significance of the prophets. It is extremely instructive to us both for where he is correct and where he is in error. He is certainly right to emphasize the inner relation between ethics and religion as represented by the prophets. Moreover, he is right to emphasize the social character of the prophetic critique. Yet on the whole, his depiction of the prophets is decidedly one-sided. To say that Rauschenbusch used the prophets to confirm a view of religion and ethics he had reached on other grounds is probably too strong, but the prophets still look far too much like what Rauschenbusch and

155

his fellow "social-gospelers" had come to believe Christianity should be about.

This is not to say that Rauschenbusch ignored the best historical scholarship of his day concerning the prophets. On the contrary, his views were determined by the scholarly consensus that had developed in his time. That such is the case is but a reminder that the "scholarly consensus" is as open to ideological distortion as is our own theology. Particularly destructive in the picture of the prophets that influenced Rauschenbusch is the inherent anti-Semitism which saw "Judaism" as the "decline" from the great heights of prophetic insight.[18]

For our purposes, at least two important lessons need to be drawn from Rauschenbusch's portrayal of the prophets. First, we should be suspicious of characterizations of prophecy that fail to appreciate the rich diversity of prophecy. If we have learned anything about the prophets since Rauschenbusch's time it is that prophetism was an extraordinarily varied phenomenon in Israel which served different purposes at different times. The prophets by no means spoke with a single voice, nor did they share the same set of theological presuppositions. Some of them, as Rauschenbusch suggests, seem to have identified more with the exodus traditions in a manner that put them in tension with the development of the kingship, whereas others drew on the Davidic covenant as central to Israel's identity. As Joseph Blenkinsopp has suggested, in the early centuries and to a limited extent in the later period, prophecy was connected with warfare and cult,[19] but such a generalization is not sufficient to characterize all prophetic activity. It does, however, help us to appreciate how extraordinary it was that Amos later suggested that Israel's warrior God had now declared war on his people.[20]

What must be guarded against is finding in the prophets a confirmation of a peculiar theological or ethical insight which one thinks particularly important for the current religious situation. This is not to say that the prophetic literature may not have significant contributions to make which challenge some of one's set assumptions, but one cannot assume that the current understanding of the "prophetic" is in fact synonymous with the role of the prophets of the Hebrew Scriptures. For example, in the current understanding, the prophets are often treated as social radicals who were willing to overthrow their social order in the interest of justice. Yet one is increasingly aware that many of the prophets were profound social conservatives who were seeking not to overthrow the status quo but to maintain it, or even to return to a prior way of life.

It is important, second, to challenge Rauschenbusch's account of the prophets primarily as ethical reformers. No doubt Gerhard von Rad's

156

stress on the centrality of the "word of God" to characterize prophetic activity may reflect more an influence of Karl Barth than an accurate account of prophecy, yet von Rad is surely right when he says that the prophets cannot be properly understood simply as moral reformers.[21] One cannot easily overlook the ecstatic and seerlike aspects of the prophets, as Rauschenbusch tries to do. Even as cautious a historian as Blenkinsopp suggests:

> The standard introductory formula "Thus says Yahweh" is taken from the established protocol of official messages and letters in the ancient Near East, pointing to the prophetic self-designation as emissary of Yahweh. The conviction of acting under such a mandate is essential to understanding how the prophets thought of their authority and role in society, and can therefore provide a starting point for addressing the central issue of prophetic identity.[22]

Rauschenbusch's characterization of the prophets primarily as ethical reformers, therefore, cannot be sustained. Or, more accurately, Rauschenbusch is right to emphasize the centrality of ethics for characterizing the activity of the prophets, but his account of ethics is far too limited. This is understandable, given the extraordinary social injustices of his own day. (I am not convinced that we face any less injustice in our day; we just fail to see it because we are less imaginative than were Rauschenbusch and his friends.) Yet when "ethics" is understood primarily as a call for justice against the status quo, we overlook those presuppositions that are necessary to sustain such an endeavor, for the question of what kind of community is necessary to sustain the task of so interpreting the world is ignored. Therefore, I have provided an account of prophecy that not only does greater justice to the full range of prophetic activity as exhibited in the Scripture, but also helps us to better understand the prophetic nature of the pastoral office.

3. The Prophetic Nature of the Pastoral Office: A Theological Proposal

I want to make clear certain methodological presuppositions about the account of prophecy I have tried to develop. First and foremost, the account of prophecy is a theological proposal which does not attempt to be faithful in every aspect to prophetic activity as we find it displayed in the Hebrew Scriptures. Certainly, any constructive theological proposal about prophecy will be accountable to Scripture, but any account or understanding of the nature and continuing significance of prophecy for the church cannot simply be an attempt to mimic the prophets of Israel.

One of the most significant reasons that our understanding of prophecy cannot help but be a theological proposal is that for Christians no account of prophecy can be divorced from Christological considerations. This is not just because Jesus is best understood, both historically and theologically, as a prophet, but also because his work has made a decisive difference in how Christians are to understand their prophetic role. Because Jesus was who he was, Christians cannot help but be prophetic, since now their very existence is a prophetic sign of God's refusal to abandon creation. If the essential role of the prophet is to interpret the world in terms of God's providential care, then the church's very existence is prophetic, for without the church we could not know who we are or in what kind of world we exist.

John Howard Yoder has suggested that the significance of the prophets can only be appreciated if we understand that Israel was constituted and existed as a people only as they gathered around events that were continually commemorated. Therefore, the prophet was uniquely important to Israel's existence because the prophet was the one who interpreted past, present, and future in the light of God's calling of Israel.

> It was he who spoke to what was going on in history and said what it means. The priest interprets nature. He speaks to what is always the same and what happens again every year. The priest manages the interpretation of the circles of the stars and the crops and flocks. He is dealing with stability—with that which is routine and recurrent. The prophet interprets events which happen but once, or if he sees pattern in the events it is a meaningful, directional, pattern. Speaking culturally, descriptively and sociologically the scholars all have to agree that Israel is the type of people that gathered around the meaning of certain events and looked in the direction which the prophets said those events were leading. We could say it as well theologically. The concept of the *word of the Lord* has in Hebrew thought a unique objective quality. The prophet is simply a channel for this word. It is spoken through him. Often, usually, it is spoken with his personal involvement. He says something he agrees with, believes and understand and cares about. But sometimes actually it is said without his personal involvement. There are times when he does not know what he is saying, or does not know what it means, or does not like it. The prophet cannot call back the word, he cannot guide it. The word is almost personalized. It goes out and it does its work. It was the word of Jahweh spoken through the prophets which makes Israel Israel.[23]

158

This interpretation of the prophetic office is confirmed by Blenkin-sopp's discussion of the profound and widespread transformation of prophecy after the loss of national independence and royal patronage.

> Increasingly reference to former prophets, occasional laments of the absence of prophetic and, not least, the well-attested practice of adapting earlier prophetic sayings to new situations (e.g., in Zech. 1–8) are symptomatic of this new situation. With the availability of prophetic material in writing, the emphasis was less on direct inspired utterance and more on the inspired interpretation of past prophecy. Correspondingly, there was an increasing sense that, in the normal course of events, God does not communicate directly but has revealed his will and purpose in past communications whose bearing on the present situation remains to be elucidated.[24]

So, the prophet remained interpeter, but now the history of the prophetic activity became the means of interpretation. Blenkinsopp notes that this extremely important shift was decisive for the self-understanding of the community that began to preserve the prophetic texts. For since the text can be interpreted in more than one way, the control of this function was also a factor in the disposal of power within the community. As Blenkinsopp suggests, "the problem for those who preserved these texts and took them seriously was: How can the word of God addressed to our ancestors who lived in a different age and faced different problems become a word of God for us today?"[25] Prophecy was no longer relegated to individuals, but now became a task of the whole community as the community sought to discern and interpret events in the light of God's past relation with them.

It is against this background that one asks in what sense was Jesus a prophet. Jesus was a prophet not only because he spoke the words of God for God, but also because in him the revealed and the revealer are one. That is, Jesus not only revealed the words of God, but his person was God's revelation as well. Moreover, it is his person that now makes possible the decisive interpretation of the world which demands the existence of a different kind of community. In fact, it is a community of interpretation that is based on the profound claim in 1 John 1:2 that he "was made manifest" not only through his words, but also in his person. " 'In many and various ways God spoke of old to our fathers by the prophets, but in these last days he has spoken to us by a son.' Not by the *words* of a son, but the being, the presence of his son. So Jesus in his person is a new kind of communication or manifesting or revealing which goes beyond what words can do."[26]

Jesus does not make irrelevant all past prophecy, nor does he render future prophecy irrelevant, but rather he now becomes the standard by which the past is understood and the future rightly anticipated. We still have much to learn, and we will continue to need prophetic figures to challenge us to see that God will often call us in unanticipated ways to be God's faithful people. Indeed, it is because of the life of this man, Jesus, that the community formed by his memory can live open to the unanticipated—open to that which may challenge it to rethink those interpretations of its past. Such a community can be open to the new, which is as common as the birth of a child, because it is sustained by the remembering that for all time God has made it safe through the life, death, and resurrection of Jesus of Nazareth.[27]

For such a community, prophecy is no longer solely the role of specific individuals, although individual prophets will, I hope, still be present. It is the community itself that is now prophetic, for it is a community formed by the life and death of Jesus of Nazareth, which means that it cannot be what it is without understanding itself to be accountable to the great prophets of Israel. Just to the extent that it holds itself so accountable by its very existence it becomes a prophetic community, as it carries in its very being the symbols that help the church to understand what it is and what kind of world in which it exists. The church is prophetic because without it, the world would have no means of knowing that it is the world; that is, the world would be without a history sufficient to understand itself as God's creation.

To stress the interpretative role of the prophet does not exclude the critical dimension of the prophetic task. The prophet still must deliver the word of judgment. The prophet still must challenge those who think that their power can make their nation safe. The prophet cannot avoid challenging the injustice that is all the more powerful because we have learned to accept it as part of the landscape. That the prophet performs such tasks, however, is but an aspect of the calling to keep the community true to the story that determines its character as the church of Jesus of Nazareth.

This is why the prophetic task is at once so conservative and yet so radical. Prophecy is meant to keep us true to the One who has made and continues to make us what we are. Just as Israel's prophets insisted that Israel be the kind of community that made it possible to remember its past, so the church must be the kind of community capable of telling the story of a crucified messiah. The task is, therefore, conservative, but the means are decidedly radical, for the very content of the story requires us to be willing to face our sinfulness as a people who constantly try to avoid the truth about ourselves and our world. As we are told in 1 John 2:9–11, we cannot say that we are in the light, that we are followers of Jesus the Christ, yet hate our brother or our sister. "He who says he is in the light and hates his brother is in the darkness still. He who loves his brother abides in the light, and in it there is no cause for stumbling. But he who hates his brother is in the darkness and walks in the darkness, and does not know where he is going, because the darkness has blinded his eyes."

The problem, therefore, with accounts such as that of Rauschenbusch that stress the prophets' ethical significance is not that the prophetic task does not involve ethics. Rather, the problem is with the kind of ethics that is entailed. The ethical is not limited to questions of justice, but involves the question of interpretation in light of the truth we are convinced has been revealed through the life, death, and resurrection of Jesus. To be such an interpretative community means that we must be a people transformed by that story. It is not simply a question of just actions and institutions; rather, we must be people who are capable of loving the stranger. This is why the subject of prophetic activity is, first of all, the community itself, not those who are not of the community.

But what does all of this have to do with understanding the prophetic nature of pastoral office? First, and most important, it means that in being prophetic the pastor stands in and for the community. It is the pastor's task to hold before the community the story that determines its existence and makes it possible, not for the pastor to be prophetic, but for the community to fulfill its calling as God's own. The pastoral task is prophetic, in so far as the means that are peculiar to the church's ministry help to remind the community of the story that makes that community prophetic. There can be no more prophetic task than the preaching of the word and the serving of the eucharist, for it is through them that the church is constituted as God's people in a world that does not know God. So, it is not a question of whether the pastor can be prophetic, but rather that the pastor *must* be prophetic, given the nature of the community that he or she serves.

Moreover, from this perspective there can be in principle no conflict between the "pastoral tasks" and the prophetic ones. Visiting the sick may appear to be mundane, but it is no less a prophetic task than protesting against the idolatry of the nation-state. Indeed, it is, in a sense, part of the protest against such idolatry, as it is one of the ways the church makes clear its refusal to let the state or wider society determine whom it will and will not serve. Thus, those who insist on caring for the persecuted, even if such care requires us to ignore national boundaries, are acting pastorally and prophetically. Or again, taking the time to talk with a couple who are seeking a divorce may be prophetic if such counseling is informed by the church's prophetic commitment to faithfulness in a world almost devoid of any sense of constancy. The only question about whether such work can be prophetic is when such activities no longer draw on the story and habits that form the church, but instead underwrite our cultural assumptions about marriage and the care of the sick and persecuted.

When "pastoral tasks" are undertaken as a means to help the church remember who it is as the church, they cannot help but serve the church's prophetic mission, for the body is built up as we learn to minister to one another in the name of Christ. The church does not give us just any peace, but the peace of Christ. Such comfort and such peace may be troubling indeed for both the church and the world, but they are no less comfort and peace for that.

The pastor, therefore, is engaged in a constant task of helping the church interpret itself and the world through the many small and great tasks that build up the people of God. It is not a question of pastor *or* prophet, but how one pastors. Pastoring will be authentic to the extent that it avoids the sentimentalities which abound today concerning what it means to be a "caring community." For the church is not just another haven in the storm to protect some from the ravages of modernity, but a people who care so deeply that they refuse to do anything else than speak the truth in love.[28]

4. Pastoral Counseling as Prophetic: An Example

Obviously, much more needs to be said to develop fully my account of the pastoral task as one of prophetic interpretation. In particular, much more would need to be said about the content of the story of Jesus which I have suggested forms the church's identity. But rather than developing my proposal in an abstract way, I have provided an example which I hope will suggest how clergy must be prophetic even in their day-to-day activities. I have purposely chosen an example from a counseling context, since so often it is in that area that it seems so difficult for the pastor to be prophetic. Another reason I have chosen such an example is because it is often claimed that in such pastoral situations it is hard to be rigorous in giving ethical advice.[29] Insofar as the prophetic is identifed with the ethical, it thus seems that no easy resolution can be effected between the pastoral task and the ethical.

During 1984, Methodism was in the throes of celebrating its bicentennial in the United States. In preparation for that event, a conference was held at Emory University, in Atlanta, Georgia, to assess Methodist theological strength for the next century. I was part of a seminar on the Methodist stress on perfection and virtue as continuing themes of church life. As some of us theorized about how sanctification might be understood in terms of the virtues, a young pastor told a story which he thought exhibited some of the difficulties of translating such theoretical emphases into practical terms.

He told of a young mother, a member of his church, who came to him concerning the possibility of an abortion. She and her husband had two children, and they had recently decided to seek a divorce; or more accurately, the husband had decided that they should divorce and she had acquiesced. The husband was a rather reserved man, an engineer with an extremely good job and income. They lived in a community of other young professionals in which divorce was common. Although the reasons for the divorce were not clear, it was obviously a situation that had been building for some time.

The young pastor, who had great sympathy for the woman, at first found her ambivalent about whether she could or should have an abortion. She had moral reservations about abortion in general and was unsure whether or not she could live with the results. She received no emotional support from her husband, who simply abandoned her in her decision making, taking no responsibility for the outcome one way or the other. The pastor said that because he did not think it right to be moralistic about abortion, he simply tried to help her reach a decision that would be best for her and her children in light of her prospective divorce. He therefore sent her to a professional counselor who would be better off to help her resolve her feelings.

Through her counseling sessions, she came to the conclusion that she would be better off having an abortion. The counselor had been particularly important because she felt supported by him. His acceptance of her seemed to give her the permission needed to have the abortion. The pastor then arranged for her to have the abortion in an appropriate medical setting and continued to support her after the abortion.

Nothing about this story is unique. It is commonplace in the professional lives of many clergy. Yet I think it is a story of failure—failure of community and failure of the pastor. It was a failure, first, because the pastor was so afraid of being "moralistic" that he could not help the woman to see how her situation was related to or involved her Christian commitments. He failed to help her interpret her situation in light of her relation to the Christian community and that community's support of her.

Because he was afraid to place any more burden on this woman, he failed to help her perceive all that was happening or to call her to have greater confidence in herself. For example, I asked him if he had suggested to her that perhaps her anger at her husband for deciding to end the marriage was involved in her contemplation of abortion. He said that it had never even occurred to him. He was trying so hard to be understanding that in being nonjudgmental he had no way of drawing on the very resources of the gospel to inform his ministry to her. It had never occurred to him that the category of sin might be relevant to such situations. We cannot know in fact whether this young woman was seeking to kill her child as a means of attacking her husband—but what could be more human? God knows the terrible irony that, for many of us, our hates are more precious to us than even our self-esteem.

Moreover, by trying to understand, the pastor asked nothing from his community. He simply accepted the assumption that the people of his church would see this woman's situation as her problem—one that had no relation to them. As a result, abortion could not help but appear "the best for all concerned." The pastor did not consider calling on the church to be a community of people who care about one another so that they might even support one another to have children under less-than-happy circumstances. Therefore, he could not relate to this mother as an officer of a community formed by a story of presence and care; he had to relate to her as one anonymous person relating to another anonymous person in need. All he represented was a vague sense of serving a community which cares about people, but not enough of a community to provide the kind of moral and physical support that might make this woman's loneliness less burdensome.

If that is an example of pastoral care, then I think it is surely right that there is a tension between being pastoral and being prophetic. For such care in no way draws on or is informed by the convictions of a community pledged to care for the widow and the orphan, for the abandoned mother, or for the poor because of the kind of God that has called it into being. Such a community cannot help but produce pastors who acquiesce to the sentimentality of a culture that assumes the way to care for people is to try to make their lives less difficult. Moreover, such a community cannot help but end with a self-hating leadership who cannot avoid despair because they know the distance between what they are and what they should be.[30] Indeed, it may be that agony will prove to be prophetic as it becomes the means by which to secure a new sense of community. What could be of more prophetic significance for the church than for the ordained ministry to recover a sense of its integrity— that the pastor, even as counselor, is such a representative of Christ's people?

I do not mean to suggest that this pastor would have been prophetic if he had responded to the woman by condemning any idea of her having an abortion; we have all the self-righteousness we need in the church already.[31] Rather, I am suggesting that what is wrong with how he proceeded is that he did nothing through his counseling to remind the woman what it meant for her to be a Christian or to be people of aid and help in such circumstances. As a result, this kind of care does nothing to help us better understand why we find ourselves in such situations. Moreover, too often the "solutions" only perpetuate the malady.

I know of no magic or easy solutions, but I do have faith in the prophetic nature of God's church. I do not believe that the church is without resources to reclaim its task of being God's presence in the world. Surely one of these resources is a faith that those who are called to the pastoral ministry will find the courage to challenge us to live up to our avowed commitments as Christians. Such a task will require nothing less than the willingness to trust our language to be a truthful account of the way we are and the way the world is. Such a trust may require that we Christians again look, as well as live, differently from most of our neighbors. We have no other choice if we are to be faithful to the prophetic task to which the Christian people are called.

NOTES

1. Joseph Hough, "The Education of Practical Theologians," unpublished manuscript, p. 23. For Hough's more developed position, see his and John Cobb's *Christian Identity and Theological Education* (Atlanta: Scholars Press, 1985). Hough and Cobb helpfully depict models of ministry, but I find myself quite unsympathetic to their own positive proposals.

2. Reinhold Niebuhr, *Leaves from the Notebook of a Tamed Cynic* (New York: Meridian, 1960), p. 74. Copyright 1929, renewed 1957 by Reinhold Niebuhr. Reprinted by permission of Harper & Row Publishers, Inc.

3. Ibid., pp. 128–29.

4. Ibid., p. 75. For a somewhat surprising account of Niebuhr as pastor, see Richard Fox's wonderful *Reinhold Niebuhr: A Biography* (New York: Pantheon Books, 1985), pp. 62–64. Fox challenges the oft-made assumption that Niebuhr's Detroit church was a working-class church.

5. There are signs of hope that this split is being healed. For example, see the essays in *Practical Theology: The Emerging Field of Theology, Church, and World*, edited by Don Browning (San Francisco: Harper & Row, 1983).

6. Walter Rauschenbusch, *Christianity and the Social Crisis* (New York: Harper & Row, 1964). Used by permission.

7. Ibid., p. 3.

8. Ibid., p. 7.

9. Ibid., p. 9.

10. Ibid., p. 10.

11. Ibid., pp. 11–12.

12. Ibid., pp. 13–14.

13. Ibid., p. 16.

14. Ibid., p. 16.

15. Ibid., p. 25.

16. Ibid., pp. 27–28.

17. Ibid., pp. 30–31.

18. For a critique of these assumptions which have dominated so much of the study of Hebrew Scripture, see Joseph Blenkinsopp, "Old Testament Theology and the Jewish-Christian Connection," *Journal of the Study of the Old Testament*, 28 (1984), pp. 3–15. Although it is difficult to prove, one cannot help but believe that our failure to appreciate the "sectarian" form of later prophecy derives partly from our inability to see the church in tension with our social order. We turn the prophets into social critics in the name of securing justice within our social assumptions. We do not, however, take the risk of thinking the prophets might well call into question the very basis of our social order, such as noting that democracy and the national purpose legitimated in its name may be fundamentally idolatrous.

19. Joseph Blenkinsopp, *A History of Prophecy in Israel* (Philadelphia: Westminster Press, 1983), p. 40.

20. Ibid., p. 90.

21. Gerhard von Rad, *Old Testament Theology*, vol. 2 (New York: Harper & Row, 1965). For von Rad's particular emphasis, see his account of "The Prophets' Conception of the Word of God," pp. 80–98.

22. Blenkinsopp, *History of Prophecy*, p. 38. Rauschenbusch's account of the prophets was in reaction to the equally distorted understanding of the prophets primarily as foretellers of the future—and, in particular, foretellers of Jesus' coming. The prophets certainly were not simply predictors of the future, but neither can that side of prophecy be ignored particularly if, as I shall emphasize below, we stress the significance of interpretation of history as definitive of the prophetic task.

23. John Howard Yoder, *Preface to Theology: Christology and Theological Method* (Elkhart, Indiana: Goshen Biblical Seminary, 1982), pp. 246–47. Walter Brueggemann's book, *The Prophetic Imagination* (Philadelphia: Fortress Press, 1978), supports this interpretation.

24. Blenkinsopp, *History of Prophecy*, p. 256.

25. Ibid., p. 257.

26. Yoder, *Preface to Theology*, p. 248.

27. For a fuller presentation of the ideas in this paragraph, see my *A Community of Character: Toward a Constructive Christian Social Ethic* (Notre Dame: University of Notre Dame Press, 1981).

28. I happened to mention to my pastor (then the pastor of Broadway) that I was working on a paper I hoped would overcome the split between the pastoral and prophetic. In response, he told a story which nicely illustrates the perspective I have been trying to develop. He said that he just left one of our elderly parishioners who was deeply concerned that after ten years the pastor was changing churches. She was particularly concerned that he should come back to bury her. He had told her he had no intention of doing so, and he thought that was a prophetic act. I think he was right, for in refusing to return to bury her, he reminded her that it is not this or that pastor who makes the church the church, but God present through this historic and particular group of people. By refusing to bury her he was reminding her of the story that will sustain her and all Christians as we face death.

29. James Lapsley has recently objected to Don Browning's attempt to understand pastoral theology as a branch of ethics, "because ethics is focused upon norms and goals

as its primary concern, and because much pastoral care is only tangentially related to ethics in any developed sense of the term. Rather the 'cup of cold water' extended in a personal relationship is generic to the gospel itself. To be sure, ethical and even disciplinary questions do explicitly arise in pastoral care (the latter when there is a 'clear and present danger' to self or others), but in the instance the theologically discerned possibilities retain status as criteria" ("Practical Theology and Pastoral Theology," *Pastoral Theology*, edited by Don Browning [Philadelphia: Fortress Press, 1983], p. 170). Lapsley's limited account of ethics prevents him from seeing that his very understanding of what constitutes a "pastoral situation" already assumes a normative stance. As a result, he fails to see that even when we begin with "suffering persons," we cannot help but try to enable them to bring their suffering in contact with the story of the gospel.

30. In his *Pastoral Theology: Essentials of Ministry* (San Francisco: Harper & Row, 1983), Thomas Oden has presented an account of the ministry that attempts to restore integrity to the ministerial office. He does so, however, by insisting that all the varied activities of the pastor must have a single center of life—life in Christ. When clergy are disconnected from this historic identity and "from the history of revelation and the capacity of God to address the heart, they easily become too cheaply accommodative to the present culture and lose the finely balanced judgment that the tradition has called wisdom" (p. 55).

31. Some think that this example necessarily presupposes a negative attitude toward abortion: I think this is not the case. Although I have argued elsewhere that abortion as a practice cannot be seen as a "good" by Christians, my depiction of this case does not depend on that analysis. Rather, all that is presupposed is the woman's own general feeling that abortion, all other things being equal, is not "a good thing." What I do think this example exhibits is the low state of moral reflection in many Protestant churches about such matters. Generally, Protestants have simply accepted our society's unthinking liberalism about abortion and the place of children in general. As a result, we flounder as pastors, since we cannot draw on any set of moral convictions to help people guide their lives. If such cases tell us anything, it is that we cannot avoid making these kinds of matters subjects that we must confront if the church is to make any pretense of being, in James Gustafson's memorable phrase, a community of moral discourse.

III
SERVING IN THE WORLD

A CHRISTIAN CRITIQUE OF CHRISTIAN AMERICA

1. Setting the Agenda: A Report on a Conversation

At a conference on narrative and virtue I had an encounter with a philosopher which raises the problem with which I wish to deal. My philosophical counterpart has been strongly influenced by C. S. Pierce and is also a committed Jew. In his paper he had argued that most of the rational paradigms accepted by contemporary philosophy cannot make sense of Judaism. We began by exchanging views about why current ethical theory seems so committed to foundationalist epistemological assumptions. We shared in general a sympathy with anti-foundationalist arguments, though neither of us wanted to give up any possibility of some more modest realist epistemology. We also found we were equally critical of liberal political theory and in particular the ahistorical character of its methodology. Then our conversation suddenly took a turn for which I was completely unprepared. It went something like this:

Philosopher: Do you support prayer in the public schools?

Theologian: No, I do not, because I do not want the state sponsoring my faith.

Philosopher: That is not the real reason. You are just afraid to be for anything that Jerry Falwell is for. You really are a liberal in spite of your doubts about liberalism's philosophical adequacy.

Theologian: That is not fair. I did not say I was against school prayer because I think such prayer is coercive, though I think such considerations are not unimportant, but because state-sponsored prayer cannot help but give the impression that the state is friendly toward religion. Moreover, prayers, insofar as they can pass muster in a religiously pluralistic context, are so anemic that they cannot help but give a distorted view of God. So I am against school prayer not because it is against the tenets of liberalism but because it is theologically a scandal.

171

Philosopher: That is not good enough. As a Christian you typically do not give a damn about the Jews. You want to create a civilization and society and then walk away from it when the going gets a little tough. Of course the prayers sponsored by public authorities are degraded but they still remind people that they are creatures. A vague god prayed to vaguely is better than no god or prayer at all. Otherwise we face the possibility of a neo-pagan culture for which liberal procedural rules of fair play will be no match.

Theologian: I am a bit surprised to hear you argue this way. After all, Christians have persecuted and killed Jews with as much enthusiasm as anyone. I would think you would feel safer in a secular culture than one that is quasi-Christian. Indeed, has that not been the dominant social strategy of Jews since the Enlightenment? The way to secure protection from the Christians is to create and support liberal societies where religion is relegated to the private sphere and thus becomes unavailable for public policy directed against the Jews or those of any other religious faith.

Philosopher: I do not deny that is the strategy of many Jews, but I think this century has shown it to be a decisive failure. Pagan societies kill us with an abandon that Christians can never muster. Christianity even in a degraded form at least has material convictions that can make the persecution and killing of Jews problematic. Paganism has no such convictions, so I will take my chances with the Christians and their societies. After all, we Jews do not ask for much. We just do not want you to kill our children. Living in quasi-Christian societies means we have to put up with a lot of inconvenience and prejudice—i.e., Christmas as a school holiday—but we Jews have long known how to handle that. We flourish under a little prejudice. What we cannot stand is the false tolerance of liberalism which relegates us to the arena of being just one religion among others.

Theologian: So if I understand you rightly, you are suggesting that you want me as a Christian to support school prayer, even if such prayers are but forms of degraded Christian religiosity, because at least that continues to underwrite the assumption we are a "religious" society. Such an assumption allows an appeal to a higher standard of justice which makes the survival of the Jewish people more likely.

Philosopher: That is about right. You Christians have to take responsibility for what you have done. You created a civilization based on belief in God and it is your responsibility to continue to support that civilization.

Theologian: But you know yourself that such a social strategy cannot help but lead to the continued degradation of Christianity. The more

Christians try to make Christianity a philosophy sufficient to sustain a society, especially a liberal society, the more we must distort or explain away our fundamental beliefs. Therefore, in the name of sustaining a civilization Christians increasingly undercut the ability of the church to take a critical stance toward this society. Even when the church acts as a critic in such a context, it cannot be more than a friendly critic, since it has a stake in maintaining the basic structure of society.

Philosopher: Why should that bother me? Christians have always been willing in the past to degrade their convictions to attain social and political power (of course, always in order that they might "do good"). Why should they start worrying about being degraded now? On that score it seems a little late. For the church to start to worry about being pure is about as realistic as Madonna to worry about being a virgin. It is just too late. So if you care anything about the Jews you ought to support school prayer.

Our conversation did not end at this point but what I have portrayed is enough for my purposes. Even though I think most of what my philosopher friend has to say is right, for theological reasons I still cannot support school prayer. That I cannot puts me at odds with the social strategy of most Christians, both liberal and conservative, in America. In the next section I will try to explain why this is the case. Then the ground will be prepared for me to suggest what a more radical Christian critique of America entails, both in terms of its logic as well as a political strategy.

2. Liberal Christianity and American Democracy, or Why Jerry Falwell Is Such a Pain

Since the turn of the century, one of the dominant themes in Christian social ethics has been the Christian's responsibility for societal affairs. Time and time again it is argued that faith and action cannot be separated. Our religious convictions cannot be relegated to one sphere of our lives and our social and political activities to another. Since the faith of Christians is a faith that does justice, there is no way we can avoid political activity. Whether the political realm is viewed Lutheran-like as a realm of lesser evil or more Calvinistically as the arena of the mediocre good, Christians cannot avoid involvement in the political process. That is especially the case in a democratic society in which the actions of

173

individual citizens can make a difference.

Armed with this set of presuppositions, Christians in the "main-stream" denominations attacked those Christians who maintained no particular social or political responsibilities. This position, they argued, pietistically relegates salvation to the individual's relation to God and thus betrays the essential Christian claim that God is Lord of all creation. What must be remembered is that Jesus came preaching a Kingdom that makes it impossible for his followers to be indifferent to the injustices in their surrounding social orders. On these grounds mainstream churches, such as those that constitute the National Council of Churches, urged Baptist and other pietistic Christians to join them in the political struggle to make this a more just society. As is often pointed out, not to take a political stand in the name of being Christian in fact is to take a polit-ical stand.

Pietists, in defense of their position, sometimes responded by appeal-ing not to their theological convictions but instead to what they con-sidered the normative commitments of the American society—namely, that our constitution has erected a "wall of separation between church and state." In the name of maintaining the freedom of religion the church claims no competency in matters political. The difficulty with this posi-tion, however, is that it attributes a perspective to the Constitution that simply is not there. Neither the free exercise clause nor the nonestablish-ment clause prohibits Christians, either as organized in churches or as individuals, from seeking to influence their society or government. Just to the extent the free-church tradition allows itself to be so excluded from the public arena, moreover, it underwrites an individualistic account of Christianity which is antithetical to its very nature.

Such was the state of the debate among Christians until recently. But now suddenly everything has changed, because the message finally got across to the pietistic Baptists. They have become politically active, seeking to influence our society and government to support causes in the name of making this a better society. Jerry Falwell represents the triumph of mainstream Christianity in America, as he is convinced, just like Martin Luther King, Jr., that Christians cannot abandon the political realm in their desire for justice. They must seek through the constitu-tionally guaranteed means to influence our political representatives to prevent abortion, to support democratic regimes around the world, to support Israel, to provide support for the family, and so on.

Therefore, the mainstream won, but it is not a victory they are celebrat-ing. For it turns out that once politically inactive Christians became active, the causes they supported were not those the mainstream wanted supported. The temptation is to try to defeat this new political activism by using the slogans of the past—religion and politics do not mix; one should not try to force one's religious views on anyone through public policy—but to do so is to go against the position the mainstream has been arguing for years.

In order to understand how we have reached this point in American Protestantism I need to call your attention to some aspects of the history of Christianity in America. I do not mean I am going to give you a rendition of Puritan America or engage in the debate about how "Christian" America has been.[1] While such studies and questions are interesting and may still have some normative importance, they are not crucial for helping us understand why Falwell presents such a challenge to mainstream Christianity. To understand that we need to appreciate why Christian theologians and ethicists in America, especially since the nineteenth century, have assumed that Christianity and democracy are integrally related.

That they have done so is because America stands as the great experiment in what Max Stackhouse has identified as "constructive Protestantism." Stackhouse notes that in *Social Teaching of the Christian Churches* Ernst Troeltsch argues that only two major Christian social philosophies have ever been developed—the Catholic and the Calvinist. Yet each of these as social philosophies no longer seems viable. "The vision of an organic, hierarchical order sanctified by objectified means of grace, and that of an established theocracy of elect saints who are justified by grace through faith, must both be judged as no longer live options for social reconstruction. This is not to suggest that these visions do not still hold power. . . But this *is* to suggest that these two forms of 'Christendom' have ended—or rather, have played their part and now must yield the stage after their immeasurable contribution to the drama of Christianity in modern culture."[2]

According to Stackhouse, the crucial question is whether Christianity can develop another "social philosophy." If it cannot, it would then seem the social ethical power of Christianity is at an end. Stackhouse argues that American Christianity has, in fact, developed a third option, which he calls "conciliar denominationalism."[3] The character of this new form of social philosophy Stackhouse sees prefigured in Walter Rauschenbusch, who held together two conflicting motifs, sectarianism and Christendom, that constitute the unique blend of "conciliar denominationalism." "On the one hand, Rauschenbusch comes from an evangelical background from which he gained a sense of intense and explicit faith that could only be held by fully committed members. On the other

175

hand, Rauschenbusch lived in the age of lingering hope for a catholic 'Christian culture' and in an age that, especially through the developing social sciences, saw the legitimacy of secular realms. He, like the developing 'conciliar denominations,' saw the necessity of the select body of believers anticipating the Kingdom in word and deed in good sectarian fashion, and of taking the world seriously on its own terms, as did all visions of Christendom. These motifs conspire in his thought to produce a vision of a revolutionized responsible society for which a socially understood gospel is the catalyst."[4]

Rauschenbusch, as the champion of liberal Christianity, could speak straightforwardly of the need to "christianize" social orders. "It is not enough to christianize individuals; we must christianize societies, organizations, nations, for they too have a life of their own which may be made better or worse."[5] On that basis he thought it quite possible to speak of saved and unsaved organizations. "The one is under the law of Christ, the other under the law of mammon. The one is democratic and the other autocratic. Whenever capitalism has invaded a new country or industry, there has been a speeding up in labor and in the production of wealth, but always with a trail of human misery, discontent, bitterness, and demoralization. When cooperation has invaded a country there has been increased thrift, education, and neighborly feeling, and there has been no trail of concomitant evil and no cries of protest."[6]

The difference between saved and unsaved social orders, from Rauschenbusch's perspective, is quite simple—saved social orders and institutions are democratic. As he says, "social sciences confirm the correctness of Christ's protest against the stratification of society in ranks and classes. What is the general tendency toward democracy and the gradual abolition of hereditary privileges but history's assent to the revolutionary dogmas of Christ?"[7] The Kingdom of God is not a concept or ideal for Rauschenbusch; it is a historical force at work in humanity. The way it ultimately works its way out, moreover, is in the form of democracy. As he puts it, "Where religion and intellect combine, the foundation is laid for political democracy."[8]

If, as Stackhouse suggests, America is the great experiment in "constructive Protestantism," it seems what is Christian about that construction is democracy.[9] For in claiming a close interrelation between Christianity and democracy, Rauschenbusch is hardly an isolated instance. As Jan Dawson has recently argued, at the turn of this century there developed a "faith in the spiritual oneness of Christianity and democracy, based on the democratic theology of Christianity and concerned primarily with the survival of Christianity in troubled modern democracies."[10] To support democracy became a means of supporting Christianity and vice versa.

Dawson quotes Lyman Abbott, successor to Henry Ward Beecher, in the liberal Christian paper *Outlook* to the effect that "Democracy is not merely a political theory, it is not merely a social opinion; it is a profound religious faith. . . To him who holds it, this one fundamental faith in the Fatherhood of God and in the universal brotherhood of man is the essence of democracy."[11] If democracy was seen as the institutionalized form of Christianity, it was no less true that democracy was dependent on religion to survive. Thus in 1907, the year following the publication of the article by Abbott, Robert Ashworth wrote in the *Chicago Divinity School Journal* that "the fate of the democratic movement rests ultimately upon religion. Religion is essential to democracy, and is, indeed, its foundation. It is based upon the New Testament principle of the equal value of every soul in the sight of the Divine Father."[12]

This kind of direct theological appeal in support of democracy becomes more muted as Christian thinkers become increasingly aware of the religious and social pluralism of America, but that does not lessen their enthusiasm for democracy as that form of society and government that best institutionalizes Christian social philosophy. Reinhold Niebuhr is certainly a case in point. Vicious in his critique of the theological and social optimism of the "social gospelers'" defense of democracy, he never questioned the assumption that democracy was the most appropriate form of society and government for Christians. What was needed, according to Niebuhr, was to provide a more adequate basis for democracy in a realistic account of human nature. Such an account, he thought, was to be found primarily in the "Christian view of human nature [that] is more adequate for the development of a democratic society than either the optimism with which democracy has become historically associated or the moral cynicism which inclines human communities to tyrannical political strategies."[13]

In effect, from Rauschenbusch to the present Christian social ethics has had one agenda: to show why American democracy possesses distinctive religious status. The primary subject of Christian ethics in America has been America.[14] This has now even become the project for Roman Catholic social ethics as exemplified in the work of John Courtney Murray. It was Murray's task to make America amenable to Catholic social theory by interpreting the separation of church and state as a confession by the state of its incompetence in matters of religion[15] and at the same time, to make Catholics amenable to America by showing that Catholics can enthusiastically support democracy as an imaginative

177

solution to the problem of religious pluralism.[16] Murray argued even a stronger case by suggesting that American democracy, whose political substance consists in an order of antecedent rights to the state,[17] can only be sustained by the Catholic theory of natural law as the only alternative to the destructive individualism of Locke and Hobbes.[18]

It is only against this background that one can understand and/or appreciate the work of Richard Neuhaus. In his much publicized book, *The Naked Public Square: Religion and Democracy in America*, Neuhaus argues that we are facing a crisis in our society. Because religious discourse has increasingly been excluded from our public life, he fears that a moral vacuum has been created. This vacuum threatens constantly to be filled by totalitarianism, as the isolation of the individual from mediating structures gives us little power to stand against the omnivorous appetite of the bureaucratic state.[19] The only way out of this predicament is to mend the "rupture between public policy and moral sentiment. But the only moral sentiment of public effect is the sentiment that is embodied in and reinforced by living tradition. There are no a-religious moral traditions of public, or at least of democratic, force in American life. This is not to say that morality must be embodied in religion nor that the whole of religion is morality. It is to say that among the American people, religion and morality are conjoined. Religion in our popular life is the morality-bearing part of culture, and in that sense the heart of culture."[20]

From this perspective Neuhaus is appreciative of the Moral Majority. For in spite of the crudeness with which they often put their position they have at least raised the issue of the public value of religion that at one time was the agenda of political liberals. Rather than condemning the Moral Majority, Neuhaus seeks to help them enter the public debate by basing their appeals to principles that are accessible to the public. "Publicly assertive religious forces will have to learn that the remedy for the naked public square is not naked religion in public. They will have to develop a mediating language by which ultimate truths can be related to the penultimate and prepenultimate questions of political and legal content. In our several traditions there are rich conceptual resources for the development of such mediating language—whether concepts be called natural law, common grace, general revelation, or the order of creation. Such a civil engagement of secular and religious forces could produce a new public philosophy to sustain this American experiment in liberal democracy. The result may not be that we would agree with one another. Indeed there may be more disagreement. But at least we would know what we are disagreeing about, namely, different accounts of the transcendent good by which we might order our life together. Contra Justice Blackmun and legions of others, democracy is not served by evading the question of the good. Democracy becomes a political community worthy of moral actors only when we engage the question of the good."[21]

Neuhaus challenges mainline Protestant liberalism to live up to its rightful commitment to sustaining democracy as the socially specific form that Christianity should take.[22] As he puts it, "The main line of the mainline story was confidence and hope regarding the Americanizing of Christianity and the Christianizing of America."[23] Indeed, he argues that in spite of their fervor for disestablishing Christianity in America, most liberals remain committed to "Christianizing" the social order, only the synonyms for "Christianize" today "include terms such as justice, equality, and sustainability."[24]

That such is the case helps explain the enthusiasm for the work of John Rawls among those working in Christian ethics. Harlan Beckley puts the matter well as he notes that the emergence of a politically powerful Christian right has made vivid a dilemma which Christian ethics has still to resolve. "The dilemma is: How can an evaluation of the distribution of rights, duties, benefits, and burdens which society necessarily imposes upon all of its citizens be faithful to Christian beliefs without forcing others to accept the distinctive moral implications of beliefs they do not and should not be required to share?"[25] According to Beckley, "This dilemma can only be resolved if the justification for principles of justice is founded upon general beliefs and values that others hold, or can be reasonably expected to hold, and which Christians can affirm on the basis of their distinctive beliefs."[26] Beckley argues to accomplish this resolution "the distinctively Christian moral ideal of love obligates those who adhere to it to embrace the beliefs which undergird John Rawls' idea of justice as fairness."[27] Rawls thus becomes the language of common grace which continues the project of Christianizing America.

Of course, there are disagreements among Christian ethicists on this score. Neuhaus, for example, thinks Rawls' theory threatens to destroy the individual "by depriving him of all those personal particularities that are the essence of being an individual."[28] As a result, Rawls' account is ahistorical, in contradistinction to the "Judeo-Christian tradition" which is "premised upon the concept of real history, real change, happening in an incomplete universe that is still awaiting its promised fulfillment."[29] What is needed, according to Neuhaus, is a recovery of some substantive account of the goods that make a good society possible through attending to the concrete desires of real people who are not required to leave their religious convictions behind when they participate in the public arena.

This same set of issues is at the center of the much-discussed and praised book *Habits of the Heart*. For the critique of "individualism" which is the hallmark of that book is but part of a larger agenda which is in essential continuity with the hope to Christianize America. As the authors suggest, in spite of our individualism, "we have never been, and still are not, a collection of private individuals who, except for a conscious contract to create a minimal government, have nothing in common. Our lives make sense in a thousand ways, most of which we are unaware of, because of traditions that are centuries, if not millennia, old. It is these traditions that help us to know that it does make a difference who we are and how we treat one another. But if we owe the meaning of our lives to biblical and republican traditions of which we seldom consciously think, is there not the danger that the erosion of these traditions may eventually deprive us of that meaning altogether? We would argue that if we are ever to enter that new world that so far has been powerless to be born, it will be through reversing modernity's tendency to obliterate all previous culture. We need to learn again from the cultural riches of the human species and to reappropriate and revitalize those riches so that they can speak to our condition today."[30] This sounds very much like a call for reconstituting Christian America.

I have no interest in trying to resolve the many disagreements among Neuhaus, Beckley, Bellah, and Falwell. Rather, what I have attempted to do is to show that the reason Falwell is such a challenge to the Christian mainstream in America is not because he is so different from them, but because he has basically accepted their agenda.[31] The Christian right and the Christian left do not disagree about the religious status of the American experiment. They just disagree about what language and/or political theory will allow them to accomplish their common goal of making American democracy as close as possible to a manifestation of God's Kingdom.

3. What a Christian Critique of Christian America Should Look Like

For most Christians in America, from the nominal Christian to the committed social activist to the theologian, it is simply unthinkable to theorize outside the tradition I have just tried to sketch. Yet my refusal to support prayer in school is because I find myself outside that tradition. That I do so is because I do not believe that the universalism that is intrinsic to the Christian faith is carried by the culture of the West, but instead is to be found first and foremost in the church.[32] From this perspective something has already gone wrong when Christians think they can ask, "What is the best form of society or government?"[33] This question assumes that Christians should or do have social and political power so they can determine the ethos of society. That this assumption has long been with us does nothing to confirm its truth.

That assumption, in short, is the heritage of what John Howard Yoder has called "the Constantinian sources of Western social ethics." It is an assumption shared by Christians and non-Christians alike, for the very logic of most contemporary philosophical accounts of ethics and social theory accepts its essential rightness only in secular terms. By calling our attention to Constantine, Yoder has no stake in determining the sincerity of Constantine's conversion or whether it was exactly at that time that a decisive shift in Christian assumptions took place. Rather, Constantine is the symbol of the decisive shift in the logic of moral argument when Christians ceased being a minority and accepted Caesar as a member of the church. It is that logic we must understand if a genuine Christian critique of Christian America is to be made.

The most obvious consequence of the change occasioned by Constantine, according to Yoder, was the change in the composition of the church. Prior to that time Christians had been a minority who at least required some degree of loyalty. After that time everyone was a member. It now takes conviction to be a pagan. As a result, Christians are now forced to develop a doctrine of the "true church" that remains invisible (p. 136).[34]

This shift is of crucial importance for how ethics is now understood. Prior to the time of Constantine, Christian belief in God's rule of the world was a matter of faith. However, with Constantine the idea that providence is no longer an object of faith for God's governance of the world was now thought to be empirically evident in the person of the Christian ruler. With this changed eschatology, ethics had to change "because one must aim one's behavior at strengthening the regime, and because the ruler himself must have very soon some approbation and perhaps some guidance as he does things the earlier church would have perhaps disapproved" (p. 137). As a result, the distinctive character of Christian life is now primarily identified with inwardness since everyone by definition is already Christian.

Once Christianity became dominant, moreover, it was now thought that moral discourse must be that which can direct the behavior of anyone. Servanthood and love of enemy, contentment and monogamy, cannot be expected of everyone. So a duality develops in ethics between "evangelical counsels" for the motivated and "precepts" for everyone else. Perhaps even a more significant change is the assumption that the decisive ethical questions become, to quote Yoder, "What would happen if everyone did it? If everyone gave their wealth away what would we do for capital? If everyone loved their enemies who would ward off the communists? This argument could be met on other levels, but here the only point is to observe that such reasoning would have been preposterous in the early church and remains ludicrous wherever committed Christians accept realistically their minority status. Far more fitting than 'What if everybody did it' would be its inverse, 'What if nobody else acted like a Christian and we did?'" (p. 139).[35]

With this new universalism comes an increasing need to test moral discourse by its effectiveness. Once the course of history is thought to be empirically discernible and the prosperity of our regime the measure of the good, efficacy becomes a decisive test for the moral rightness of our action. Self-sacrifice that is not tied to some long-term account of result becomes irrational. This is particularly important in assessing the validity of violence and the Christian's participation in war.

What is important about Yoder's depiction of the change in moral logic occasioned by the Constantinian turn is that the effects he describes are still with us. With the Renaissance and Reformation "Christendom" was replaced by the nation-state. Christians, however, did not respond to this change by maintaining the cosmopolitanism of the Holy Roman Empire, but rather now maintained that Christian societies could wage war on one another in the name of preserving their Christian culture. With the Enlightenment, the link between church and state was broken, but the moral identification of Christians with the state remained strong. This has been especially the case in America where "once the separation of church and state is seen as theologically desirable, a society where this separation is achieved is not a pagan society but a nation structured according to the will of God. For nearly two centuries, in fact, the language of American public discourse was not only religious, not only Christian, but specifically Protestant. Moral identification of church with nation remains despite institutional separation. In fact, forms of institutional interlocking develop which partly deny the theory of separation (chaplaincies, tax exemptions)" (p. 142).

If there is to be a genuine Christian critique of Christian America, I am convinced that this habit of thought, which Yoder calls Constantinianism, must be given up. Otherwise, we Christians remain caught in the same habits of thought and behavior that implicitly or explicitly assume that insofar as America is a democracy she is Christian. As a result Christians lose exactly the skills necessary to see how deeply they have been compromised by the assumption that their task is to rule, if not the government, at least the ethos of America. That is why Christian social strategy in America continues to be caught in a fateful ambiguity— namely, Christians claim that Christianity, or at least religion, should be more present in public life yet they want to make government itself religiously neutral. The history of the Supreme Court decisions on church/state issues should be enough to convince anyone that there is no easy way to resolve this tension in the American legal system, much less the social and political systems.[36]

Am I therefore suggesting that Christians must "withdraw" from the social, political, and legal life of America? I am certainly not arguing that; rather, I am trying to suggest that in order to answer questions of "why" or "how" Christians participate in the life of this country we do not need a theory about the Christian character of democracy. Rather, I am suggesting, with Yoder, that as Christians we would "be more relaxed and compulsive about running the world if we made our peace with our minority situation, seeing this neither as a dirty trick of destiny nor as some great new progress but simply as the unmasking of the myth of Christendom, which wasn't true even when it was believed" (p. 158).

As Yoder argues, since almost all rulers claim to be our benefactors in order to justify their rule, there is no reason that Christians cannot use that very language to call their rulers to be more humane in their ways of governing. Moreover, if we are lucky enough to be in a situation where the ruler's language of justification claims to have the consent of the governed, we can use the machinery of democracy for our own and our neighbor's advantage. But we should not, thereby, be lulled into believing that "we the people" are thereby governing ourselves. Democracy is still government by the elite, though it may be less oppressive since it uses language in its justification that provides ways to mitigate oppressiveness. But that does not make democracy, from a Christian point of view, different in kind from states of another form (pp. 158–159).

Perhaps the hardest habit to break deriving from our Constantinianism is the assumption that if we do not govern then surely society and/or government will fall into anarchy or totalitarianism. But I notice no shortage of people willing to rule nor any absence of ideologies for rule. The problem is not Christians disavowing ruling, but rather that when Christians rule they tend to create international and national disorder because they have such a calling to make things right. To quote Yoder for the last time, if Christians "claim for democracy the status of a social institution *sui generis*, we shall inflate ourselves and destroy our neighbors through the demonic demands of the claims we make for our system and we shall pollute our Christian faith by making of it a civil religion. If, on the other hand, we protect ourselves from the Constantinianism of that view of democracy, we may find the realistic liberty to foster and celebrate relative democratization as one of the prophetic ministries of a servant people in a world we do not control" (pp. 165–166).

I am aware that the position I have taken will be a surprise to most Christians schooled on the assumption that there is an intrinsic relation between Christianity and America. Yet I suspect the position will be equally unwelcomed by many who dislike calls like that of Neuhaus for a recovery of the role of religion in American life. They want people who still use their private time to entertain religious convictions to be willing to work to create a social order and corresponding government that relegates those convictions to the private sphere. That is done, of course, in the name of creating a democratic society that is based on universal claims justified by reason qua reason.[37] Constantinianism is a hard habit to break even for those who no longer understand themselves to be religious.

From this perspective the problem with Yoder (and Falwell) is their refusal to find a neutral or at least nonconfrontational way to state the social implications of their religious convictions.[38] That is not playing the game fairly, as it makes religion more public than is healthy for an allegedly pluralistic society. After all, there have to be some limits to our pluralism.

Of course Yoder might well respond that he is willing on a case-by-case basis pragmatically to use the allegedly more universal language of our society. But for many, I suspect, such a pragmatic approach would be insufficient. It is not enough to be willing to play the game of the putative neutral or objective language and procedures of pluralist democracy: one must be willing to believe that such language and procedures are truly the form of the society any people anywhere would choose if they had the material means, institutional creativity, and philosophical acumen. To challenge that presumption, as Yoder has, is I think the necessary starting point for any genuine Christian critique of Christian America.

4. On Being Christian in America

But where does this leave us? If America is not the "new Jerusalem," does that mean Christians must seek to make America live consistent with secular presuppositions? In order to make the line between being Christian and being American clear, must we side with those who wish to force any religious phenomenon out of the public arena? Should we rejoice in the destructive kind of individualism which is so graphically displayed in *Habits of the Heart*? Do we not have a stake in sustaining a public ethos that might make the rise of paganism, which might well use the language of Christianity, less likely?

I see no reason that the position I have taken would make me give an affirmative answer to these questions. I believe that Christians should not will that secular society be more unjust than it already has a tendency to be. Therefore, we have a stake in fostering those forms of human association that ensure that the virtues can be sustained. Virtues make it possible to sustain a society committed to working out differences short of violence.[39] What I fear, however, is that in the absence of those associations we will seek to solve the moral anomie of the American people through state action or by a coercive reclaiming of Christian America.[40]

Therefore, if I refuse to support prayer in the public school it becomes all the more important that I urge Christians to learn to pray authentically as Christians. For if Christians reclaim prayer as an end in itself rather than a way to confirm the "Christian nature" of our society, we will perform our most important civic responsibility. As Origen argued, what more important public service can we render than to pray that the emperor recognize his or her status as a creature of God? Such a prayer is no less significant in a society that believes "the people" have in fact become the emperor.

NOTES

1. For an extremely interesting approach to this latter question see Mark Noll, Nathan Hatch, and George Marsden, *The Search for Christian America* (Westchester, Illinois: Crossway Books, 1983). In summary, their position is that "a careful study of the facts of history shows that early America does not deserve to be considered uniquely, distinctively or even predominantly Christian, if we mean by the word 'Christian' a state of society reflecting the ideals presented in Scripture. There is no lost golden age to which American Christians may return. In addition, a careful study of history will also show that evangelicals themselves were often partly to blame for the spread of secularism in contemporary American life. We feel also that careful examination of Christian teaching on government, the state, and the nature of culture shows that the idea of a 'Christian nation' is a very ambiguous concept which is usually harmful to effective Christian action in society" (p. 17).

2. Max Stackhouse, "Introduction" to Walter Rauschenbusch's *The Righteousness of the Kingdom* (Nashville: Abingdon Press, 1968), p. 21.

3. Ibid., p. 22.

4. Ibid., pp. 22–23.

5. Rauschenbusch, *The Righteousness of the Kingdom*, p. 102.

6. Walter Rauschenbusch, *Theology for the Social Gospel* (Nashville: Abingdon Press, 1917), pp. 112–113.

7. Rauschenbusch, *The Righteousness of the Kingdom*, p. 199.

8. Rauschenbusch, *Theology for the Social Gospel*, p. 165.

9. For Stackhouse's own constructive efforts to extend Rauschenbusch's program, only now in terms of human rights, see his *Creeds, Society, and Human Rights* (Grand Rapids: Eerdmans, 1984). In defense of his position Stackhouse provides a history of the joining of Puritanism and liberalism to create the universalistic creed of rights that culminated in the United Declaration on Human Rights. He notes these "principles could not be articulated in the particular language of Christian piety which had shaped both the Christian and secular liberal philosophers who had first developed them. Representatives from many cultures and religions would have resisted overt theological formulations in christological or deist terms. The principles had to be stated in 'confessionally neutral' terms. But even at this point we see the triumph of the basic assumptions of the Liberal-Puritan synthesis. The state itself should not be 'religious.' In this view the theologically and morally valid state is one limited by righteous principles and one that allows other organizations to define what is religiously valid. In brief, the 'godly state' is a secular state" (p. 103). Stackhouse's account seems far too sanguine about how the obvious tensions between the Puritan sense of community can be reconciled with the individualism of liberalism. But even if that were not a problem, one cannot help but wonder what has happened that a "secular state" by definition can be called "godly."

10. Jan Dawson, "The Religion of Democracy in Early Twentieth-Century America," *Journal of Church and State*, 27, 1 (Winter, 1985), p. 47.

11. Quoted in Dawson, p. 48.

12. Ibid., p. 48.

13. Reinhold Niebuhr, *The Children of Light and the Children of Darkness* (New York: Charles Scribner's Sons, 1944), p. XIII. In fairness to Niebuhr, it should be pointed out that he wrote *The Children of Light* at the end of World War II in the interest of trying to deflate some of the more enthusiastic celebrations of democracy the war had occasioned. Yet Niebuhr remained throughout his life a firm supporter of democracy as that social system that best embodies the Christian understanding of man. Richard Fox observes, "What is still surprising about *The Children of Light* is that the author of *Moral Man*, even if older and wiser, could have become so complacent about democratic processes in advanced industrial society. The book elevated gradualist experimentation and piecemeal reform to the level of a basic axiom" (*Reinhold Niebuhr: A Biography* [New York: Pantheon Books, 1985], p. 220).

14. For a more complete development of this claim, see my *Against the Nations: War and Survival in a Liberal Society* (Minneapolis: Winston-Seabury Press, 1985), pp. 23–50.

15. This part of Murray's work is often, unfortunately, ignored. One of the reasons for this may be that these were articles published in *Theological Studies*, 13 & 14 (1953), called "The Church and Totalitarian Democracy" and "Leo XIII: Separation of Church and State." They are still worth reading.

16. This is, of course, the main argument of Murray's *We Hold These Truths* (Garden City, New York: Image Books, 1964).

17. Murray, *We Hold These Truths*, p. 308.

18. In his *An American Strategic Theology* (Ramsey, New Jersey: Paulist Press, 1982), John Coleman provides the best Roman Catholic attempt to continue Murray's project. Coleman, however, is much more interested in how Catholicism can act to renew the ethos or civil religion of America than the more strictly constitutional issues with which Murray was concerned.

19. Richard Neuhaus, *The Naked Public Square: Religion and Democracy in America* (Grand Rapids: Eerdmans, 1984), pp. 83–86. Charles Taylor rightly argues that no one saw this problem more clearly than did Hegel — namely, that "absolute freedom requires homogeneity. It cannot brook differences which would prevent everyone participating totally in the decisions of the society. And what is even more, it requires some near unanimity of will

to emerge from this deliberation, for otherwise the majority would just be imposing its will on the minority and freedom would not be universal. But differentiation of some fairly essential kinds are ineradicable. Moreover they are recognized in our post-Romantic climate as essential to human identity. Men cannot simply identify themselves as men, but they define themselves more immediately by their partial community, cultural, linguistic, confessional and so, on. Modern democracy is therefore in a bind. I think the dilemma of this kind can be seen in contemporary society. Modern societies have moved towards much greater homogeneity and greater interdependence, so that partial communities lost their autonomy, and to some extent, their identity. But great differences remain; only because of the ideology of homogeneity these differential characteristics no longer have meaning and value for those who have them. Thus the rural population is taught by the mass media to see itself as just lacking in some of the advantages of a more advanced life style. Homogenization thus increases minority alienation and resentment and the first response of liberal society is to try even more of the same: programs to eliminate poverty, or assimulate Indians, move populations out of declining regions, bring an urban way of life to the countryside. But the radical response is to convert this sense of alienation into a demand for 'absolute freedom.' The idea is to overcome alienation by creating a society in which everyone, including the present 'out' groups, participate fully in the decisions. But both these solutions would simply aggravate the problem, which is the homogenization has undermined the communities or characteristics by which people formerly identified themselves and put nothing in their place. What does step into the gap almost everywhere is ethnic or national identity. Nationalism has become the most powerful focus of identity in modern society. The demand for radical freedom can and frequently does join up with nationalism and is given a definite impetus and direction from this" (*Hegel and Modern Society* [Cambridge: Cambridge University Press, 1979], pp. 114–115). Neuhaus' point is profound, but I do not see how he provides an adequate response since he continues to support the political and economic presumptions that are the source of the difficulty.

20. Neuhaus, p. 154.

21. Richard Neuhaus, "Nihilism Without the Abyss: Law, Rights, and Transcendent Good," paper delivered at 1985 conference on Religion and Law at Catholic University Law School. Unpublished manuscript, pp. 14–15. For a similar claim, see *The Naked Public Square*, p. 36. While agreeing with Neuhaus that religion needs to help our society discover or create a moral discourse for the public sphere, John Coleman rightly raises questions about the assumed neutrality or objectivity of that discourse. Thus he criticizes Brian Hehir for requiring Christians to come to the public arena shorn of their particularistic commitments. As Coleman says, he does not think it possible to escape "the 'permanent hermeneutical predicament' of particular languages and community traditions in a conflict of interpretive schemes through the emergence of a common universal language. I fear that this proposal could court the risk of a continuation of the pernicious intertwining of an ethics of deep concern with an ethic of looking out for number one. But finally, and most persuasive for me, I simply do not know anywhere else to look in American culture besides to our religious ethical resources to find the social wisdom and ethical orientation we would seem to need if we are to face as Americans our new context of increasing interdependence at the national and international level" (*An American Strategic Theology*, pp. 197–198). Thus Coleman, like many Protestant thinkers, calls us to renew the biblical and republican-virtue tradition against contemporary liberalism. (This is, of course, the main theme of William Sullivan's *Reconstructing Public Philosophy* [Berkeley: University of California Press, 1982]). It is a strange social order indeed that makes Catholics so committed to making America work that they accept the project of constructive Protestantism. For a provocative article of the destructive results this process has had on orthodoxy, see Vigen Guroian, "The Americanization of Orthodoxy: Crisis and Challenge," *The Greek Orthodox Theological Review*, 29, 3 (1984), pp. 255–267.

22. Neuhaus, *The Naked Public Square*, p. 121.

23. Ibid., p. 220. In an unpublished paper, "Democratic Morality—A Possibility," Neuhaus

responds to this essay and qualifies the starkness of this claim. As he says, "I count myself among the many Christians, perhaps the majority of Christians in America, who have the gravest reservations about the idea of 'Christian America.' It makes sense to speak, always cautiously, of America as a Christian society in terms of historical forces, ideas, and demography. But no society is worthy of the name of Christ, except the society that is the church, and then it is worthy only by virtue of being made worthy through the grace of God in Christ" (p. 6).

24. Ibid., p. 230. For one of the ablest critiques of Neuhaus see George Marsden, "Secularism and the Public Square," *This World*, 11 (Spring–Summer, 1985), pp. 48–62. Marsden challenges Neuhaus' contention that religion is the morality-bearing part of our culture thus denying Neuhaus' statement of the problem. As Marsden says, "Non-theistic secularism also promotes a morality. The problem regarding public philosophy is not simply that of whether or not we have morality in public life. More basically, it is a problem of having competing moral systems and hence less of a consensus in public philosophy than we might like. Putting more religion into public life would not resolve this problem unless we decide first whose religion it would be. In fact, there is even less consensus regarding religion than there is on public philosophy; it is difficult to see how adding more religion would increase the needed consensus" (p. 59).

25. Harlan Beckley, "A Christian Affirmation of Rawls' Idea of Justice as Fairness – Part I," *Journal of Religious Ethics*, 13, 2 (Fall, 1985), pp. 210–211.

26. Ibid., p. 212.

27. Ibid., p. 212.

28. Neuhaus, *The Naked Public Square*, p. 257.

29. Ibid., p. 258. Neuhaus' criticisms are broad strokes of the much more detailed and refined criticism of Rawls offered by Michael Sandel in *Liberalism and the Limits of Justice* (Cambridge: Cambridge University Press, 1982). Yet Neuhaus does not explain how he can at once criticize Rawls on such grounds and yet continue to underwrite America as the exemplification of what a Christian social order should look like. For whether Neuhaus likes it or not, the public philosophy of America is liberal and Rawls in many ways is its most eloquent spokesman. In recent essays Rawls has begun to reinterpret *A Theory of Justice* more in terms of political strategy for pluralist democracies that may at once make it less philosophically compelling for philosophers but more socially significant. See, for example, his "Justice or Fairness: Political Not Metaphysical," *Philosophy and Public Affairs*, 14, 3 (Summer, 1985), pp. 223–251. In spite of his qualifications the question still remains whether any account of justice can be intelligibly abstracted from a conception of the virtues integral to the pursuit of goods in common.

The very fact that many Christian theologians such as Beckley feel the need to adopt Rawls in order to have a comprehensive theory of justice may mean that something has already gone wrong in Christians' understanding of the social and political role of the church. Put overly simply, one needs a theory of justice when one no longer assumes that the very existence of the church is a social stance. Christian thinkers obviously must test various accounts of justice offered by different societies in order to find areas of common cause. But it is quite another matter to assume that in order for Christians to act politically they need a theory of justice such as Rawls' that claims to order the basic structure of society. In that respect Beckley's contention that Rawls' theory does not pretend to comprehend all of morality fails to denote adequately the tendency of Rawls' account to render some goods, such as the family, problematic. See, for example, *A Theory of Justice* (Cambridge, Massachusetts: Harvard University Press, 1971), pp. 511–512. I am indebted to Mr. Greg Jones for helping me see this.

30. Robert Bellah, et al., *Habits of the Heart: Individualism and Commitment in American Life* (Berkeley: University of California Press, 1985), pp. 282–283. For Bellah's more explicit views, see his "The Revolution and the Civil Religion," in *Religion and the American Revolution*, ed. by Jerald Brauer (Philadelphia: Fortress, 1976), pp. 55–73. There Bellah observes that when his original article on civil religion was published (1967), it came just as the

existence of civil religion was becoming questionable. He observes, "Only the biblical religions can provide the energy and vision for a new turn in American history, perhaps a new understanding of covenant, which may be necessary not only to save ourselves but to keep us from destroying the rest of the world" (p. 73).

For a thorough discussion which raises doubts about the extent of the influence of civic republicanism in America, see John Patrick Diggins' *The Lost Soul of American Politics: Virtue, Self-Interest, and the Foundations of Liberalism* (New York: Basic Books, 1984). Equally interesting is Arthur Vidich's and Stanford Lyman's *American Sociology: Worldly Rejections of Religion and Their Directions* (New Haven: Yale University Press, 1985). They document that the birth of sociology in America has been, even in its most secularized and scientific form, a continuation of the project to form civil society on the basis of religious values. They argue "the problems of American sociology emanate from the dilemma and contradictions in the relationship between God, the state, and civil society. In America's Puritan heritage there is envisioned a society composed of a voluntaristic covenant of believers, exercising mutual watchfulness over one another, acceding to legitimate civil authority but recognizing the ultimate sovereignty of God over all affairs. The nation would take form as a democratic commonwealth. However, in America the promise of this democratic commonwealth was threatened by new forms of worldly success and failure and new modes of social differentiation. American sociological thinkers were the moral successors to the earlier Puritan theologians. Convinced that America was destined to be the redeemer nation for the world, these sociologists took as their project the inner-worldly perfection of American social, economic, and political institutions. Implicit in this project was the belief that a covenanted national community could be established within the boundaries of the United States. Virtually all the American sociologists converted issues of theodicy into problems for sociodicy. Instead of vindicating the ways of God to man, they sought to justify the ways of society to its members" (p. 281). They point out also that as sociologists noted the inability of Protestant churches to provide a moral framework for civil society, sociologists tended to center on the state itself as the only institution with the moral authority to guide society. Sociology as a "policy science" thus becomes the new priestly craft necessary to help the modern bureaucratic state "manage" society.

31. Falwell is particularly interesting when he wanders into questions of international relations. Suddenly he no longer makes direct biblical appeals but, rather, sounds like any good American realist accepting consequential calculations for determining the right moral policy.

32. For an attempt to develop this position, see my *A Community of Character: Toward a Constructive Christian Social Ethic* (Notre Dame: University of Notre Dame, 1981) and my *The Peaceable Kingdom: A Primer in Christian Ethics* (Notre Dame: University of Notre Dame, 1983).

33. John Howard Yoder, *The Priestly Kingdom: Social Ethics as Gospel* (Notre Dame: University of Notre Dame, 1984), p. 154. When Christians ask such a question they assume a majority status. In contrast, Yoder's view, as well as my own, is that Christians cannot help but be a minority if they are being faithful to their basic convictions.

34. All references to Yoder will appear in the text. It should not be thought that Yoder is committing the genetic fallacy by his appeal to the early Christian community. He is not saying that because the early church was a minority it should always be a minority, but rather in this context he is working descriptively to show the change in the logic of moral argument when this occurred. Of course, he will argue that the form of the early church is normative for Christians, not because it was the early church but because what the early Christians believed is true and results in Christians taking a critical stance toward governmental authorities. I share that view but I cannot here adequately defend it.

35. Connected with this reversal is what happens once the ruler is let into the church, for then the ruler, not the average or weak person, is the model for ethical reason. Thus, the rightness of truth telling or the wrongness of killing is tested first by whether a ruler can meet such standards. Yoder, however, does not mean to exclude rulers from the church

189

but rather he expects them to act like Christians. Thus, "Caesar would be perfectly free (for a while) to bring to bear upon the exercise of his office the ordinary meaning of the Christian faith. It might happen that the result would be that his enemies triumph over him, but that often happens to rulers anyway. It might happen that he would have to suffer, or not stay in office all his life, but that too often happens to rulers anyway, and it is something that Christians are supposed to be ready for. It might happen that he would be killed; but most Caesars are killed anyway. It might happen that some of his followers would have to suffer. But emperors and kings are accustomed to asking people to suffer for them. Especially if the view were still authentically alive, which the earlier Christians undeniably had held to and which the theologians in the age of Constantine were still repeating, that God blesses those who serve him, it might also have been possible that, together with all of the risks just described, most of which a ruler accepts anyway, there could have been in some times and some places the possibility that good could be done, that creative social alternatives could be discovered, that problems could be solved, enemies loved and justice fostered" (p. 146).

36. For a romp through church/state issues, see George Goldberg, *Reconsecrating America* (Grand Rapids: Eerdmans, 1984).

37. It is interesting to observe that most Americans, whether religious or secular, continue to take a missionary stance for democracy. Americans criticize our government's support for nondemocratic regimes around the world to the point of sometimes advocating intervention against nondemocratic regimes. As Yoder observes, "after the 'Christian west' has lost the naive righteousness with which it thought it should export its religion around the world, we still seem to have a good conscience about exporting our politics" (p. 151).

38. By associating Yoder and Falwell at this point, I do not mean to deny their obvious differences. Yet they both use primary religious language in the public arena without apology. The problem with Falwell is not that he uses Christian appeals but that his understanding of Christianity is so attenuated.

39. Of course, some accounts of what it means to be virtuous require violence as a necessary correlative—the just person must envisage the possibility of using coercion if he or she is to be just and to do justice. To be persuasive, therefore, my claim requires a substantial account of the content of the virtues— e.g., why the virtues of patience and forgiveness are central to the moral life. I have tried to provide such an account elsewhere in this book.

40. George Hunsinger, for example, has argued that we live in a time not unlike the situation that confronted those who produced the Barmen declaration. See his "Barth, Barmen, and the Confessing Church Today," *Katallagete*, 9, 2 (Summer, 1985), pp. 14–27. See also my response, "On Learning Simplicity in an Ambiguous Age," *Katallagete*, 10, 1–3 (Fall, 1987), pp. 43–46.

VIRTUE IN PUBLIC

I want to address two issues raised by the recent conference, "Virtue: Public or Private."[1] The first is the relation of the virtues and politics—that is, whether an emphasis on the virtues requires a withdrawal or at least a deemphasis on the political—and the second, the relation of virtue and grace. Though I have strong views about these questions, some of which I shall develop here, my primary interest is to clarify exactly how the issues should be stated. Such clarification is necessary, for, as I hope to show, the way the issue is stated often presupposes mistaken views about virtue and politics.

For example, the alternative, pitting public versus private, is a mistake from the perspective of an ethics of virtue. That way of putting the issue presupposes a view of politics that stress on the virtues is meant to challenge. The idea that some significant distinction can be drawn between public and private reflects a political theory that assumes the political realm is not dependent on people of virtue. Such an assumption, moreover, is modern, as in the past it was assumed that a person of virtue, even if not directly involved in politics, served a political function. The person of integrity was and is a political resource, for his or her character makes possible a society that would otherwise be impossible. When we are not able to count on the other to be virtuous we must then rely on institutions, most often the state, to compensate for this. The more we rely on the state to sustain the relations necessary for social life, the less it seems we need people of virtue—and so a vicious circle begins.

Of course, no social order avoids entirely recommending and/or supporting some virtues. Even in a liberal society dedicated to the freedom of the individual, virtues are still encouraged, though such encouragement may not be acknowledged. For example, in our society we are taught in untold ways that we are to be tolerant, sincere, and fair—these are our procedural virtues which we assume are necessary to make social

191

life possible in a society that shares no good in common. Procedural though they are, they are nonetheless no less virtues as they are perduring dispositions and habits which form people to see and act in specifiable and predictable ways. Moreover, they seem unobjectionable from a liberal point of view, as no one is forced to be tolerant, sincere, or fair. Rather, these virtues make possible the choice of more substantive virtues but they entail no account of what the individual must choose.

This account of the virtues, however, is insufficient, if not self-deceptive. For the very notion that these "procedural" virtues can be divorced from some more determinative conception of the good is itself a substantive claim. As a result, the nature of the moral life is distorted as virtues such as humility, temperance, courage, and prudence are made secondary to these truly "public" virtues. Indeed, the situation is worse, since by definition the more "procedural" virtues undercut the social significance of virtues such as humility by suggesting that these virtues cannot be supported socially because any support would violate the individual's freedom. As a result, however, the liberal often fails to see that they are training people to be virtuous which in their own terms is coercive since they claim to be creating a social order that respects the "right of everyone to be virtuous in their own way."

No society and corresponding government can avoid training people to have virtue. That is not even a very interesting observation, since it is obvious. The virtues are not something we choose to have or not to have. The only interesting questions have to do with which virtues we acquire, how they are acquired, and what they tell us about the kind of social order in which we exist. It must be remembered that there is no one "theory of virtue and the virtues," but rather how a community understands and relates the virtues reflects its convictions. Indeed, the very distinction between virtue and the virtues entails a quite different understanding of the nature of political society.

For example, Aristotle maintained that one could not become virtuous simply by copying the actions of a virtuous person, but rather one could only become virtuous by acting in the manner that a virtuous person acts. Crucial for Aristotle was that what we do must come from a firm and unchangeable character. That is, virtuous persons are those who would not choose to do other than what they have or have not done, since what they have or have not done is consistent with who they are. Their actions, so to speak, are not what they do but confirm what they are. Thus, virtuous persons do not feel what they do to be onerous, though in fact it may involve hardship and may even be life threatening, because what they do is commensurate with what they are. They could not nor would they want to choose to be or do other.

Therefore, for Aristotle, simply providing a list of the virtues was not sufficient to indicate what is required for a person to be virtuous. Rather, becoming virtuous requires long training, as it is an esoteric achievement not accomplished by many. In particular, it requires apprenticeship to a master who can initiate one into the painful process of becoming a person of character—that is, someone capable of becoming virtuous. Yet according to Aristotle, without such people, few though they may be, politics is impossible. For politics, like ethics, involves judgments about contingent matters and thus requires people of wisdom which comes only by being well formed through the virtues.

In contrast to Aristotle, the Stoics tended to ignore questions of how one becomes virtuous in favor of providing the standards necessary to produce people with the appearance of virtue. They were not interested in questions of how one could be a person of character, but were content to produce lists of virtues with sets of correlated duties. They assumed if one fulfilled these duties it was sufficient to acknowledge that one was a person of virtue. They did so because politically they were concerned to produce people capable of governing an empire that was more concerned with order than goodness. For such a task the appearance of virtue was enough.

I suspect also entailed by the Stoic view was a sense that the person with political responsibility might be called to do certain things they might not do as private citizens. Thus, political actors are often called on to say less than the truth if they are to fulfill their political responsibility. It is often alleged, therefore, that a tension exists between political responsibility and the life of virtue. Thus, the distinction between public and private virtue is required if we are to make sense of political life.

Yet, again, such a way of characterizing the limits of the virtues for politics presupposes an insufficient account of virtue and politics. For the very characterization of political responsibility presumes persons of extraordinary virtue—namely, persons capable of disinterestedness so they are capable of making decisions when there is no good to be done but still a decision must be made. Rather than there being a discontinuity between their private and public self there is a strict continuity, as only a person of virtue would be capable of such disinterestedness. It may be objected that to put the matter this way invites us to mistake disinterestedness for political expediency. No doubt at times we may not be able to tell which is the more apt description, but that such is the case does not undercut the point that we can only trust a person of virtue to operate in the sphere of the political if, in fact, the political is constantly open to the temptation of expediency. If "dirty hands" are unavoidable in the political realm, then we can only trust to such offices those who can recognize the moral ambiguity of much of what they must do without thereby excusing their actions in the name of "politics." This is not only because otherwise the political would be corrupting for the person of virtue, but, more importantly, we would otherwise abandon the political to a cynicism that would reduce politics to nothing more than a clash of power. Perhaps that is why those polities are more nearly just in which political actors can perform their tasks so they are morally made better through the performance of their duty.

Put in terms of the contrast I have drawn between Aristotle and the Stoics (a contrast that would need much qualification to be historically accurate), one cannot preserve the polity that the Stoics were trying to serve without an account of virtue such as that of Aristotle. The appearance of virtue cannot be long sustained without some persons being genuinely virtuous. Moreover, no society can claim to be good that does not require such people to be present. That does not mean that it is incumbent on the state to make people virtuous—to put the matter that way is to underwrite the assumption that the appearance of virtue is sufficient to sustain a good society. Rather, it is the function of the state to encourage those institutions and communities within society to produce people whose virtue is the resource that makes possible a non-coercive society.

The charge is often made that those who would emphasize the importance of the virtues for politics in the modern world are hopeless romantics who want to recall the modern world; or worse, they are sectarians who must retreat from significant political engagement in the interest of preserving their moral purity. What must be faced is that the Greek polis is no more, and we have no possibility of reconstituting it. Therefore, to claim political significance for the virtues is at best an act of political irrelevance and worse, raises the specter of totalitarian imposition. The former is particularly feared by religious people who think an emphasis on the virtues may force Christians to withdraw from political responsibility.

It is hard to know where or how to begin to answer such charges. I hope at least some of what I have said above may be of some use in dispelling such fears. It is interesting to note that Aristotle, in fact, did not presume the existence of the polis, as with his customary realism he knew he lived in a time when the polis was gone. Yet still he wrote of virtue on the presumption that no polity is possible without some account of the good and how the virtues constitute as well as provide the

194

means of becoming good. Courage is required not when it is no longer costly, but exactly when we cannot afford to be cowardly as otherwise we abandon our societies to their worst impulses.

Yet I cannot deny that liberal democratic societies present a particular challenge to any attempt to recapture the political significance of the virtues. For democratic societies tend to underwrite the assumption that the moral life is immediately accessible and requires no training of the self. The citizens of such a society, it is assumed, are naturally moral or at least have a natural desire to be moral. In contrast, the emphasis on virtue assumes that the moral life is a strenuous affair which entails a lifetime. For democracies it is sufficient to be moderately good, to have the appearance of virtue, but if we are to be truly virtuous we cannot help but seek to be good through and through.

I do not believe, however, that intrinsic to the nature of democracy is a downplaying of the significance of virtue. That is, I do not believe it, if democracy is understood as a system of social relations and institutions to encourage the discussion necessary for the articulation of the good a people can share in common. The question, however, is whether such an understanding of democracy is even a possibility in a society such as ours. Moreover, such a view of democracy is no longer articulated even in our theories of democracy, so it is not even any longer held out as an imaginative ideal.

Yet if the church, which after all is a public institution, can be the kind of community that manifests the political significance of virtue, then the church may well have a political function not often realized. Moreover, to be such a community is not to withdraw from "society" but rather to stand within our society making present what would otherwise be absent. If politics is defined as that realm of conflict where force is the ultimate determination of right, then the church must "withdraw" from such politics. But that very "withdrawal" is a political act as we hold out for a richer understanding of the political.

In this respect, it seems that many "neoconservatives" are caught in a particular bind. They want society to recover "traditional values," which they rather uncritically identify with virtues, yet they adhere to an ideology that undercuts the very values they hold. They want a society that makes freedom of the individual the supreme value, but they are upset when some use that freedom to sell and buy pornography.

This becomes particularly apparent in matters of foreign policy, where the virtues of liberal society are thought to legitimize anything we must do to oppose the Soviet Union. Yet at the same time those very "virtues" have an acid effect on the values that legitimize the condemnation of the

Soviets. I do not doubt that it is a fearful thing to live in a totalitarian regime, but it at least seems a matter of honesty that the very criticisms that neoconservatives make against our society's moral laxity should temper somewhat their enthusiasm for the righteousness of America. In particular it is difficult to understand how neoconservatives can call for a return to "republican virtues" while advocating a capitalist economic system which clearly seems to undermine those very virtues. How does one seek one's own interest economically yet think that the public good may require us to qualify that interest? Finally, some suggest that the emphasis on the virtues may lack, or at least overlook, the Christian concern to maintain the priority of grace. As Meilaender notes, the imitation of the virtuous is never sufficient to make one virtuous.[2] Rather, becoming truly virtuous is more like a moment of felicity—like something that comes as a gift—than something we do. Moreover, it is crucial that this gift, like character, be preserved. Otherwise, we have no sense of transcendence which makes us too likely to become self-righteous, or worse, such communities of virtue risk becoming ends in themselves rather than having the virtues render them open to the God that has called them into existence.

This is, no doubt, one of the deepest issues that can be raised about the attempt to develop an ethics of virtue in the theological context. I know no easy or quick response. Yet I think, generally speaking, there is no reason to think that in principle there is some ultimate incompatibility between a stress on virtue and the maintenance of a doctrine of grace. The virtues are possible because they are a response to another. Put even more strongly, our character, at least as I tried to argue in *The Peaceable Kingdom*, is more like a gift from another than something we have done.[3] For only as we are so formed do we have a self capable of being formed by the virtues in a manner that makes us capable of continued growth in virtue. Perhaps that is the ultimate challenge of facing the political implications of the virtues, as any genuine account of the virtues ultimately must entail an affirmation of God's mercy which at once judges and makes possible our attempts to be communities in which virtue can flourish.

NOTES

1. The essays and a summary of the discussion of the conference are now published in *Virtue: Public and Private*, edited with a foreword by Richard John Neuhaus (Grand Rapids: Eerdmans, 1986).

2. Gilbert Meilaender, "Virtue in Contemporary Religious Thought" in *Virtue: Public and Private*, pp. 7–29.

3. (Notre Dame: University of Notre Dame Press, 1984). See also the third printing of my *Character and the Christian Life* (San Antonio: Trinity University Press, 1985). That book contains a new "Introduction" in which I deal explictly with this issue.

HOPE FACES POWER

Thomas More and the King of England[1]

Rarely are we able to be the intelligent spectators of an historical event, more rarely still its actors. At such times the darkness lightens and the space contracts until we apprehend the rhythm of our daily actions as the rhythm of a much larger scheme which has included us within its composition.

Iris Murdoch[2]

1. Hope and Power in More's Witness

The seduction of power is as perennial as the threat of power spurned. Power is a medium for good and evil. Lawyers and politicians and their victims—Nixon and his cronies, for examples—come and go; but the moral problems of how to use power, how to live with it and leave it behind, remain.

One way to look at the moral problem of power is to ask how a virtuous person uses power, and lives close to power, without losing the sense of self that is necessary to negotiate the temptations of power. We propose to ask that question with respect to Thomas More, in this 500th year of his birth, particularly with respect to the Thomas More of Robert Bolt's play, *A Man for All Seasons*.[3] We propose to offer an account of the character necessary to maintain what Bolt's More called "that little area in which I must rule myself." We contend that consideration of More's character is a way to learn how to be honest about power and still to hope. We will try to show how More's hope involved moral and intellectual skill—skill in the use of power, skill in serving power in such a way that he was not consumed by it, and skill in knowing when to spurn power and to accept the consequences.[4]

199

More was attractive to the dramatist because More's public life was a puzzle. There does not seem to be any satisfactory explanation for his decision to spurn power when he did—in the midst of a hard-won and successful public career at a time when men of moral substance all around him adjusted themselves to the demands of the new English nation-state. The task of that generation of leaders was a titanic task. They learned how to live with a concentration of national power which had begun in More's childhood and which has maintained itself for five centuries. They learned how to live with the central fact of modern history, and More, it seems, did not. More, who was a practical, political man, a subtle political schemer, a loyal servant of Cardinal Wolsey, Henry VIII, the principal actors in the polity of his time, declined the opportunity to be a Titan. His spurning of the patronage of king and archbishop seems arbitrary if not perverse. The conventional way to account for it has been to explain it as martyrdom—that is, as an admirable stubbornness which is not quite accessible to practical reason.

A modern way to deal with the absurdity of More's "exit" from power is to regard it as eccentric—to view More as an existentialist hero defending an "adamantine sense of self."[5] That explanation is as inaccessible to practical reason as martyrdom is; the difference, perhaps, is that the martyr hears the voice of God and the existentialist hero hears only his own voice. We contend that it is possible to suggest a deeper account for More's spurning of power. If one attends to the kind of hope that formed More's life, one can, we think, sketch a continuity between More's legal and political life and his turning away from power. Martyrdom, or the adamantine sense of self, is then a consequence of More's life rather than an explanation for it.

The crucial point to be made is that none of us can afford to be without the kind of hope that formed More's life. Few of us will be called to do what More did, but hope is important to any moral life, and to all moral lives. More and those like him remain our masters in learning how to hope. We are not likely to learn enough about how to hope by reflecting abstractly on what hope is or on how hope relates to other virtues (such as faith and love). We can learn—we do learn—more when we look to those whose lives were hopeful; we learn not whether to hope, but how to hope.[6]

There is a difference between hope and optimism. Optimism is not hope as we mean to talk about hope. Optimism differs from hope in that optimism can exist without truth. Because it can exist without truth it is defeated and perverted by power. Hope, when seen as optimism, is, in the poetic phrase, dashed.

An optimistic person whose "hopes are dashed" becomes a cynic. He becomes a cynic because he still needs some way to locate and protect "that little area in which I must rule myself." Cynicism gives him a way to do that without requiring that he worry about the truth. Cynicism thus promises a check against power, against the persons, institutions, and roles that claim our lives. Both the hopeful person and the cynic have found a way to stand back from their engagements; but cynicism stills the imagination against the possible, and therefore protects the cynic without requiring that he be truthful. The price of cynical protection is self-deception. The cynic abandons the human burden of deciding what is true and what is not; he does this by refusing to believe in anything. His optimism is lost because he lacks the skill to turn optimism into hope; his refuge is a state in which he deludes himself into thinking that neither hope nor truth is necessary. He comes to believe that the moral life can be lived on negative premises.

Cynicism leads to despair, because it is impossible to live a life based on negative premises. Despair is to hope what hypocrisy is to truth: hypocrisy proves how much we need truth in our lives; despair proves how deeply we need hope.

In this way, despair can be seen as the result of hope out of control, of the overextension of hope, of absolutizing the range of hope,[7] of having so much need for hope that one is willing to trick oneself into being optimistic when, with skill, one might have learned how to be optimistic and truthful at the same time—to be, in a word, hopeful. This is, perhaps, what Aquinas meant when he numbered among the temptations to despair "the mere excess of good," which makes "the difficult good impossible to obtain."[8]

Despair is the condition in which one no longer looks for alternatives. Cynicism leads to despair because cynicism does not look for alternatives truthfully. Optimism leads to cynicism because it does not pay attention to truth. Hope, as we are talking about it, is based on truth and forces the imagination to look for alternatives.[9] If we are unable to look for alternatives, we are forced to rely on power. Hope is therefore an alternative to reliance on power.

We mean to suggest here that More's life illustrates how hope is an alternative to reliance on power. The point can be made in a preliminary way by comparing More's behavior in Bolt's play with the behavior of Cardinal Wolsey, Thomas Cromwell, and the Duke of Norfolk. All four men lived in circumstances in which power was available to them, but only one of them ultimately refused to rely on power. In all four cases, opulence, arrogance, "clout," and received deference tempted powerful men to a narrowed sense of what was possible. It was thus that power corrupted and, in the case of a fifth character, the King, absolute power corrupted absolutely. As Camus has said, "the truth is that every intelligent man . . . dreams of being a gangster and of ruling society by force alone."[10] Hope varies inversely with the extent to which power seems to be the answer—as it seemed to be the answer to Wolsey, Cromwell, the Duke, the King, and Camus' gangster. This is not to say that hope varies inversely with the attainment and exercise of power; those who hold and wield power can be hopeful people, as More was. What we mean to say is that hope varies inversely with the absoluteness of one's *trust* in power. Hope declines as trust in power increases, and this seems to happen because hope declines as one's sense of alternatives narrows.

Our thesis is that More's response to power is a paradigm of the hopeful life—the life lived truthfully and therefore with hope rather than with optimism; the life lived with a broad sense of alternatives to power and therefore without reliance on power. Bolt's play is the story of a hopeful life. Moreover, we think More is particularly interesting because he was both a Christian and a lawyer. The molding of a Christian lawyer's life is a power-centered task, and for this reason moral admonition addressed to the powerless—in, for example, St. Paul's Letter to the Christians in Rome—at first seems useless. And such moral admonition addressed to lawyers as there is—in, for example, the American Bar Association's *Code of Professional Responsibility*—tends to a narrow sense of alternatives to power. Being a Christian and a lawyer seems to be a matter of learning about power and conscience, since lawyers wield power, even when they do not have it, and Christians wield conscience. Bolt's story is a story about power and conscience.

The lawyer's life is a problem when subjected, as a Christian life, to the New Testament. The New Testament is not about using power, but about how God provides the means to live hopefully rather than powerfully. "What it impels the church towards—and it is the Holy Spirit moving in it who does this—is agreement with the direction in which it looks itself. And the direction in which it looks is to the living Jesus Christ."[11] But Jesus was not a lawyer (anything but), and almost none of the Christian lives traditionally given as examples for Christians were lawyers; almost all of these lives were lives of powerlessness. It is important that lawyers and anyone who thinks about the way power is used in the United States (i.e., by lawyers) seek such examples as there are of the limits and possibilities of power in a Christian lawyer's life. More's life is a Christian lawyer's life. His martyrdom, in that respect, seems—and is—a paradox but our idea is that his martyrdom was a consequence both of his being a Christian and of his being a lawyer.

More was finally crushed by power, but we are attracted to him because he more than most seems to have had the ability to be the intelligent spectator and actor which Iris Murdoch suggests is so rare. His hope and his life, both of which he fought with every possible technique, to save, were finally sustained by what Aquinas called the "arduous good" which the world's possibilities cannot encompass. And thus More learned to hope, and the hope that guided his life gave him the freedom to see the world as it is and as it might be. This is demonstrated by his response to the Act of Supremacy:

Roper:	There's to be a new Act through Parliament, sir!
More:	. . . Act?
Roper:	Yes, sir—about the marriage!
More:	Oh.

* * *

Margaret:	(Puts a hand on his arm) Father, by this Act, they're going to administer an oath.
More:	. . . An oath? . . . On what compulsion?
Roper:	It's expected to be treason!
More:	(Very still) What is the oath?
Roper:	(Puzzled) It's about the marriage, sir.
More:	But what is the wording?
Roper:	We don't need to know the (contemptuously) wording—we know what it will mean!
More:	It will mean what the words say! An oath is *made* of words! It may be possible to take it . . . . Then let's get home and look at it. . . . God made the angels to show him splendor—as he made animals for innocence and plants for simplicity. But man he made to serve him wittily, in the tangle of his mind. . . . Our natural business lies in escaping—so let's get home and study this Bill.

As we shall see, More's hope allowed him to "escape" and thus "to act" more than most of us can do. But finally it also helped him know when escape was impossible if he was to secure that area in which he had to rule himself.

So long as truth is possible, hope is possible and, from the perspective of a lawyer like More, skill is possible; skill is hope and hope is skill. We examine this proposition in the following section. We then contrast the life of hope as skill with lives in which there was despair of skill. We next turn to More's curious surrender of power—which to his contemporaries looked like a surrender of hope—and suggest that More's resignation as chancellor demonstrates the facts that hope is built on truth and that hope's dependence on truth is a political reality as well as a moral reality. In discussing the political dimension of hope, we propose to demonstrate a framework for the ideas of hope as skill and hope as truthful.

2. Hope and Skill

The ordinarily hopeful way to deal with power is to apply to it the arts of the mind. Since More was a lawyer, this meant in his case meeting power with analysis and with knowledge. This approach was manifest in More's confidence in his own ability to outwit his persecutors. He saw this ability as important, so important that he was willing to extend the protection of the law (that is, of analysis and knowledge) to the devil himself. He was willing, as a modern would say, to extend "due process of law" all the way to hell. One reason he was willing to do so was that he needed legal protection for himself. If legal protection was left intact for everybody, even the devil, then More's own persecutors would never be able to get him. That is a familiar argument for those who want citizens to support the rule of law.

Bolt sees More as doing more, however, than trying to save himself:

Margaret: Father, that man's bad.
More: There is no law against that.
Roper: There is! God's law!
More: Then God can arrest him.
Roper: Sophistication upon sophistication!
More: No, sheer simplicity. The law, Roper, the law. I know what's legal not what's right. . . . The currents and eddies of right and wrong, which you find such plain sailing, I can't navigate. I'm no voyager. But in the thickets of the law, oh, there I'm a forester. I doubt if there's a man alive who could follow me there, thank God.

This view is more than survival. Lawyers, too, were among the witnesses to the word of God in the world, and this attitude of More's is a kind of witness. More, as lawyer and as witness, had hope not only for himself but for his time and for his society. It was a lawyer's hope. One could sum it up by saying that he, like almost any lawyer at almost any time, hoped that his society would preserve law—that is, government under law. Government under law was, and is, a radical idea. In England it finally led to the spectacle of the king himself being torn from the seat of power, deposed, and killed, because the king himself (Charles II) was seen as lawless. When More says, in the play, that "the law is a causeway upon which, so long as he keeps to it, a citizen may walk safely," he aspires more than describes, but he does aspire; he does have hope for his country.

The fact that More had this hope, that it was more than a hope for his own survival, and that it was a lawyer's hope, is enough to make him a hero. (His use of cleverness to save himself, even to save his truth to himself, would perhaps not be enough to make him a hero.) But there is a further sense in which More's witness was both lawyerlike and heroic. More was bearing witness to the truth about the nature of power in the world. His witness went beyond the procedural idea that every person should have the full benefit of due process of law. His witness was to the truth that human governments are limited, that however much power they—King Henry VIII—may have, they have less power than they think they have. "The King in Parliament cannot bestow the Supremacy of the Church because it is a Spiritual Supremacy!" After he finally says that much, and only after he makes that principal point, does More add that the Act of Supremacy also violated English law.

In any event, so long as the state followed the law, More was confident that he could cope with its power—to save himself, to save a fundamental legal principle, and to save the idea that governments, too, should be truthful about themselves. He was confident because he had hope *as skill*. Skill does not confront power; it calls power to rationality. It does not appropriate power either. Lawyers rarely *have* power; they *use* it. They do not possess power; they manipulate it. One reason Bolt's play is so popular among lawyers, particularly among American lawyers, is that it exalts this use of lawyer skill.

This lawyer skill is not a matter of principles. Lawyers use legal principles, but they use them more to garnish their work than to carry it out.[12] Lawyers, when being candid, admit scant regard for legal principles.[13] Laypersons—clients of lawyers, for example—sometimes think that this scant regard betrays cynicism, but lawyers do not think of themselves as cynics. A client will ask a lawyer a "legal question," about what the law is on some set of facts which is important to the client. And the lawyer will answer, in effect, "Tell me what you want the answer to be and then I will answer the question." Nonlawyers may think that the lawyer's request exhibits disdain for principles, or that it exhibits disdain for the idea of government under law. But the lawyer thinks of legal principles as something to be taken apart and made to fit the client's needs. The lawyer thinks this work *is* government under law. Principles and

205

facts are the lawyer's raw materials. What is sacred in the law is not legal principles. The sacred thing in the law, to a lawyer, is the fact that those who have power are bound to respect skill and knowledge in the wielding of power—skill and knowledge even among those who merely wield power, but who do not have it.[14] That is, we think, the political side of a respect for character:

> [W]hen people rebel against the tyranny of rules, they often forget that there is an alternative. Under the alternative view, you can have rules . . . but in special situations the virtuous person would take special action. Hence the ultimate standard is the virtuous person: what he or she would do is the test of what is right.[15]

With regard to what is *legal*, principles come last. More understood that. It was important to him. He lived it. Bolt understands that; it is part of the reason he thinks that More's life might stand up as an illustration of the courage to preserve one's soul—one's unbudgeable self—in the modern world.

Skill seen as hope is both larger than itself and smaller than itself. Larger, because skill seems here to be exalted into virtue, and, beyond any particular virtue, into character. The idea of skill, which might suggest facility at making omelettes as well as facility at making arguments, seems unable to bear this much moral weight. But skill can be made to bear moral weight when it is seen in the life of a person who is both skillful in hope and hopeful about his skill. More's was such a life, as were the lives, say, of Daniel Webster who, as in Benet's play, could draw goodness from the depths of hell, or of Abraham Lincoln, whose aspiration for government *for* the people is precisely this idea of skill as hope at the service of an entire culture, a *people* (in the biblical sense).

Skill is also smaller than itself. It is a matter of craftsmanship, about which the craftsman will have standards which are aesthetic—matters of taste. It is important, particularly when one thinks of lawyers, to see skill, lived with hope, as character. And it is useful, again when talking about lawyers, to narrow the focus and analyze skill as a matter of craftsmanship and taste. Much of Bolt's genius as the teller of More's story consists in his way of describing More as a person who dealt with power, habitually, as a craftsman. And craftsmanship is important. A lawyer's craftsmanship calls for some of the best that is in him and some of the best that the grace of God adds to what is in him. Bolt's More had a respect for craftsmanship as a matter of taste; he disdained its absence as a kind of stupidity. He also had a respect for craftsmanship as a matter of hope—of the virtue of hope—and disdained its absence as a kind of despair. Both points are illustrated, in the play, when More tells Wolsey that Wolsey's Machiavellian diplomacy is not necessary:

More: [after reading, at Wolsey's request, a letter from Wolsey to the Vatican] (Crisply) It's addressed to Cardinal Campeggio.
Wolsey: Yes?
More: Not to our ambassador [which would have been proper; ignoring the ambassador was improper].
Wolsey: Our ambassador's a ninny.
More: (A smile) Your Grace appointed him.
Wolsey: (Treats it at the level of humor, mock exasperation) Yes, I need a *ninny* in Rome! So that I can write to Cardinal Campeggio!
More: (Won't respond; with esthetic distaste—not moral disapproval) It's devious.
Wolsey: It's a devious situation!
More: There must be something simple in the middle of it. (Again this is not a moral dictum; it is said rather wistfully, as of something he is beginning to doubt)

To More, Wolsey's use of deviousness seems distasteful and his behavior evidences a lack of craftsmanship. But Bolt directs the actor to suggest a deeper regret, too. There is more here than craftsmanship and good taste. The theme of the play is in this scene. More is beginning to doubt the sufficiency of lawyer skill in the matter he and Wolsey are discussing, the King's marriage. More's hope is that the use of skill more than craftsmanship will save something. He thinks of saving his own life and of saving a way of life.

Another art of the mind that can cope with power is knowledge—knowledge in the sense of an intellectual command which liberates, makes one less afraid and therefore better able to look power in the eye. English law in More's day was a recondite and complex body of knowledge—as, perhaps, law always is, since its office is to analyze principles and principles do not yield easily; they offer too much security for that.

More knew that knowledge can often confound power, even when knowledge has no power of its own. An anecdote illustrates this. When More was a law student at Bruges, one of the professors there invited any comer to debate him. He would, he said, dispute any question in any science. More asked him whether beasts of the plow, taken in withernam, were capable of being replevied. The professor could not deal with that recondite bit of English common law; Erasmus, who was present, said that the professor retired "with his withers wrung and More's withernams unwrung."[16]

Knowledge, in situations like that, is not power; it is a way to deal with power. More, who had that sort of knowledge and knew he had it, could find what he had more useful than his belief in principles of right and wrong: "The currents and eddies of right and wrong which you [Roper] find such plain sailing, I can't navigate. I'm no voyager. But in the thickets of the law, oh, there, I'm a forester."

So long as law is able to hold power at bay, More was dead certain that he and his way of life would be all right; he had humility about himself as a lawyer—humility which, in this case, means that he saw himself, without illusion, as a superb lawyer. He also had humility about law itself. He knew that the time must come when the law itself would not protect him.[17] Late in the play power is brought to bear on him lawlessly, i.e., through perjury, planned and executed by the state itself. Early in the play More knew that this time might come. That is possibly the meaning of his hint to Wolsey that he was beginning to doubt whether the simplicity of skill and knowledge is dependable. More sensed a swelling of power which his skill would not be able to contain. In that swelling, of which Wolsey and Cromwell would be victims as much as More would be, power would destroy unless it is appropriated. This new power would not yield to law; it would be popular and irrational. (It would be—and is already—the power of nationalism.) Bolt illustrates this point in the character of the Common Man. When Roper said to More that all of England is buzzing over the matter of the King's divorce, More replied, "The Inns of Court may be buzzing. England doesn't buzz so easily." When England buzzes, More's humility told him, discussions of the writ of replevin will not hold power back.

The point is that analysis and knowledge will go a long way toward containing power. That is the most elementary hope that law has—law as something to live, as lawyers live it.

Despair decides that the mind and the arts of the mind will not be enough when with hope they might be enough. (An American example of hope is Thurgood Marshall and the small group of lawyers who in the early 1950s assembled precedents and set out to demonstrate that *the law* required an end to school segregation.) This despair shows up in other characters in Bolt's play. Bolt uses them to give background to More's hope, and to make More, *as a lawyer*, interesting. For example:

(1) Bolt's Wolsey, naked to his enemies, no longer has power. He struggles to save himself with old arts of deviousness which are not only unattractive and unnecessary but also futile. Deviousness is despair; it

is untruthful (because unnecessary and futile); it is contrasted in the play with More's character. More's character is fashioned with habits of skill as hope and of hope as skill.

(2) Bolt's Roper—who was, as a matter of history, clever enough to save some of More's property from the relentless Cromwell—yields to the despair of violence. In Bolt's drama he holds the place of the Zealots in the Gospel. More's (and Jesus') lives are lives of hope and therefore of peace. This life of peace is not so much a matter of convictions and certainties as it is a matter of *character*. More says to Roper, "Will, I'd trust *you* with my life. But not your principles. You see, we speak of being anchored to our principles. But if the weather turns nasty you up with anchor and let it down where there's less wind, and the fishing's better. And 'Look,' we say, 'look, I'm anchored . . . to my principles.'"[18]

(3) Thomas Cromwell was an abler man than Bolt portrays him to be. He followed More to the block, but his family held high power in England through the reigns of the next half-dozen kings and queens. The curator at the Frick Museum probably showed a better historical understanding than Bolt does, when he put Hans Holbein's More on the left side of the fireplace, Holbein's Cromwell on the right side, and El Greco's St. Jerome above them in the center. (More would have enjoyed that arrangement.) But for Bolt, Cromwell is a study in the despair of corruption. Cromwell destroys people, destroys character in people, and that is about as despairing as a person can be. Cromwell's is the delusion Karl Barth calls "the syndrome of the two kingdoms";[19] Cromwell seems to suppose he can lead a decent life in private which in public follows "chance or laws of its own." Bolt's Cromwell speaks of "the constant factor" of giving the powerful what they want; government is more accommodation, he says, than corruption. "Our job as administrators is to make it as convenient as we can." Bolt is an old-fashioned (and, we think, accurate) moralist when he portrays that delusion as the essence of evil.

(4) The Common Man, not a historical figure—or, rather, the most historical of them all—despairs of virtue and lives as if the only value were survival. It is he who keeps the world going, who says at the end, "if you must make trouble, make the sort of trouble that's expected." He proves that evil is banal.

In each of these cases, the absence of hope is despair about skill and knowledge. In a narrow, dramatist's sense, Bolt makes More's story interesting and finds it meaningful by touching on More's lawyer qualities and making them resound far beyond themselves, so that they approach what St. Paul meant when he told the Christians in Ephesus

209

that his prayer for them was that they realize the hope to which they were called and the power which was theirs by virtue of hope. "This power in us is the same as the mighty strength which he used when he raised Christ from death, and seated him at his right side in the heavenly world" (Eph. 1:20).

3. Truth, Hope, and the Confrontation with Power

Bolt's More had three critical moments in his hopeful dealing with power. The first occurred when he was faced with the King's and bishop's decision, as he put it, "to declare war on the Pope." The second occurred when the power of the state began to be applied to force him to take the oath. The third occurred when the state, sunk in the despair of corruption and of the delusion of the two kingdoms, concocted perjured evidence – gave up the game, so to speak – and confirmed More's martyrdom.

More reacted differently to each of these events. When the state applied pressure (the second crisis), he used the skills and the hope we have talked about in terms of analysis and knowledge. His reaction to this pressure is the main focus of Bolt's play and it is what makes the play, and More himself, interesting to modern American lawyers. When the state corrupted its use of force with perjury (the third crisis), More responded (in fact and in the play) as Christian martyrs always have. He knew how to act, because his hope was faithful. In a sense, his reaction then was based on faith more than hope, faith, in Barth's phrase, as "hope against hope." More saw God –"love right through"– reaching to draw down the curtain. He proclaimed the Kingdom, as his Lord had, and he accepted his happy sentence with relief. The climax of the drama, and of his life, was the realization of the glory he had avoided: "If he suffers us to fall to such a case that there is no escaping then we may stand to our tackle as best we can, and yes, Will, then we may clamor like champions . . . if we have the spittle for it. *And no doubt it delights God to see splendor where he only looked for complexity.* But it's God's part, not our own, to bring ourselves to that extremity! Our natural business lies in escaping . . . " When the time came, More spoke his mind about the King and the Act of Supremacy, and Cromwell (and the world, as it always does) said: "Now we plainly see that you are malicious!" And power killed him. More's sentence of death is not the climax of the play, though, because his death is – even in Bolt's view – a settled matter of

Cross and Resurrection. The climax of the play is the clash between hope and despair.

The first of the three crises, the resignation, is the one that interests us as we consider a different way in which hope deals with power—the way of *confrontation*. More resigned as chancellor rather than get involved in the case of the marriage. In our reading of the play (and of More's life), that was a matter of his refusing to "work within the system." There seems to have been no need for him, as a matter of conscience, to step out of his position so early in the game. He did so against the King's urging. It was possible, at that point, that the case might still have been resolved—as so many royal marriages had been with Rome—without the Act of Supremacy and the creation of a separate English church. It was nothing new for a king to declare war on the pope, and few Christians felt it necessary, as Christians, to take sides in such wars. There was in the marriage case room for the application of the hopeful skills of analysis and knowledge, both with regard to the King's attitude (what lawyers call counseling) and on behalf of the King (what lawyers call advocacy). Why, then, did More resign with such imprudent finality, and, even then, say that he would be willing to speak his mind to the King about the marriage?

The reason seems to be that More knew that hope required his retreat from that situation. Optimism was possible, for all the reasons mentioned in the last paragraph. But those reasons could not survive the *real* test of hope in the face of power, the test that says hope must be truthful. Hope must keep a sense of the alternatives to power. Optimism—hope without truth—is not sufficient for dealing with the pretentious powers that determine a person's existence in the world. The use of power can be a hopeful art, but only so long as the use of power is not an end in itself. Hope—that is, the person who lives a hopeful life and lives it well—knows the limitations of power. It knows that optimism needs the truth and that hope is schooled in faith and love. The hopeful life must bend to the demands of truth or it will, by a paradox as certain as the fact that power corrupts, lose its hope, become mere optimism, then turn to cynicism, and finally issue in a despairing life.

We have been talking about power as if it were often a clear menace or, at best, a circumstance. Power may also be an incentive to delusion, a subtle temptation. Power as delusion is a particular risk for lawyers, especially modern American lawyers, because power seems to offer a way to improve society.[20] Lawyers are always being asked to bend a little so that power can work and society can be made better; lawyers are always being told—are always telling one another—that the essence of their profession (what we have been calling the hopeful skill in it) lies in working within the system. They are always being told that someone has to do the job and that if they don't do it, someone less moral. Things have to be done as an official that cannot be done with moral comfort in private life, but that is the way office (including the license to practice law) is. The words for *that* play are "Somebody has to do it," or "What else are you going to do?" This is a play about the syndrome of the two kingdoms. It is interesting to us that Thomas More declined the temptation even when he knew—or maybe *because* he knew—that he would be good at acting in that play.

Some distinctions may be useful. It is important, first, to notice that we are talking about a compromise with truthfulness, a compromise demanded of public persons, which comes about because the person who makes the compromise is optimistic. It is important, second, to know what we mean by compromise. It is not compromise, in the sense we have in mind, for the public person to adjust his view to the views of others when there seems to be no clear right or best thing to do—when, in other words, he needs their views as much as they need his, when all of those most immediately involved are seeking truth. It is not compromise, as we mean it, to commit oneself to the discovery of the truth through a willingness to share the variety of ways people discover for leading good lives. What we mean by compromise is an agreement to bracket one's basic convictions in order to achieve certain limited ends. Compromise, as we mean it here, assumes that *the good society is based on power*. Compromise is what we talked about, above, as the despair of Thomas Cromwell. It needs to be distinguished from respect and civility and even from concessions made when people work together on the assumption that *the good society is based on truth*. As Bolt states in the preface to his play, and illustrates in the play, compromise asks the loss of self; it also destroys the possibility of good societies.

Compromise is destructive because it becomes institutionalized and accepted as a proper way of life. When that happens, the distinctions between the public and the private, between the kingdom of the world and the Kingdom of God, become a sign of despair. The distinctions come to say that the social world cannot be held together by truth. A society afflicted by the syndrome of the two kingdoms raises up leaders who have trained themselves to believe that their public roles *are* their selves, who define themselves by roles (e.g., "lawyer").[21] They are compromised before they enter the fray. When this happens, as it may well already have happened to us Americans, it is no longer honest to distinguish between the public and the private person. Privacy has

212

already been voluntarily offered to feed the public role. There is no private person left. Power, as requiring the surrender of the private person, is that with which Bolt saw More struggling. Power threatens the private, adamantine sense of self which More sought to save. "There's a little . . . little, area . . . where I must rule myself."

Here, virtue is a tangled trail through a dark forest. The man or woman of affairs tends to believe that it is egocentric not to make such a compromise. Refusal seems to them to betray hope (optimism), for to be unwilling to compromise is to cease to be effective, and it is important to them to be effective. (The way power corrupts is by gradually convincing those who have power that the most important thing is to be effective.) Thus, for most of More's contemporaries in the English establishment—including even Alice More, his wife, and Margaret Roper, his daughter—More's refusal to remain in office seemed to be a betrayal of hope; he seemed hopelessly to abandon his public role, the possibility of reform in the government, and the possibility of saving England from schism over the marriage.

More's choice to resign seems to us, though, to witness that a choice against compromise is a hopeful choice. Hope, unlike optimism, retains a sense that there are alternatives to power. Hope, unlike optimism, is truthful. Hope, like love, rejoices in the truth. Compromise would have required delusion. Beyond that, More's choice seems to say that living hopefully, that is truthfully, has social consequences *beyond* his sense of self. These social consequences are dependent upon the maintenance of the self—on, that is, a decision to live truthfully.[22]

Our conclusion from this interpretation is that More's hope was formed by faith and love; it knew the limits of optimism, because it was based on the truth that effectiveness cannot justify power. Only goodness can justify power. Faith and love form hope because the truth is that God is "love right through." Because this is the truth, St. Paul sees the Roman Christian, in a sweeping paradox, as "rejoicing in hope" (Romans 12:12): "The great hope which God sets before men compels them to demonstrate against the course of the world. But is there any one who does not hope? What is it that makes of our hope an ethical action? Surely, it is our rejoicing!"[23]

More's quiet confrontation, when he resigned as chancellor, was not quiet at all. All that followed was implied in the resignation, so that the resignation itself, as well as More's willingness at that point to speak his mind to the King (that is, to speak the truth about the marriage), *was* a confrontation with power rather than a choice to exercise skill in wielding power.[24] That would seem to have involved More's own realization that hope, because truthful, cannot avoid confrontation with the power of the world. Bolt seems to understand the point. He wants More to have that realization early in the drama. He hints at More's limited expectations for craftsmanship when More talks to Wolsey about the letter to Rome and when More intimates to Roper that lawyers' gossip is not serious but that gossip that "sets England buzzing" will be serious and a force that cannot be contained by skill or knowledge.

The point is that the powers of the world fear the truth and fear those who trust in truth to guide their way. Power sustains itself, ultimately, by resorting to violence (as in the play), which means that it always fails to sustain itself. Power cannot face its own powerlessness,[25] and truth's (hope's) demand is that power face its own powerlessness. The incongruity between truth's demand and power's need is the reason people such as Thomas More become martyrs; they are, as Cromwell would have put it, an administrative inconvenience. They too vividly remind those in power that their pretensions to rule the world are just pretensions. The Gospel seems to pose an alternative: those who wield power must either comprehend that God is the Lord of our lives or resort to violence as a means for denying that God is the Lord of our lives. The truth is that the Kingdom is here, whether the world says so or not.[26]

Speaking of hope as a virtue that depends on truth and of confrontation with power as an inevitable necessity in the lives of those who wield power while trying to live truthfully may suggest that the hopeful person is one who forces the world to violence. We must deal with this issue. If More was one who forced the world to violence, then he was deluded when he said, "I am the King's true subject, and pray for him and all the realm . . . I do none harm, I say none harm, I think none harm. And if this be not enough to keep a man alive, in good faith I long not to live . . . And therefore, my poor body is at the King's pleasure. Would God my death might do him some good."

It is not the *intention* of the hopeful person to force those who would rule to resort to violence. To live so as to force violence would be itself to fall into despair. It would be self-righteous and anarchic. That view of the hopeful person would deprive us of needed heroes, from Socrates to Martin Luther King, Jr. and Cesar Chavez. But, at least for Christians, hope does not provoke violence because our hope is grounded on the conviction that in the life and death of Jesus Christ, God has shown once and for all that his love is deeper and more profound than the evil we find in the world. We trust that this is the case. Not to trust that it is would abandon the world to sin and thus deny that *God's work* has been effective.

214

Viewed this way, More can be understood as knowing that a refusal to "work within the system" is not only a matter of conscience (which is always admirable but sometimes seems to suffer from a tinge of solipsism), but a *social* responsibility. More's act of conscience was not something discontinuous with his work as a lawyer or as chancellor. He saw the act of conscience as required by and consistent with the character of his public commitment. More trusted the law because he insisted that he must be able to live in a society that could be trusted, and he had an obligation to stand by what he knew as the truth because the truth is finally the only safeguard a society can have. Societies need a trust that is grounded on truth. Without it, violence comes all the sooner.[27]

More could equivocate on much of the conceptual content in the issues he faced — or, at least, he played a diplomatic game of disguising truth in ambiguity. But he refused to take the oath. Equivocation stopped there. That was because for him oaths reach to the heart of what society is, to truthfulness itself. "When a man takes an oath he's holding his own self in his own hands." A society that does not demand truthfulness is a society that cannot be trusted. In our view, More's understanding of the necessity to maintain a sense of selfhood —"that little area in which I must rule myself"— was not so much the unique act of the existentialist, the authentic man, as it was the normal obligation of all people who seek to live in a truthful society. An untruthful society is not only dangerous but corrupting. It encourages those who live in it to distrust one another.

And the reason why More, the statesman who resigns, cannot forsake his own conscience for the sake of public duties is not only to maintain personal integrity, but because personal integrity is a public duty. A leader who does not insist that we be truthful leads us to moral chaos. He may trade in optimism but he does not trade in hope. His leadership may take the appearance of stability, but that is only because optimism trains people for roles in which they are not capable of being truthful and are therefore incapable of hope.

The truthless society is organized despair. It is a place where people cannot be sure that there are any grounds for hope. It is a world described by John LeCarre, where the last illusion of the illusionist man is that he has no illusions.[28]

4. Conclusion

More's hope was built on the conviction that truth finally transcends power. His hope insisted that our existence, in particular our social existence, is held by a power beyond that of the state. Because of that conviction he was schooled in hope and his hope was not diluted by those who were optimistic. The time for him to begin refusing to use power was the moment he began to have to be untruthful, to sacrifice the truth that was the ground of his hope. Two generations later English lawyers would remind the king of Bracton's thirteenth-century principle, "non sub homine, sed sub Deo et lege," but it may have taken the blood of More and other lawyers for England to get that far.

More's claim that God is "love right through" was not only a "religious claim," but a political statement. Such love, which is beyond skill and knowledge, is a necessary condition for society because it provides the self with the depth necessary for social order. It is important that we understand this point, because it is the answer to the common misinterpretation of More's refusal to condemn anyone who did take the oath. It is at best anachronistic to make the liberal assumption that More thought that a good social order should allow freedom of conscience in the sense that each conscience is private. (And Bolt is not so naive as to suppose otherwise.) The reason that the first duty of every loyal subject is to be loyal to his conscience is not because conscience is an end in itself, but because the subject's failure to be true to himself is a failure to be true to the love that provides us a basis for being able to trust and share ourselves and to accept the trust of others.[29]

More would say that the reason that one must stand on one's conscience is not because the state is just, but because it is not just. Thus, his response to Margaret's argument that he is trying unnecessarily to make himself a hero is as follows:

More: That's very neat. But look now . . . if we lived in a state where virtue was profitable, common sense would make us good, and greed would make us saintly. And we'd live like animals or angels in the happy land that needs no heroes. But since in fact we see that avarice, anger, envy, pride, sloth, lust, and stupidity commonly profit far beyond humility, chastity, fortitude, justice and thought, and have to choose, to be human at all . . . why then perhaps we must stand fast a little—even at the risk of being heroes.

Margaret: (emotionally) But in reason? Haven't you done as much as God can reasonably want?

More: Well . . . finally . . . it isn't a matter of reason. Finally it's a matter of love.

Thus, More's confrontation with power came about because he was truthful, and because he insisted on hoping that truth is deeper than the

216

optimism of those who too quickly resolve differences through the use of power. More was not seeking martyrdom. He was not even seeking an argument—the issues, as he saw them, were too serious for that. He was seeking, insisting on, the existence of the truth. The fact that the truth led to his death is not an indication that More's convictions were mistaken. It is an indication of how deeply our world is built on fear.[30]

NOTES

1. This essay is co-authored with my good friend Thomas Shaffer, Professor of Law at Washington and Lee Law School.
2. Iris Murdoch, *The Red and the Green* (New York: Viking, 1965), p. 113.
3. We have concluded after some investigation that Bolt's More is an accurate picture of the historical More. Colleagues more steeped in English history, particularly Marvin O'Connell and Robert E. Rodes, Jr., disagree with this in some respects, but not, we think, in matters essential to our thesis here. The text we are using is Robert Bolt, *A Man for All Seasons* (New York: Random House, 1962). Historical sources include William Roper, *The Life of Sir Thomas Moore, Knighte* (1556); Harpsfield, *The Life and Death of Sir Thomas More* (1550–53); R. W. Chambers, *Thomas More* (Ann Arbor: University of Michigan Press, 1973); and E. E. Reynolds, *St. Thomas More* (New York: Image Books, 1958).
4. The word "skill" as used here may appear to have two senses—moral and intellectual. We contend that the two are distinguishable but need not be separated. The language of skill is deliberately chosen; it reflects our conviction that the moral life and "morality" cannot be treated independently from the life of wisdom. Hauerwas has argued elsewhere that Aristotle's and Aquinas' understanding of virtue as habit is best understood in terms of the acquisition of skills for discrimination and action (*Character and the Christian Life* [San Antonio: Trinity University Press, 1975], pp. 35–82). Moreover, the significance of language for the shaping of such skills makes it impossible to separate the moral from the intellectual. Prudence, the central moral virtue for Aquinas, is best understood as "knowing how" rather than "knowing." For a fuller development of this point, see Stanley Hauerwas, *Truthfulness and Tragedy* (Notre Dame: University of Notre Dame Press, 1978), pp. 82–98. Even though More's powerful intellectual and legal skills are not obviously "moral," we contend that they are in fact moral. They are sustained by and give shape to the hopeful form of his moral character.
5. This view of More is probably Bolt's (see his "Preface" to *A Man For All Seasons*).
6. The theoretical assumptions behind this paragraph should be mentioned, if not defended here. Our claim is this: Not only does hope employ and give the basis for certain skills, but it is a skill. It is a skill which one learns. We do not learn to lay bricks without guidance from masters; neither do we learn how to hope without guidance from masters. The acquisition of a skill involves, usually, an initiation into a way of life. A master, who has gone before, usually presides over the initiation. Put in language Hauerwas has used elsewhere, we need a *narrative display* in order to understand how it is we should hope (*Truthfulness and Tragedy*, pp. 15–39). From this perspective, the traditional theological virtues—faith, hope, love—are best understood as reminders of the narrative of the master Jesus, a narrative that schools the self to serve God rightly. Such virtues become distorted if they are treated as independent norms for behavior. If the moral life is inseparable from the life of wisdom, then, in spite of modern philosophy's attempt to secure an independent status for "morality," our moral lives as lived continue to depend on the existence of masters. This paper does not try to argue this point directly; we seek here to exhibit it by calling attention to More's hopeful life.

7. William Lynch, *Images of Hope* (New York: Mentor-Omega Books, 1965), p. 43. We are sympathetic with Lynch's view of hope and particularly with his stress on the significance of imagination in the practice of hope.

8. Thomas Aquinas, *Summa Theologica*, vol. I (New York: Benziger Brothers, 1947), pp. 759–64.

9. Lynch says: "One of the best safeguards of our hopes is to be able to mark off the areas of hopelessness and to acknowledge them, to face them directly, not with despair but with the creative intent of keeping them from polluting all areas of possibility. There are thousands of things that man cannot do, thousands of things that some can do and others cannot. To keep the two, the possible and the impossible, in place is to stay free of intolerable burdens" (op. cit., p. 51). The trick is to know how and when to make such discriminations, especially when that which is "impossible" points to the limitations of one's character. More provides an example, we think, of how one man learned to hope rightly. His hope gave him the means to preserve his sense of self when he was confronted with that which he could not change. He might have sought change with optimism but not, as we are using the term, with hope.

10. Albert Camus, *The Fall* (New York: Knopf, 1957), p. 55.

11. Helmut Gollwitzer (ed.), *Karl Barth, Church Dogmatics: A Selection* (New York: Harper & Row, 1961), p. 73.

12. John Dewey, "Logical Method and Law," *Cornell Law Quarterly*, 10 (1924), p. 17.

13. David Riesman, "Some Observations on Law and Psychology," *University of Chicago Law Review*, 19 (1951), p. 30.

14. Too often considerations of the relations among "law," religion, and morality concentrate on law as a system of rules, rather than as an activity. As a result, claims of moral or religious support for the law have little to do with law as it is practiced by citizens and by lawyers. These accounts ignore the soil in which law grows—the lawyer and the lawyer's character meeting the client and the client's character (Louis M. Brown and Thomas Shaffer, "Toward a Jurisprudence for the Law Office," *American Journal of Jurisprudence*, 17 [1972], p. 125; Thomas Shaffer, "Christian Theories of Professional Responsibility," *Southern California Law Review*, 48, 721 [1975]; Thomas Shaffer, *Legal Interviewing and Counseling* [St. Paul: West Publishing Company, 1976], pp. 39–63).

15. Philip Rhinelander, unpublished remarks to the American Society of Newspaper Editors, March 12, 1977. Professor Rhinelander, Professor Emeritus at Stanford University, kindly provided the authors with a copy of these remarks.

16. The anecdote is from a memorandum to students written by our colleague, Edward F. Barrett. See William Blackstone, *Commentaries on the Law of England*, vol. 3 (New York: Bancroft-Whitney, 1916), p. 148.

17. When this point comes will vary from one legal system to another. Some legal systems are so corrupt, or serve such a corrupt political system, that they make it impossible to serve the law at all. The position of the legal profession in the Union of South Africa is an example of where the line between the possible and the impossible might lie. The system of law presupposed in this paper is one in which people have both a means to control and limit power and a means to resolve conflicts short of violence. Our view of law here is similar to that described in Robert E. Rodes, Jr., *The Legal Enterprise* (New York: Kennikat Press, 1976). In contrast to the analytical approach to law, which assumes that the only legally relevant community is the one created and defined by the law itself, Rodes argues that, "All the law we actually experience is addressed to an ongoing community. It takes its place in a matrix of different human relations, only part of them legal. To my mind, what defines the relevant community is history. This is of course true in the trivial sense that the existence and effect of a law is a matter of historical fact. But more important, the very coherence of the community in which laws operate seems to depend on some common experience or common consciousness of history" p. 14. From this perspective, the recent attempt by both natural-law and positivistic theorists to secure the "autonomy" of the law from the vicissitudes of history can be interpreted as an attempt to save the morality of the

law in a community that no longer shares a common interpretation of its history. We sometimes admire the attempt, although it seems to us to be destined to fail and, worse, it seems
to prevent lawyers from facing the moral challenge of practicing law in a society as complex
as ours (Thomas Shaffer, "Guilty Clients and Lunch with Tax Collectors," *The Jurist*, 37
[1977], p. 89).

18. J. Scarisbrick, "Thomas More: The King's Good Servant," *Thought*, 52 (1977), pp. 249,
267–68.

19. Karl Barth, *Evangelical Theology* (London: Fontana, 1965), pp. 122–24.

20. C. P. Snow's *Corridors of Power* (New York: Charles Scribner's Sons, 1964) is a political
example. Thomas Shaffer shows how this point operates within a law practice, "Justice in
Everyday Life," *Res Gestae* (September, 1978), and in a law-school setting in Thomas Shaffer,
"Moral Moments in Law School," *Social Responsibility: Journalism, Law, Medicine*, vol. III
(Washington and Lee University, 1978).

21. Shaffer, *Southern California Law Review*, note 13.

22. It is interesting to notice that More was a conventional holder of power as chancellor—then and now the highest judicial office in England, and then, if not now, "the
King's conscience"—and not, apparently, a reformer. Before he became chancellor,
More had been an unremarkable aide-de-camp to Wolsey (see Scarisbrick, op. cit., and
Chambers and Reynolds, op. cit). While he pursued this more or less ordinary political
career, he earned membership in the humanist intelligentsia of sixteenth-century Europe
and assayed political reform, in fancy at least, in his *Utopia*. But he seems not to have
sought reform through his office holding. Scarisbrick finds some evidence that More may
have been a compromiser. We are inclined to contend that More was a reformer in that he
was honest, publicly and privately; this honesty was both unusual and promising. Compare his career as a chancellor to that of Francis Bacon, less than a century later (Bowen,
Francis Bacon: The Temper of a Man [Boston: Little, Brown and Company, 1963]; Thomas
Shaffer, "Book Review," *Yale Law Journal*, 73 [1963], p. 537).

23. Karl Barth, *The Epistle to the Romans* (trans. Edward Hoskyns, 6th ed.; London:
Oxford University Press, 1968), p. 457.

24. More's position on the King's marriage derived from his moral convictions, we think,
rather than from a loyalty to the church as contrasted with loyalty to the King. His position
was not political. More was aware that the church had often found ways to compromise
on issues involving royal marriage. He had no illusions about the righteousness of the
papacy. It is important to remember that he identified, in fact, with humanist and
spiritualistic movements which were calling for church reform. We contend that (1)
whatever decision was reached on the marriage could not have been a decision based on
honest argument; and (2) More knew this and acted accordingly.

25. Power resorts to violence when power lacks authority—a point made often by
political theorists. See, for example, Hannah Arendt's *On Violence* (New York: Harcourt,
Brace, and World, 1969), pp. 35–36. The Gospel seems to us to display the relation of power
to violence more radically. It assumes that all power not based on recognition of God's
authority can only provide the semblance of order.

26. A forceful presentation of this view is John Howard Yoder's *The Politics of Jesus* (Grand
Rapids: Eerdmanns, 1972).

27. The relation among trust, truth, and cooperation is one that can be studied in small
settings (Morton Deutsch, "The Effect of Motivational Orientation Upon Trust and
Suspicion," *Human Relations*, 13 [1960], p. 123). Thomas Shaffer and Robert S. Redmount,
Lawyers, Law Students, and People (Colorado Springs: Shepard's-McGraw-Hill, 1977, ch. 8),
contains examples from legal education.

28. See John LeCarre's novel, *Tinker, Tailor, Soldier, Spy* (New York: Knopf, 1974).

29. Barth, *The Epistle to the Romans*.

30. We are grateful for the suggestions and criticisms of James Childress, Edward M.
Gaffney, Thomas Ogletree, Robert E. Rodes, Jr., Nancy Shaffer, Mary Jo Weaver, and John
Howard Yoder.

TRUTH AND HONOR

The University and the Church in a Democratic Age

1. What is the Christian University?

Many excellent historical and critical essays have been written about what kind of relation has and ought to pertain between the church and the university. Yet this question, like so many other kinds of perennial questions, has remained unresolved. Moreover, it is not even clear how one can make any progress toward resolution since it is seldom clear exactly what are the issues involved.

Part of the difficulty in this respect is that the question about how the church is or is not related to the university changes from one period to another as the relative strengths, social standing, and character of the respective institutions change. For example, it is interesting how seldom we now discuss whether academic freedom is possible at church-related institutions. Rather, the issue that seems to confront us now is what justification, if any, can be given for the continued existence of Christian universities.

But again it is not clear what kind of question this is. Sometimes it seems born of grim necessity. For historical reasons Christians have found themselves inheritors of institutions of higher learning to which they continue to have financial relations and supply students. But the current financial condition of many of these institutions makes us ask why Christians have a stake in maintaining these schools. Though such schools continue to exist at great personal and financial sacrifice for many, they are not able to provide an education that is in any way superior to that of the local branch of the state college.

Of course, we are all familiar with the answers that have been given to justify the continued existence of the Christian college. The Christian college is justified because it alone is committed to providing a liberal arts curriculum that is commensurate with Christian and humanistic convictions. Or, the Christian college is concerned with the "whole student," which at least means that good counseling service is provided as well as is the opportunity to get to know the professors outside the classroom. Or, the Christian college offers value education by requiring religion and philosophy courses as well as providing a general atmosphere that fosters the development of moral responsibility. In other words, St. Alonzo of the Left Elbow of the Immaculate Conception on the Mount may not be a multiversity such as Indiana University and we thank God for it.

Even though these answers are often given, their frequency does not make them any more persuasive. We know that the liberal arts curriculum does not make one liberal — even if we knew what being liberal meant or we could show that to be such was an inherently good thing. Indeed, we know that the relation between course work and the development of a particular kind of person is far too subtle to be reduced to any formula. In such a context the Christian colleges' proclamation of the importance of the liberal arts appears as an ideology which attempts to hide the fact that they cannot afford to do anything else. Moreover, the liberal arts college has recently discovered that if it is to compete with other colleges for students it must water down the requirements that have traditionally been associated with a liberal arts education. For example, it is amazing how quickly Christian colleges are willing to cancel a liberal arts requirement when they find out they can attract students by offering courses in nursing and/or computer science.

In addition, our reputed care or personal regard for students, even when manifested with the best intentions, is interpreted as an unwarranted attempt to control the student's personal life. Also, it is not clear what rationale can be given for much of what has come to fly the flag in the name of student services at our supposedly academic institutions. Often our services only act as a way to delay the student's growth out of adolescence.

If we take our refuge in the justification of Christian colleges on the basis of value education, we are left holding an even weaker reed. After all, Jeb Magruder of Watergate fame did take an ethics course under William Sloane Coffin. Of course, this is but a trivial example of the more profound Platonic insight that goodness or virtue is not something that can be taught — or, if it can be taught, the teaching of it is a much more subtle process than the simple expediency of taking an ethics or values course. But even if this were not the case, we find ourselves in the

222

embarrassing position of not being sure what values we want or should want to recommend. To be sure, it is a good thing to be honest, but we are not sure what that means or how it is to be done today.

The kinds of problems with this set of justifications for the existence of the Christian university, however, may help us see that perhaps we have the wrong question. For to ask why the Christian university should continue to exist presupposes that we have some sense of what a Christian university is. But I think that is just the matter at issue—namely, the reason that we have trouble in saying why the Christian university should exist is that we remain unsure what distinguishes such an institution from other universities. This is particularly true since secular institutions have become increasingly regarded as paradigmatic for all universities. The Christian university thus seems left with a dilemma of wanting to measure up to the paradigm—we are just like them (perhaps with a little something added)—while at the same time being forced to realize that the more it fulfills the paradigm, the less distinctive its own contribution becomes and the less reason there is for its continued existence.

I think, however, that the Christian university can be distinctive and that there is good reason for it to exist. I have no grand idea or definition of what a Christian university is, but rather for me a university is Christian if it receives its financial and moral support from the church. In other words, I am enough of a realist to assume that whoever pays the bills will determine the character, for better or worse, of an institution. The issue is not, therefore, whether there is such a thing as a Christian university, but rather *do we have a church that is distinctive enough that it can set priorities and purposes for its universities?*

Generally my answer to this last question is no, but the reason for this, I think, helps illumine what distinctive character a Christian university should have. For it is my thesis that the university as an institution that is characterized by the virtues of honor and truthfulness has been undermined by certain democratic values. This has happened not only to the university but also to the church. If my analysis is correct in this respect, then I think we will also have a sense of how the church and university may renew their ancient bond—namely, that the church supports the university by developing a people capable of bearing the burden of honor and truthfulness, a people without which the university (and, interestingly, democracy), as I conceive its task, cannot exist.

This is obviously as complex and obscure a thesis as it is controversial. To try to bring greater clarity to it I will first analyze the meaning of honor, suggest why it is such an important virtue for universities, and

223

show how truthfulness gives form to honorable behavior in the university. I will then try to suggest how this analysis helps us see why the institutions that support the university financially and morally (and in particular the church) are so crucial for its character.

2. The Meaning of Honor

I must admit I did not develop my sense of the importance of honor for the university by chance, but rather because I was asked to serve on a committee at Notre Dame to investigate why the honor system had failed and what the possibilities were for its reinstitution. Generally, serving on committees is a beneficial experience, as it gives one a healthy sense of the limits of human rationality. However, much to my surprise, serving on this committee jogged me from a kind of dogmatic slumber as I became aware that the concept of honor, especially in relation to the university, is much more important than I had assumed.

Initially, I had strong reservations about the idea of honor, since historically and sociologically I associated it with forms of life for which I have little sympathy. That my reservations in this respect are not just a personal quirk is suggested by how little honor is used as a working word in our everyday speech — we no longer think of our moral behavior as a matter of honor, but doing the right, performing praiseworthy actions, or "doing one's own thing." The contexts in which honor is still used are highly regimented and associated with institutions that seem to imply that honor consists in uncritical obedience to the commands of superiors. Thus, to defend the idea of honor or to reassert its importance seems to be either hopelessly naive or perversely conservative and authoritarian.

However, these sociological considerations are misleading, since the idea of honor suggests important aspects of our moral life that cannot be lost without our lives becoming poorer. I think this is especially true for institutions like the university that cannot long forget what they are about without becoming perverted. The skill to articulate such purpose involves the idea of honor, since honor is a moral bridge between the self and its society. To be honorable requires an effort of will from the agent, but honor has significance for the social order beyond an individual's possession of it. Grammatically, therefore, honor is one of those interesting notions that are at once related to the moral agent and his or her social contexts. Our ability to display it in our lives depends on being

224

able to strike the right balance between the agent and society, to preserve their interdependence without reducing one to the other.

It is instructive to look at the institution of dueling to understand better the nature of honor. I am aware that more compelling examples could be chosen to recommend the idea of honor, but dueling has the virtue of not biasing the moral case too quickly. What is particularly interesting about duels is that they were often fought over what we today would consider arbitrary or insignificant insults which were dignified by being described as "affairs of honor." But it is exactly the insignificance of the insult and the willingness to risk one's life to redress the wrong that makes the whole institution of dueling intelligible. For the concern the "gentleman" showed for such matters is exactly what made him a gentleman—namely, someone who was to be granted special treatment due to his station in society.

This point, I think, is analogous to Veblen's explanation for the necessity of the American rich to consume. The rich do not buy expensive, extravagant, and nonutilitarian goods because they can, but to mark themselves off as rich in a society that has no established criteria for a leisure class. The rich must consume not because they are rich, but because if they did not engage in consumption of unnecessary goods there would be no way to establish their status in a democratic society that ideologically claims to be classless. The gentleman was insulted by what we would regard as insignificant acts because that is exactly what made him a gentleman. If he was not willing to fight the duel he was a traitor to his class, since he refused to perform the action necessary to reinforce his social position and its advantages. It was the gentleman's willingness to die for the insignificant that at the same time established and communicated that he was not like other men.

Put more theoretically, *honor is morally significant as a means to mark off those forms of behavior that are to be done as ends in themselves*. This is a bit misleading, however, as these referential acts cannot be abstracted from their societal context; such acts are significant exactly because they are the way a particular society reinforces and articulates to itself the forms of life that give that society its reason for being. The concept of honor and its associated practices in a society are not important because without them that society could not exist, but rather because without them the reasons that make that society what it is would not be present. In other words, it is exactly the nonutilitarian aspect of honor that makes it so important for a society's understanding of itself.

This point is consistent with De Tocqueville's insight that "there is a close and necessary connection between what we call honor and inequity of condition."[1] It is the dissimilarities among people that give rise to the notion of honor, and thus "as such differences become less, it grows feeble; and when they disappear, it will vanish too" (p. 627). It is therefore especially important, if a class is to maintain its dominant position, to honor and emphasize those virtues that have their "share of magnificence and renown and which easily go with pride and love of power" (p. 627). Such a class must be bold to invert the commonsense assumptions about how best to survive to give those virtues that legitimate their position precedence over all others.

The concept of honor thus does not operate like the more or less common assumptions shared by all persons about right and wrong. The forms of honor usually presuppose an established society in which the moral conditions for the survival of that society are well set. The concept of honor in its particular manifestation is therefore more characteristic of one age or one country or one class. Thus, in the feudal world an act that would have no importance if done by a commoner would be considered dishonorable for the noble, since the aristocracy was exactly that class that could afford not to be subject to the forms of convention ordered by the necessity of survival. Honor is a correlative of aristocracy, as the latter would rather have the general society ruined than see the values they embody lost.

Even though De Tocqueville associates honor with aristocracy, he makes the broader claim that "every time men come together to form a particular society, a conception of honor is immediately established among them, that is to say, a collection of opinions peculiar to themselves about what should be praised or blamed" (p. 620). Society, on this view, cannot exist without established distinctions among classes. That is why democracy presents such an interesting test case for De Tocqueville, for even though he finds that honor still plays a part in the American ethos, he suggests its form and practices will become increasingly ambiguous. For as a society erodes all class distinctions, the precepts of honor will be fewer and fewer, and such precepts will draw continually closer to the moral custom accepted by the population at large.

. This perhaps helps explain why the idea of honor appears so often as an ideological leftover "in the consciousness of obsolete classes, such as military officers or ethnic grandmothers."[2] Berger associates the decline of the age of honor with the use of the idea of dignity with its anti-institutional and individualistic assumptions. Like De Tocqueville he associates honor with groups that retain a hierarchial view of society, such as the military and traditional professions like law and medicine. "In such groups honor is a direct expression of status, a source of soli-

226

darity among social equals and a demarcation line against social inferiors" (p. 340). Thus, the concept of honor is inextricably linked with institutional roles. However, dignity relates to the intrinsic humanity of each person, divested of all socially imposed roles or norms. To have dignity pertains to the self as such, to the individual regardless of his or her position in society.

In a democratic age which adheres to this individualistic conception of dignity, it is not surprising that the concept of honor appears morally doubtful. The past conceptions of honor appear to us as arbitrary forms of class distinctions which unjustifiably robbed some people of their due rights. Moreover, the concept of honor seems rooted in an understanding of the human being that places far too much emphasis on social context for the definition of each person's identity and moral worth. The concept of dignity suggests that identity is achieved exactly as we express ourselves against our institutional roles.

Berger argues, however, that there are anthropological constraints on our age's peculiarly strong stress on dignity. For the concept and ethics of dignity, if pressed too consistently, finally begin to erode the essential sociality of the human on which any sense of identity is possible. I will not try to suggest the complex causes that underlie our current sociological situation; it is sufficient to indicate that the institutional fabric, whose basic function has always been to provide meaning and stability for the individual, has become incohesive and deprived of its plausibility. "The institutions then confront the individual as fluid and unreliable, in the extreme case as unreal. Inevitably, the individual is thrown back upon himself, on his own subjectivity, from which he must dredge up the meaning and the stability that he requires to exist. Precisely because of man's intrinsic sociality, this is a very unsatisfactory condition. Stable identities can only emerge in reciprocity with stable social contexts."[3]

Therefore, the ethics of dignity, with its strong anti-institutional bias, has paid a costly price for whatever liberation we may have achieved. Berger thus suggests that a rediscovery of honor in the future development of modern society is both empirically plausible and ethically desirable, as this can be done without sacrificing the conviction that the weakest member of society has an inherent right to protection and dignity. "Man's fundamental constitution is such that, just about inevitably, he will once more construct institutions to provide an ordered reality for himself. A return to institutions will, *ipso facto*, be a return to honor. It will then be possible again for individuals to identify themselves with the escutcheons of their institutional roles, experienced now not as selfestranging tyrannies but a freely chosen vehicle of self realization. The ethical question, of course, is what these institutions will be like. Specifically, the ethical test of any future institutions, and of the codes of honor they will entail, will be whether they succeed in embodying and in stabilizing the discoveries of human dignity that are the principal achievements of modern man."[4]

3. Honor, Truthfulness, and the University

This analysis of the idea of honor helps explain why it is both so important and yet so difficult to use the concept of honor to discuss many of the problems of the modern university. For the university is an institution of aristocracy in a democratic world. As Frederick Olafson suggests, "In the eyes of many—both supporters and critics—the university is still an essentially medieval institution in its formal institutional structure and in its dominant conception of knowledge and culture. In both domains it still bases itself on a conception of hierarchy—that is, of an ordering of academic life and of the corpus of knowledge and culture through a system of ranks within which certain fixed attributions of authority to the superordinate ranks exercise a controlling role in the life of the university."[5]

The nobility of the university is not, however, that established by birth. Rather, those who occupy the hierarchy of the university are there because they are distinguished by their willingness to expose themselves to the truth by developing the skills of critical intelligence. It is important, however, to note that such intelligence is not the same as intellectual cleverness. Indeed, one of the marks that the modern university is in trouble is that it selects students primarily on the basis of intelligence, determined by skills measured in terms of standardized tests. Yet we know that the intellectual life or the life of wisdom demands courage and other virtues which guide the inquiring mind. The university is an inevitably elitist institution but it should not be an elite determined by I.Q. but rather by the willingness to expose our ignorance in the search for wisdom.

An institution formed to train the critical mind must be formed by a shared past that creates present expectations that determines matters of honor. For the university is not waiting to be created; it is an institution that knows why and for what purpose it exists: the development of the critical person who would rather know than not know. We know that the willingness to expose ourselves to critical scrutiny is no easy task, as we

228

all prefer to rest content on the conventional wisdom of the past,[6] especially as it assumes the status of scientific or scholarly knowledge. Thus, the university is that institution we depend upon to honor those who provide us with more truthful ways of understanding and knowing.

Berger suggests, however, that the values of democracy have tended to undermine the university as an institution of honor committed to truthfulness. The university's attempt to maintain and impose a code of conduct that is commensurate with its purposes appears to result in an arbitrarily established difference among people rather than a context for their equality. That this should be viewed negatively is inevitable if, as the democratic model seems to demand, the task of the university becomes the enhancement and the fulfillment of the individual's desires—e.g., "What do you want to learn about?" or "That course is no longer relevant since it does not help me in my chosen profession"[7]—than the creation of a class of people distinctly marked by their love of truth.

Thus, the idea of the university as a society dedicated to providing people with the skills to articulate truthfully what they know and should know has shifted to the idea that the university's primary task is to serve the needs of the individual and society as immediately experienced. Such needs can come in the form of training for the job market or the military, or in helping solve the problem of dignity. For the "interest model" rests on the assumption that the university should not only serve a democratic social order,[8] it should *be* one and thus subject to the interests of those that make it up. Without an institution like the church that provides the space and time necessary for people to engage in the work of the mind, the university can only exist in spite of, rather than because of, its social purpose.

Connected with the democratization of the academy is the tendency of college graduates to claim that though they have a college education, they have not been essentially changed by the experience. But universities necessarily pass on and investigate what Olafson has called the "high culture" of our civilization, which certainly has roots in our everyday life[9] but which one does not come in contact with without it affecting our "natural and parochial selves." Thus, Olafson suggests that "much of the frantic current emphasis on ethnicity and 'pop' culture by people in the universities appears to be an attempt on their part to assure themselves that exposure to intellectual life has not really changed them and that they retain the myopic parochialism of their origins."[10]

To be sure, the ethic of individual dignity has helped eliminate many unjustified impositions on students and faculty which were inconsistent

229

with or not necessary for the university's purpose. However, this ethic is ultimately not sufficient for the university if the university is an institution committed to a task not subject to those who currently happen to be associated with it. For the purpose of the university is not subject to democratic vote nor is it legitimated by the amount of participation of its constituent members in the processes that give form to that purpose.[11]

Of course, since one of the main things that those who work toward skills of truthfulness learn is that they have no corner on truth, the citizens of a university community tend to place great value on the importance of discussion for giving the university direction. This does not mean, however, that the university must assume that all behavior that takes place within its bounds deserves to be regarded as part of that dialogue. If the university community has become so unsure of its purpose that it no longer feels able to articulate acts of dishonor for those participating in its work, then it is not worthy of surviving as an institution dedicated to learning and scholarship.

The task of the university is not one that everyone is called upon to perform, though of course everyone must be truthful, but rather it is the duty of those with the intellectual and moral virtues necessary for this kind of task. For though we assume that all people wish to know rather than not know, we generally fear the truth like the plague. We prefer our illusions, which are often rooted in our concern not to hurt others or ourselves rather than risk encountering the wildness and unpredictability of reality which ultimately defies our categories. Those called to such a task cannot afford to be deficient in intellectual or moral virtue, as the absence of one without the other will leave us prey to the conventionalities we are always tempted to call the truth because of the sheer weight of their general acceptance.

Contrary to much of the reigning thought about universities, truth is not something we learn simply by perceiving or analyzing further; it requires the qualification of the self. To know the truth requires correspondence to the truth. Most of us are rather lacking in this regard, but the pervasiveness of our failure must not be allowed to blind us to this requirement for those who pursue academic study—whether they be students or professors. Such moral commitment is not to be equated with the mediocrity and triteness of the reigning piety; rather, it has more to do with such virtues as integrity, honesty, justice, humility, humor, and kindness.

It requires integrity, for those who labor in the academy are constantly tempted to sell their wares at the current cultural store. It requires honesty, because learning is essentially a matter of recognizing our

230

limitations. It requires justice in the sense that we must learn to gaze fairly at reality as it is, not as we wish it to be. It requires humility, as we recognize that we can never contain the truth within our conceptualizations. It requires humor to guard us against the most dangerous of all intellectual sins, the temptation to take ourselves too seriously. (To have humor is to recognize that the viability of truth does not rest on our particular formulation of it.) Finally, it requires kindness and mutuality, as the demands of truth can be so hard and destructive that only the love of others can sustain us in the endeavor.[12]

It is therefore to be expected that the university, as the institution that provides for the class of people to do this kind of work, defines some behavior and practices as honorable and others as dishonorable. Since the ability to know the truth in its many and various contexts and levels is always a process rather than a status, it is necessary to establish conditions for the process. These conditions at least are the faithful reporting of what we have learned in a way that clearly distinguishes one's insights from those of others. There are definite acts we can associate with this condition that should not be done—e.g., using another person's work as representative of one's own. Cheating is thus a class term which judges the individual as engaging in behavior inconsistent with the ends of the university, regardless of the motivation or excuses the agent might give to explain such behavior. The university's concern with cheating is not a moralistic attempt to restrain petty immorality but is the articulation to itself of what it is about. The reasons why certain persons cheat may be of interest to their welfare or even indicate some problems in the university's social fabric, but such response cannot qualify the meaning and significance of cheating itself.

It is one of the ironies of the current situation that it is assumed that one of the marks of the Christian university is to be understanding and forgiving to those who have cheated or engaged in other activities detrimental to the university's purposes. The campus chaplain's office too often becomes the comfort station to protect the student from the demands and consequences of undertaking the task of the university. What must be remembered is that before the church becomes a dispenser of comfort to the afflicted, it must first be a dispenser of truth.[13] When the church's rightful ministry of forgiveness is turned into a cheap policy of understanding and acceptance, both church and university have compromised their commitment to truth.

The church's stake in the university is that we believe that the God we find and worship in Jesus Christ is the true God. Christians thus believe that they have no fear of the truth, but rather they have a stake in having

231

the truth of our existence stated as clearly as possible. We do not assume that such truth will make us whole, for the truth can be as destructive as it can be healing, but rather we seek the truth because it is our duty. If we compromise our duty because we are gripped by sentimental accounts of Christian kindness, we neither serve the church nor the Gospel well.

Do not think I am suggesting that it is or should be the task of the university to be the church—that is, to preach the Gospel. For the university to do this would be presumptive and destructive, because the task to which the university is committed does not save. Rather, I am arguing the church must charge the university to do what it can—namely, to develop people of critical intelligence—for it is just such a people the church requires for its purpose. But the church must also support the university by providing the resources necessary for the university to continue its work in a world that generally only wants truth on the world's own terms.

Some may object that the position I have developed is far too severe, given the ambiguity of the university as an institution dedicated to the pursuit of truth—i.e., that what I have said may be theoretically accurate, but the university that I defend simply does not exist. We know the university is full of teachers who have little sympathy with the purpose of the university as I have stated it. We also know that few students come to the academy to learn as an end in itself, but instead see the university as but one more hurdle toward the securing of a better job. We know that too many of our classes are taught with no more purpose than the allocation of grades at the end of the semester. Moreover, the competitive nature of the current university, with its constant demand of good grades for admission into good professional and graduate schools, seems to warrant for many a less rigorous stance about dishonorable behavior.

Such a list could be extended almost indefinitely, but it would serve no useful function. For no one would argue that the university is free from hypocrisy or that as a multiversity it assumes tasks tangential to or even antithetical to its essential purpose. Yet this kind of point does not mean that the university should not be concerned about whether its constituents engage in dishonest behavior. There are no pure institutions in this world—not church, not state, not family, not university. Because the church often fails to preach the gospel with integrity does not mean it makes no difference that we try to live true to the gospel. Because the state does not always seek justice does not mean that we should cease to work toward a more just society. How poorly the university would train if it assumed the cynical position that since we are all in sin, there

232

is no way to expect anything good of anybody! Surely the university, as still one of the least ambiguous institutions of our society, can require its constituents to act honorably even if it is necessary to exclude some who act dishonorably.

The university has the task of educating young people to bear the burden of truthfulness in a world of ambiguity and hypocrisy. For the university to excuse dishonorable behavior or to expect less than honorable behavior because of its own inconsistencies is to fail in this task. It is each person's duty to decide to be trustworthy regardless of the conditions that surround him or her. To suggest that our honesty is always relative to the moral status of our surrounding environment is a formula of moral cowardice which cannot sustain the work of the scholar or the citizen. Moreover, it is to fail to see all people with the dignity that Berger suggested must be preserved, as it assumes that people cannot rise higher than their social conditions. There is no greater dignity than to treat another as if he or she is capable of honorable behavior.

The moral authority that grounds this kind of ethic at the university is not the administration, or the faculty, or the students, but that band of scholars who are true to the university's purpose. Just as the church's authority rests on the witness of the saints so the university's authority to articulate and embody the ethics of honor peculiar to itself rests on those scholars who have so completely embodied it in their person and work. To be sure, there can be no honor at a university (or in any other society) that does not have in its past and present paradigms of moral and intellectual excellence—that is, people who willingly sacrifice their self-interest for the sake of knowing better and more truthfully. That is why it is so important that the university have not only criteria of dishonor, but ways of recognizing those in its midst who do honor to its purposes.

4. The Christian University

In conclusion, let me try to be as clear as I can be about what implications this analysis might have for how we think about the Christian university. First and foremost, I have not said that the university is just another extension of the church. The university is not, cannot be, and should not be in the business of holding out the salvation that only the church can properly proclaim. Nor can the Christian university simply be the church's institution for inculturation to the intellectual and social culture of the church's surrounding society.

Rather, I have tried to suggest that the church has a stake in the university because the church has a commitment to the development of critical intelligence. For we exist as a people who have been formed by a gospel that assures us that we have no fear of the truth. We all learn to say this easily, but we know in fact that it is an extraordinary assumption. As Ernest Becker has suggested, it may well be that a full apprehension of the human condition would drive us mad.[14]

Yet if my suggestions above are correct, the university is that institution that values the development of the rational life above all else. Such a life is not identified with any specific curriculum or administrative division or academic discipline. Rather, the rational life is that one in which appearances and plausibilities are relentlessly tested in the hope that the realities will be truthfully disclosed in the process. It cannot be the special possession of any one area or discipline.

Nor is the rational life one that is devoid of value or emotive concerns. As Julian Hartt has suggested, "the rational life stands out against the life of spontaneous enjoyment either of weal or woe, bane or blessing. And it also stands out against abstract understanding of what is and what is good. The rational life is one in which the right rights are rightly enjoyed."[15] The university has no unique claim to achieving such a life, but it does claim to be the place that strives the hardest to support those who wish to develop such a life to do so.

But such an institution is not easily sustained. Financially it is not easy to sustain, for societies have much to fear from the development of such people and therefore prefer to support the university on their own terms. Nor is it easy to attract students and faculty, as few willingly expose themselves to such institutions. And finally, it is not easy to sustain morally and intellectually, for few of us have the moral courage to believe that the truth is worth pursuing.

Thus, the church is important to the Christian university by providing the money to sustain its existence so that the university will not have to sell out to its society's needs. It sustains the university by producing people who are willing to stand the rigors and the demands of such an institution. But finally and most importantly, the church sustains the university by keeping alive the story and the rituals that assure us that falsehood is finally bounded by the power of truth.

NOTES

1. Alexis De Tocqueville, *Democracy in America*, translated by George Lawrence (Garden City: Doubleday, 1969), p. 626. Further references in text.
2. Peter Berger, "On the Obsolescence of the Concept of Honor," *Archives of European*

Sociology, XI (1970), p. 339. Reprinted in *Revisions: Changing Perspectives in Moral Philosophy*, edited by Alasdair MacIntyre and Stanley Hauerwas (Notre Dame: University of Notre Dame Press, 1984), pp. 172-181.

3. Ibid., p. 344.

4. Ibid., pp. 346-7.

5. Frederick Olafson, "Democracy, 'High Culture,' and the Universities," *Philosophy and Public Affairs*, 2, 4 (Summer, 1973), p. 386.

6. For an account of our capacity for self-deception, particularly as it is reinforced by our assumption that we desire to know the truth, see David Burrell and Stanley Hauerwas, "Self-Deception and Autobiography: Theological and Ethical Reflections of Speer's *Inside the Third Reich*," in my *Truthfulness and Tragedy* (Notre Dame: University of Notre Dame Press, 1977), pp. 82-98.

7. This is not to deny that questions of relevance are unimportant to scholarly activity. In fact, one of the difficulties of contemporary universities is how the separation into disciplines has encouraged the growth of hardened orthodoxies about what are and are not areas and methods for scholarly concentration. It is my contention that the Christian university should be that institution with the courage to hire scholars who can challenge the "professionalized" paradigms of academic "specializations." We need to recover the idea that there just may well be something called Christian sociology, economy, etc.—not in the sense that Christian convictions provide special knowledge inaccessible to others, but rather that being Christian may well bring certain interests and concerns to the fore that have been ignored or are not in the province of the sociologist or the economist.

8. Of course, we should not be surprised that the modern university takes as its primary task the training of people for the tasks of democracy. The university always has served the social orders in which it exists. I am suggesting, however, that the ends of the church and the ends of democracy are not necessarily compatible. Therefore, at least conceptually, though I despair at the practical possibility, I assume theoretically that a university supported by the church should provide people with skills that universities supported by the wider society do not.

9. This is important, of course, because an aristocracy of the mind must be seen as important to all people in the society that supports it. Thus, though not every Christian would be called to the university, every Christian must see that they have some stake in what goes on there. As important, then, as the church is for the kind of people that it sends to the university, is the kind of welcome it provides for those it receives back from the university.

10. Olafson, "Democracy, 'High Culture,' and the Universities," p. 402.

11. In the past, the position I am trying to represent has been identified with those who have assumed that truthfulness is only associated with those disciplines that deal with truth as an end itself—democratic models of the university are all right if one wants the university to pursue disciplines that provide practical results. However, I refuse to accept the distinction between theoretical and practical truth such a division implies. It seems to me that a Christian university might well encourage the growth of certain practical disciplines—e.g., nursing—but what becomes important is *how* it encourages reflection in its students and faculty in nursing.

12. See my "Problematics of a 'Christian College'," *The Cresset*, XXXIV, 7 (May, 1971), p. 7.

13. Julian Hartt, *Theology and the Church in the University* (Philadelphia: Westminster Press, 1969), p. 156.

14. Ernest Becker, *The Denial of Death* (New York: Free Press, 1973), p. 27.

15. Hartt, p. 34. I think this provides the basis for why liturgy is so important for the university's own purposes. Unfortunately, the "college chapel," under the burden of providing worship bland enough for anyone, provides poor faith to sustain and train our desires to enjoy the right things rightly.

HOW UNIVERSITIES CONTRIBUTE TO THE CORRUPTION OF YOUTH

1. The Current State of the "Christian University"

"The aims of Duke University are to assert a faith in the eternal union of knowledge and religion set forth in the teachings and character of Jesus Christ, the son of God; to advance learning in all lines of truth; to defend scholarship against all false notions and ideals; to develop a Christian love of freedom and truth; to promote a sincere spirit of tolerance; to discourage all partisan and sectarian strife; and to render the largest permanent service to the individual, the state, and the nation, and the church. Unto these ends shall the affairs of this university always be administered."

So reads the bronze plaque that rests in the middle of Duke University. Yet at the recent inauguration of the president of Duke University, the chairman of the board of Duke read this statement leaving out "set forth in the teachings and character of Jesus Christ, the Son of God." That he did so is certainly appropriate, as there is no visible evidence that teaching or scholarship at Duke is decisively determined by adherence to Jesus Christ. To be sure, Duke Chapel continues to stand in the middle of the campus and is used as the symbol of Duke on most of the campus publications, but that it does so is more a witness to its aesthetic than its Christian nature.

Christians built and supported universities because they thought them important for enabling us to live better as Christians. Yet now statements such as that on the bronze plaque at Duke are often seen by those who make up the modern university as, at best, quaint sentiments from the past or, more likely, potential threats from the religious right. For example, one seldom sees emblazoned on Harvard's shield its full motto—i.e., *Veritas: Christo et Ecclesia. Veritas* is quite enough challenge for the contemporary university.

237

Why and how this transformation took place no doubt involve complex social and intellectual issues. Even if I had the competence to account for the loss of Christian control of their universities, that is not my primary concern. Rather, I am only interested in noting this change insofar as it helps us now to face the issue of how as Christians we are to understand our commitment to, and participation in, the life of the modern university. I certainly do not believe it is possible or desirable to recapture Duke or Harvard as Christian universities. The question is not whether Duke can be Christian; but rather how Christians should understand what they are doing as teachers, administrators, and students at Duke, Harvard, and the University of North Carolina.

Of course, some may well think they do not need to have the issue put so contentiously, as they support or teach at less secular universities. The possibility of being a "Christian college" still exists at smaller schools that specialize in liberal arts or pre-professional education. In such contexts it not only remains possible to assert the union of knowledge and religion as set forth in the teaching and character of Jesus Christ, but a genuine attempt to determine the morals and character of students can be made. Thus, the mission statement of Anderson College in Anderson, Indiana, reads "Our mission is to be an institution of Christian higher education at its best. We understand this to mean building that quality program which will enable each member of the campus community to become stronger in body, mind and spirit; to experience what it means to love God and 'neighbor'; to purposefully adopt a style of servanthood in all of life (Based on Mark 10:35–45; 12:28–33)."

It is not for me to judge how well or completely Anderson and the many schools like it accomplish this purpose. I am sure it differs from school to school. Yet I do have general questions about the coherence and/or practicality of such mission statements in the society in which we live. Such statements confirm and comfort those who work to maintain such colleges, but I suspect the reality often belies the stated ideal. That it does so is not because anyone is being willfully deceitful, but because we are dealing with fundamental issues and conflicts which are not easily resolved.

For the problem with bronze plaques such as the one in the middle of Duke is that they give the impression that there once was a golden age when it was possible to maintain "Christian universities." Due to the pluralism of our culture that time may have passed for such universities, but now that mission can be carried on by smaller colleges which have a more homogeneous constituency. Yet I think questions of how Christians are to be related to universities and colleges were in fact no clearer in the "golden age" than now. The only difference now is that living in a more secular culture means we are less able to avoid such issues.

For example, in Anderson College's mission statement we are told that as a "Christian institution of higher education" they are committed to building a "quality program." Yet the nature of that "program" is not spelled out. It usually takes the form of some pledge of commitment to the "liberal arts," which assumes that there is some intrinsic connection between being Christian and having a "well-rounded" education. But I know of no theological justification for such an assumption. After all, a "humanistic education" does not necessarily insure more humane students. Even more important the sense of "humane" sponsored by such an education may undercut the student's being Christian.

It is perhaps unfair to single out bronze plaques and mission statements, as they are meant to be written at the highest level of generalization. Yet such generalizations can too easily become ideologies that repress rather than encourage the kind of critical questions we must ask as Christians if we are to understand our commitment to "higher education." For example, why was it assumed by those who wrote the words on the bronze plaque at Duke that advancing all forms of learning is compatible with the teachings and character of Jesus Christ? To be sure, such learning is done in the name of truth but as those of us in the university know, that is an essentially contested notion. Or why was it assumed that advancing such truth will necessarily be of service to the state, nation, and church, or even why those three social realities should necessarily exist in harmony with each other?

In truth, we must say that as Christians we have not thought hard about what intellectual difference Christian convictions might make for what is considered knowledge. As a result, our universities and colleges increasingly look like any other.[1] Thus, "Christian liberal arts colleges'" curriculum looks like any liberal arts college's curriculum. When asked what makes it Christian, administrators appeal to campus atmosphere or to the convictions of those teaching. But what is not clear is how those convictions, which no doubt are often quite real and genuine, make a difference for the shape of the curriculum and/or the actual content of the courses. After all, why should it, since those teaching at such schools did their graduate work at universities where they were taught to honor the autonomy of their field? It is good to have Christians teaching sociology or history, but we would be very doubtful of them if they claimed that their being Christian made a significant difference in the content of their courses. The same basic textbooks in economics, political science, and biology are used in Christian colleges just as much as they are in more secular institutions. It would be a terrible thing, would it not, if Christian students lacked the intellectual frame of reference to be actors in our society?

Moreover, I think it is clear that those who support Christian universities and colleges would be quite upset if the qualifier came to mean that the education students received might put them at a disadvantage for being a success in America. For education, no matter how much supporters of liberal arts might protest, is meant to give students power that they would not otherwise have. It is not simply the power to have a job, but the power that comes from being introduced to the high culture of a civilization which underwrites and legitimates those who rule through education. In the absence of any epistemological and social alternative, the Christian university has no choice but to perform that task.

2. Moral Education in an Allegedly Pluralist Culture

That Christian universities and colleges have found it difficult to maintain intellectually and institutionally their identity as Christian is at least partly the result of having to work in an allegedly pluralist society. I emphasize "allegedly," as I think it doubtful if genuine pluralism—that is, the belief that the unity of political community will not be endangered by allowing the proliferation of groups—has ever been the working policy of America.[2] Obviously, America is a nation that has a plurality of religious groups, which made it necessary to avoid any established religion as well as to provide freedom of religious groups. But this does not insure that our social policy in fact is pluralistic.

For example, consider the strange results this has had in matters of education. John Westerhoff points out that since the national government took no responsibility for education, "Church-supported schools, with clear religious identities and orientation, were expected to induct persons into life in the new nation. However, the increasing need for national unity, loyal citizens, and common values combined with a growing rationalism, skepticism, and empiricism to give the original principle of separation of church and state a new meaning. What occurred was understandable, but not expected. Freedom in education for religious identity (so long as it did not promote separatism) became freedom from religious identity on behalf of civil harmony. Thus the doctrine of separation of church and state had come full circle. Not only was the right to teach religion and interpret life and history from the perspective of a religious tradition prohibited from state schools, but public support of church-related schools was denied. A national commitment to the education of the public had become identified with public education. The state's right and duty to encourage higher education became the right and duty to educate. The result was a functional elimination of religion from its original place of central importance in higher education."[3]

In principle, pluralist social strategies are meant to reinforce the ability of religious groups to maintain their own integrity but in fact the result is the opposite. For as Westerhoff points out, the "church's interest in pluralism locates in freedom which is necessary for faithful life in loyalty to God alone. The state, on the other hand, defends pluralism from the point of view that order and loyalty are necessary for its survival and health."[4] This contrast becomes particularly critical in relation to the church's educational institutions, which often are justified insofar as they serve what our society and state understand by pluralism rather than the church's understanding of pluralism.

In such a situation the role of the "religious college or university" becomes that of training students in virtues necessary to sustain not the church — but the society and the state. When religious colleges do so, however, they are not so much reinforcing the particularistic identity necessary for a pluralistic society, but rather educating people to live in an open society. The latter differs from pluralism, as it assumes that a good society is one in which positions and associations are open to anyone regardless of ethnic, racial, or religious convictions. As Thomas Green has observed, what is often "described as an increasingly pluralistic society is in fact only an increasingly open society in which status is determined less by ascription and more by achievement or some other criteria."[5] As a result, Christian colleges which were built and supported in the interest of maintaining the integrity of religious groups, become the means of assimilation in the name of creating a society in which "differences between people are simply irrelevant as long as they do not inconvenience the conduct of affairs either in the polity, in the economy, or in the family."[6] This is "make-believe pluralism" which results in producing people who live by an equally make-believe morality.

This is not to say that contemporary universities and colleges, Christian or secular, do not morally train students. Contrary to the often-made claims that the university today is at best amoral, I find that most higher education does a good job of initiating, or at least reinforcing, in our students the dominant morality of our culture. It does this not by explicitly teaching courses in "ethics" but by the very way colleges and univer-

241

sities structure their curricula. Of course, I believe the morality thereby embodied to be corrupt and corrupting, but it is nonetheless a morality.

It is important that I not be misunderstood. By suggesting that the Christian college corrupts the youth, I am not suggesting that higher education has that much power. Rather, I think it is the case that the university simply reinforces the corruption that has already been well begun. Quite simply, the university underwrites the assumption that morality is something we create through individual choice rather than it being the shaping of our lives through the disciplined discovery of the good. No better example of this assumption can be found than those who want the contemporary university to teach values. Used cars have some value, but I suspect that values have very little to do with any substantive account of morality. For universities to teach values—or to help students clarify values—only reinforces the idea that the moral life is but another form of consumer choice.

Of course, that is exactly what we would expect a capitalist society to suggest as the basic form of morality. Thus, the modern university or college depends on convincing those who come to it that any need they have can be met. In such a context, the university or college cannot help but appear as a gigantic cafeteria. The student comes to it as a cipher to be filled up by pushing trays along the line, taking a salad of math or computer science, some potatoes of philosophy (just to be sure they are introduced somewhere along the way to some "big ideas"), little corn of literature (to insure they will be recognized as "educated" people), and finally some meat: a major in business, physics, or history (the traditional pre-law major) which puts one on the appropriate career track.

Moreover, individual courses assume the same structure. The idea that a course might actually attempt to initiate students into practices that make the students more truthful is thought to be oppressive. Rather, each course should present various alternatives so that in the process the students can "make up their own mind." Of course, the teachers may want to argue that one position is better than another but in doing so they must make clear they are only giving "their own opinion." For example, would it not be shocking for a philosopher or theologian to argue that modern ethical theory is corrupt or corrupting and thus refuse to have students read modern theory? A curriculum made up of courses that only present "alternatives" confirms the moral assumption that we are or should be autonomous consumers whose power is increased by providing us increased choice in the market.[7] In the name of objectivity we refrain from trying to shape the lives of our students in a manner that might change their image of what they are or should be about. The most teachers can hope for is that some student becomes so interested in their subject he or she might decide to major in it or even to pursue it in graduate school. But the notion that we ought to teach or shape our curricula in a manner that might actually change a student's funda-mental moral stance is unthinkable. As a result, we more or less leave students morally exactly the way we found them – i.e., people who pride themselves on their autonomy and who are increasingly aware that all moral positions are "relative" or "subjective" because they are matters of choice.

3. The Problem of the Socratic Ideal for the University

Some may well think that the critique of the modern university I have made here is grossly unfair.[8] Of course the university reflects the primary moral values of its society, they would argue. There is nothing peculiar about that, as the university has always more or less mirrored the social order in which it exists. Those who would hold up as a goal, the liberal art curriculum of the past and its correlative model of gentleman-scholar as teacher fail to realize that such curricula and teachers served to reinforce a class bias which we now believe unjust. Contemporary curricula may be less coherent but they also are more open to the democratic ethos of our society.

This line of defense usually goes on to suggest that the task of the university is not moral formation but rather the introduction of students to critical inquiry and questioning. In support of such a task, Socrates' method is often called forward as the standard or ideal of what univer-sity education ought to be about. The universities' task is not so much to give students answers as it is to make them relentless questioners of every unexamined assumption or piece of conventional wisdom. There is a sense in which this is seen as a moral task, insofar as this kind of education makes people more aware of themselves and others. The university is morally justified in the sense that the examined life becomes our ideal.

It is certainly not my intention to argue for a return to a liberal arts curriculum as more appropriate to Christian commitments. I do not believe that such a curriculum ever existed as coherently as its defenders presuppose, nor do I believe that a return to such a curriculum would be a moral advance. I do not think there is anything inherently incom-patible between more practically oriented education and Christian commitment to the university. Yet I do not think that that justifies

243

the failure of the modern university to provide any rationale for the education it provides other than the assumption that by taking a variety of courses students will be better informed and possess more inquiring minds.

Please note I am not suggesting that the university fails in its task to initiate students into the Socratic task of critical inquiry; rather, I am suggesting that the Socratic method itself is suspect for moral development. No one has made this case more clearly than has Martha Nussbaum in her article, "Aristophanes and Socrates on Learning Practical Wisdom."[9] Noting that Aristophanes failed to understand the difference between Socrates and the Sophist, Nussbaum argues that Aristophanes rightly criticized Socrates' teaching for its largely negative effect. It is one thing for Socrates to try to show that conventional morality and virtue lacked reasoned defense, she argues; it is quite another to engage people in dialectic when one has no substitute to offer, as Socrates often confessed he did not, other than the examined life itself.

What Aristophanes saw, according to Nussbaum, is that Socrates was negligent in his indifference to the antecedent moral training of those he engaged in dialectic. In Aristophanes' view, Socrates mocked "habituation without acknowledging that it might be essential in forming a pupil's moral intuitions to a point at which the search for justification can appropriately begin. He entrusts the weapons of argumentation to anyone who will expose himself to teaching, without considering whether he is one of the people who will be likely to put the teaching to good use. He implies that teaching is sufficient and habituation is irrelevant. This intellectualism is what Socrates' pupils retain from his teaching: this insistence that moral teaching is the business of experts, not elders, that a technical training enables one to scoff at ordinary norms" (p. 80).

The problem with Socrates' strategy was that even though Socrates said his interest was not in undermining conventional morality, that was its inevitable effect. Because he emphasized argument rather than character, an inference can be drawn that any belief is permissible as long as one is clever enough. Aristophanes (and Aristotle) therefore criticized Socrates for failing to make clear the difference between his ironic aloofness and the immoralism of those who conclude from his method that conventional morality lacks adequate rational defense. What Socrates failed to see is his very method of inquiry requires an account of the virtues that he failed to give. That he did so is due to his assumption that virtue is like an expert craft or skill which can be gained only by the

244

dialectic engendered by an expert teacher. Preceding or further training, apart from the teaching itself, is not required.

Yet as Nussbaum points out, the assimilation of morality to an expert craft is questionable. "It neglects, as Aristotle points out, the crucial importance of early habituation and the training of desires; dispositions to behave morally are not like capacities to perform. A craft can be separated from the desire to use it well; a good doctor is also a good poisoner. It fails to identify with sufficient precision the aim or end of morals, that of which the expert is an expert producer. In most of the Socratic dialogues we find no positive account of the human good" (p. 84).[10] Socrates' failure to attend to virtue as a form of habituation accounts, moreover, for the irresponsible manner by which he selected his dialogue partners and students. For he made no attempt to determine his students' prior training or beliefs. As a result, his method of questioning often had unanticipated results as his students too easily concluded that they must create their own morality.

Though it is not crucial to my case whether in fact Nussbaum's defense of Aristophanes' critique of Socrates is fair to every aspect of Socrates' position, I think the most obvious objection should be met. For who gives a more impassioned defense than Socrates of living virtuously? Nussbaum agrees that Aristophanes certainly overlooked much that is favorable to Socrates, but she maintains that "Socrates' concern with virtue and its justification, at least as depicted in Plato's early dialogues, leads to no clear or obvious results. In the one place, where the theory of the good does become more concrete, it is in a form that invites, rather than prevents, confusion with immoralism. It would not be unfair to say that most of Socrates' concern for virtue remains in the realm of personal choice and good intentions for others" (p. 86). Thus, Socrates' prestige and influence had helped to undermine conventional standards no matter whether he intended to do so or not.

Moreover, Nussbaum argues that the direction of Plato's more mature work suggests he had come to understand this. "Plato, from his perception of the great threat that open dialectic poses to social stability, and his belief that without social stability men cannot live good lives, infers the necessity of restricting dialectic to those who are both initially well-trained and outstandingly intelligent" (p. 88). In short, Plato came to understand that Socrates was too optimistic about the potential of the common man for moral growth and understanding. Unless we are well prepared, Socratic dialectic can as easily be destructive as therapeutic.

As an alternative to Socrates, Nussbaum defends an Aristotelian view of education. Aristotle was no less concerned than was Socrates that the virtuous must not only know they are virtuous but be able to justify their convictions. Yet in contrast with Socrates, Aristotle argued that the virtues are neither natural capacities nor pieces of learned wisdom, but habits formed by practice in choosing and doing the appropriate actions. Natural appetites are not bad, Aristotle thought, but through training the young must learn to find pleasure in the things that reasonable adults agree are right; "a pre-rational training must prepare the soul for the full reasoned understanding of virtue. The good city, ruled by men of practical wisdom who have a clear and explicit picture of their concept of the good, will establish a system of training which makes use of traditional methods—but in the service of the full life of virtue to come" (p. 90). Such an ethos therefore depends on the existence of men of practical wisdom. For the good can be discovered only through the deliberations of virtuous people weighing the appearances in an effort to achieve the most nearly true judgments about matters that matter.

Aristotelian justice is therefore not an underwriting of the conventional, since the wise person can give reasons for preferring his or her way. Nor is justice thought to be determined by some transcendental standard. Rather, the standard is the judgments of people who have proven themselves wise. They are not "experts" in the sense of knowing something we do not know, but rather they are special because they see "better and more clearly what we all, collectively, know. Thus moral argument and moral change will take place within a climate of reasoned debate, and will represent an attempt to reach the best possible ordered articulation of our moral intuitions" (p. 91).

What is problematic about Aristotle's views is that they are not easily applied to political reality where reason is seldom sufficient to settle conflict. Aristotle thought that a system of early education that imparts to all citizens a shared concept of the good at least holds out some hope of moderating such conflicts. Moreover, the system of laws that summarizes the decisions of people of practical wisdom will also help provide sanctions to chasten hedonism which threatens disorder. The process of legislation itself will also help train many about the good life. But most important of all is the ruler(s) must foster "friendship among men in the polis qua citizen, so that, even if a law seems repugnant to an individual or a group, those men will be inclined to obey it out of good will to the regime itself and to their fellow citizens who are benefited by it" (p. 93).

All of this about Socrates and Aristotle may be interesting enough, but it may be thought to have little to do with the modern university. But I think the implications are direct and significant. For if Socrates' method subtly led to the corruption of the youth of Athens, the contemporary university's degraded form of the Socratic method does so in a more direct and almost inevitable manner. In the name of exposing students to critical questions through a chaotic curriculum filled with equally chaotic courses, we only reinforce the disdain for reasoned discourse. Our students are even less prepared than were Socrates' interlocutors to begin the demanding task of engaging in reasoned discourse to know better the good and true. They lack the virtues necessary for sustaining the life of the mind, as there exists no community capable of directing them to the good in the first place.

Put differently, the very idea of university education as moral education becomes problematic in our culture, which not only does not require the development of virtue but sees such development as an impediment to freedom. We lack a community of law and/or friendship that gives direction to such education. The contemporary university not only does not challenge that set of conventional assumptions but in the name of the Socratic method underwrites a false sense of objectivity, believing that objectivity is insured by giving every position a hearing. Thus the Socratic method, in the name of being anticonventional, underwrites the conventional morality that is based on the inviolability of each person's subjectivity. The only interesting question about our situation is whether our culture possesses the resources that might make something like the Aristotelian alternative a real possibility.

4. On Being Christian in the University

I know that I have, to this point, painted a fairly stark picture. I also know that in some ways it is an exaggerated depiction. I know that much good education does go on at both Christian and secular universities.[11] I know that students continue to find teachers who provide them with visions of the good which become habitual ways of responding to the world. I know that teachers discover students who have moral convictions and intellectual commitments that startle and almost frighten the teachers with their seriousness. Yet on the whole I think the picture I have drawn is largely correct. Even more troubling, however, is that I have no ready solution to offer.

I think my analysis, however, has not been without benefit, as we now better know how to state the problem. Moreover, the analysis I have provided is some comfort for those like myself who are identified with the university. For if I have been right, the problem is not only in the

247

university, but in wider society and the church. Thus, it would seem that the result of my analysis is to shift the responsibility away from the university, since the university can only be as good as the community that sustains it.

I am not satisfied, however, with that conclusion. Indeed, I think those of us committed to the university as Christians can do better, and I think we may be doing better than we can say. In a way, the situation of the university is a bit like the lives of the people described by Robert Bellah and his coauthors in *Habits of the Heart*. For the authors note that the common difficulties their respondents face in justifying the goals of a morally good life point to a problem for all people in our culture— namely, "for most of us, it is easier to think about how to get what we want than to know what exactly we should want."[12] They go on to suggest that too often people lack sufficient moral language to describe the good they do or want to do and instead must interpret the good they do in terms of "expressive individualism." In like manner, I suspect, the good that the university does or that those in the university want to do fails to be acknowledged because we lack the common language to celebrate that good.

For example, universities of all kinds still give some people the time and resources to do nothing but study and teach the debates about the Trinity. That they are allowed to do so is right and good, as it is through such study we maintain the essential memory necessary for us to under- stand the moral and theological commitments of our forebearers. Our difficulty is that we cannot lift up such activity as crucial to the univer- sity's moral task, because it lacks "relevance." As a result we have to justify the university in terms that will insure success in our society, in the hopes of sustaining the study of the Trinity.

This is an odd situation for the university, since the university more than any institution in our culture is committed to maintaining the habits necessary for reasoned discourse so we can better understand what it is we should want. In the terms I used above to describe the Aristotelian perspective, the university is the place where we should train those with the wisdom to help us all know better what is best about us. Such train- ing comes by the discipline of confronting texts and figures of the past and present in the hope of continuing discussion of our forebearers. For, finally, the university is the way a culture insists that its forebearers have not lived (or died) in vain. That does not mean they must agree with their forebearers; they just must remember that they are part of the conversation.

Such a perspective, moreover, helps us see why it makes sense to think of a university that avows Christian identity. Such an avowal is nothing other than the claim that certain past and present conversation partners are crucial for this community to know what is its good. To say that an institution is Christian is to say that certain matters cannot be left out of the conversation if we are to know better what it means to be Christian. Thus, it might be expected that the curriculum of a college that claims Christian identity would look different from those that do not. But even more important, it means that what is taught as history, or psychology, or sociology at such schools, and how they are taught, might be different. That is the most decisive challenge facing us as Christians if we in the university are to be able to claim we are serving well the church and, ultimately, our society. The temptation, even at more conservative Christian colleges is (in the name of being Christian) to be enamored with pragmatic causes—"living simply, feeding the hungry, banning the bomb, challenging abortion—than with learning to think seriously and theologically" about every subject.[13]

In that sense I think we must think seriously about how the continued existence of the Christian college or university's nominal identification with its Christian past may in fact allow us to avoid dealing with the hard intellectual issues facing us as Christians. We must recognize that the very existence of Christian colleges and universities is the result of the hegemony of Christians in this culture that was acquired and is sustained by force and power. The temptation will be to try to count on that culture to sustain the Christian educational enterprise. But if we do that, then we will fail to face our challenge and equally fail to serve the church or our culture. For, as I have tried to suggest, that culture itself is now in very deep trouble.

Let me try to make this as concrete as I can. I recently met a colleague leaving his office from which was coming a strong smell of incense: I asked him what he was doing and he answered that he was meditating, as he was about to teach certain Hindu texts and of course to do that well he ought to pray before doing so. He could get away with such prayer as someone teaching a non-Western religion because such a tradition never had power in our culture. No one teaching New Testament today in a Christian or secular university, however, could do that, because of the power the church has used in our society to force others to attend to our Scripture. We do not trust ourselves with our own heritage because we have used distrustful means to sustain it.

But perhaps the increasing secularism of our culture presents us with a new opportunity in this respect. As Christians lose power they also gain the freedom to call on their convictions to challenge the reigning intellectual paradigms, not only in the study of religion but in other disciplines as well.[14] Or they may even find that they have the freedom to make their own colleges more intellectually interesting, as no longer are they used to train people to be like everyone else but rather to sustain our difference as Christians. In doing so, moreover, we believe that we serve our society well, as our difference becomes a reminder of what a genuine pluralism might look like.

I am aware that such a position cannot help but appear to many as a self-destructive formula. What secular university is going to hire economists who maintain that their Christian convictions make a difference for how they do economics? Where is the kind of Christian college I describe going to get financial support and even students? I have no ready response to such questions, though I think there is a more positive response than we imagine. I am convinced, however, that only when we ask such questions will we be on the way toward being institutions that not only do not corrupt our students (and ourselves) but may even help form them virtuously.

Yet finally I must admit that I think there is no solution to the primary moral issue I have drawn. Universities are not primary moral institutions but must draw on the wisdom of a good society that initiates the young into the practice of virtue. Though the university is integral to the sustaining of that wisdom, the university is not well constituted for primary moral training. That must come from elsewhere. If the church is to be serious about the character of its educational institutions, it can do nothing more important than to attend to the character of its youth.

NOTES

1. George Marsden notes how the rise of specialization contributed to the trend of even evangelical colleges losing control over their curricula. "The Ph.D. thesis, a demonstration of technical expertise in an area accessible only by specialists, became the prerequisite for entry into academic life. By contrast, nineteenth-century evangelical colleges had been havens for generalists, theologian-philosophers who provided the community with advice in economics, politics, morality, and often in natural science. The new specialists who were taking over by the end of the century could usually outclass the old-time teachers in any of the specialties. Moreover, their new concept of being scientific meant simultaneously to specialize and to eliminate religiously derived principles from their disciplines. The technical achievements of this new specialization thus reinforced prejudices against evangelicalism, which had been heavily committed to the older generalist approach." Marsden goes on to note that the solution to this potential conflict was "to grant the authority of the new science and history, but to emphasize that this authority was limited to certain secular domains. Picking up and vastly accentuating a theme present in the thought of evangelical predecessors they now rested the entire weight of their apologetic on the point that Christianity went far beyond that which mere scientific reason could reach. They differed from most of their predecessors in suggesting that Christianity had to do only with the aspects

of things wholly immune from scientific or historical inquiry" ("The Collapse of American Evangelical Academia," in *Faith and Rationality: Reason and Belief in God*, edited by Alvin Plantinga and Nicholas Wolterstorff [Notre Dame: University of Notre Dame Press, 1983], pp. 221–223).

2. For the most penetrating analysis of the different meanings of pluralism in relation to education, see Thomas Green, "Education and Pluralism: Ideal and Reality," *The J. Richard Street Lecture* (Syracuse: Syracuse University School of Education, 1966), p. 10.

3. John Westerhoff, "In Search of a Future: The Church-Related College," in *The Church's Ministry in Higher Education*, edited by John Westerhoff (New York: UMHE Communication Office, 1978), p. 198.

4. Ibid., p. 199.

5. Green, "Education and Pluralism," p. 19.

6. Ibid., p. 23.

7. In a review of recent books on the state of higher education in America, Andrew Hacker reports "A recent survey of liberal arts graduates revealed that over half of them had taken no work at all in economics or philosophy or, for that matter, chemistry. Frederick Rudolph says he encountered 'evidence of decline and devaluation' at virtually every campus he visited. Higher education, he asserts, has become 'a supermarket where students are shoppers and professors are merchants'" ("The Decline of Higher Learning," in *New York Review of Books*, XXXIII [February 13, 1986], p. 35). Hacker notes that this tendency is reinforced as "undergraduate courses now reflect the way disciplines are conceived at the doctoral level. This has been the real academic revolution," and has done more than anything to undercut the liberal arts. "Faculty members, to be true to their callings, feel they must spend much of their time discussing the work of their fellow professors" (p. 37).

8. For an even a stronger critique, however, see Harold McManus, *Community and Governance in the Christian University* (which can be obtained through the Committee of Southern Churchmen, Post Office Box 140215, Nashville, Tennessee 37214). Dr. McManus' paper was written as a challenge to developments at Mercer University. He quotes Professor Ted Nordenhaug's comparison of the modern academy to a tower of Babel, to the effect that "the Babel-academy is characterized by the following depressing conditions: First, there is no common intellectual language in which ideas, ends, purposes, can meaningfully be discussed. No language in which inquiry and its results in the various fields can be shared. Secondly, in the absence of a common language of inquiry and ideas, we have only a shared technical language, the language of means and mechanisms that refers to the organization of the academy. Thirdly, this mechanical language has come to conceal the Babel-academy's inability to talk about its intellectual ends by confounding these with its means. This has resulted in a sophistical transformation of normative standards into descriptions of average practice. Today the academy lacks a common intellectual life, i.e., a common or public language in which its members can share the process of inquiry. Not being able to inquire together, we cannot therefore justify the corporate purpose of the academy" (pp. 4–5). McManus notes that this condition has been the occasion for the rise of adminstration in the university, for if the university does not have a purpose it at least has purposes. In order to organize the university's many purposes, however, there is the need for bureaucracy to coordinate the university's many activities.

9. Martha Nussbaum, "Aristophanes and Socrates on Learning Practical Wisdom," *Yale Classical Studies*, 26, edited by Jeffrey Henderson (Cambridge: Cambridge University Press, 1980), pp. 43–97. Additional references to this article will appear in text.

10. Nussbaum's use of the notion of "expert" in this context seems anachronistic, but I suspect she has in mind MacIntyre's characterization of the expert in his *After Virtue* (Notre Dame: University of Notre Dame Press, 1984), pp. 79–87. MacIntyre argues that the rise of the authority of the expert is correlative to developments in epistemology that require a hard distinction between fact and value in the interest of creating predictive sciences. Thus, the modern university is built on the assumption that what is needed is the training of experts rather than people of wisdom. The latter derive their authority from the knowledge

of the unpredictability of our existence. If, as MacIntyre argues, the world is inherently unpredictable, then students of the modern university are not only being morally corrupted but misled by the reigning epistemological presuppositions of the university. In this respect it is interesting to note how recent work in epistemology increasingly has undermined the foundationalist assumptions that have been used to justify, particularly in the social sciences, the methodologies of academic disciplines. I am not sure if Nussbaum was trying to suggest this critique by her use of the language of expert in reference to Socrates, but I think she is at least correct that Socrates' (and Plato's) attempt to ground ethics in a metaphysics of necessity, while certainly different from modern epistemologies, still shares the desire to avoid unpredictability as an integral aspect of knowledge and morality.

11. For a thoughtful discussion of what it means for Christians to teach at secular institutions, see Kenneth Hermann, "Beyond the Hothouse: Higher Education Outside the Christian College," *The Reformed Journal*, 35, 11 (November, 1985), pp. 19-23. Hermann notes that Christians "must not view the university as merely a convenient place for evangelism or a fate to be endured while resting periodically in the oasis of fellowship meetings. It is certainly not an institution which Christians can justifiably abandon. It must be challenged on its own terms as an academic institution from a Christian perspective" (p. 22). I think he is right about this; for all of its faults the university continues to offer one of the few places in our society for the development of civil discourse about the good. It is less clear, however, what it means to speak to the university "on its own terms," for, as I have tried to suggest, it is by no means clear today what those terms are.

12. Robert Bellah, et al., *Habits of the Heart: Individualism and Commitment in American Life* (Berkeley: University of California Press, 1985), p. 21.

13. Nathan Hatch, "Evangelical Colleges and the Challenge of Christian Thinking," *The Reformed Journal*, 35, 9 (September, 1985), p. 15. As Hatch argues, "The battle for the mind cannot be waged mobilizing in the streets or on Capitol Hill; not by denouncing more furiously the secular humanists. If evangelicals are to help preserve even the possibility of Christian thinking for their children and grandchildren, they must begin to nurture first-order Christian scholarship, which means of course freeing Christian scholars to undertake what is a painstakingly slow and arduous task—and one that has almost no immediate return on investment" (p. 11). In order to drive that point home Hatch asks, "How many Christians do you know who would tithe so that a Christian scholar can go about her work?" (p. 12).

14. As Thomas Green suggests, "The educational function of the public schools is in relation to the efforts of public education. It is to assist in developing a sense of self-identity through historical memory and contemporary participational roles. The only difference is that in relation to public education the role of religion is to contribute to the sense of historical identity with the civic community and to prepare for the participation in the polity, economy and the professions. In relation to its own members the educational task of the Church is to develop the sense of historical identity with the worshipping community in such a way that the participational roles in the civic community do not become idolatrous, that is, so that the way society is, is never confused with the only way it can be, so that the establishment in short can never be quite secure. Religious institutions, of course, do not do this now. It is doubtful that it ever could be done except in an advanced secular society in which common education is possible in such a way that people are not religiously and politically illiterate as they are now. That is why religious leaders should encourage the growth of a secular society. But to say that is a bit like asking them to commit suicide. There is, however, an old biblical idea which is germane here. It is that a man may have to lose his life in order to gain it" (op. cit., p. 35).

TAKING TIME FOR PEACE

The Ethical Significance of the Trivial

1. On Learning to Live with the Bomb

In the July 29, 1985, issue of *Time*, which contained a special section called "The Atomic Age," we are told that the Bomb's presence abets, if it does not exclusively account for, much of what is nerve-racking and unsatisfactory about our lives. According to *Time*, that includes feelings of dislocation, aimlessness, and loneliness, as well as dim perceptions of unidentified dangers. "When the Bomb dropped, people not only saw a weapon that could boil the planet and create a death-in-life; they saw yet one more proof of their impotence. 'We live in a world of virile weapons and impotent men,' wrote the French historian, Raymond Aron, shortly before his death in 1983. We saw a vision of the future in Hiroshima, but we also saw ourselves, and (again) we did not like what we saw."[1]

This analysis of what nuclear weapons do to us is not unlike that of Jonathan Schell in *The Fate of the Earth*. As Schell suggests, "When one tries to face the nuclear predicament, one feels sick, whereas when one pushes it out of mind, as apparently one must do most of the time in order to carry on with life, one feels well again. But this feeling of well-being is based on a denial of the most important reality of our time, and therefore is itself a kind of sickness. A society that systematically shuts its eyes to an urgent peril to its physical survival and fails to take any steps to save itself cannot be called psychologically well. In effect, whether we think about nuclear weapons or avoid thinking about them, their presence among us makes us sick, and there seems to be little of a purely mental or emotional nature that we can do about it."[2]

253

Time agrees with Schell's rather pessimistic assessment, as its essayist asks, "So what is there to do about the Bomb, which may be reduced in numbers but not removed? The answer seems to be: nothing. The only maneuverability given ordinary people is how they may think about the Bomb. Is it possible to do that less fearfully and more clearly? Americans do not really believe in the Apocalypse, no matter how many movies we watch. One way or another in the next few years, we will want to stop looking too indirectly or too directly, and quietly come to terms with the Bomb."[3]

But what could it possibly mean for us "to come to terms with the Bomb?" Does that mean we must come to terms not only with our own death, but also with the fact that our survival as a society depends on our willingness to possess and use such weapons as the preeminent means of self-preservation? To suggest that we must come to terms with the Bomb is not only nonsensical, it also seems nothing less than absurd and immoral. For it asks us to learn to live essentially as people who cannot face or acknowledge our responsibility for creating such a world; it asks us to abandon our own moral agency to a technological imperative. Thus, it implies that the best among us are not satisfied with "nothing" but instead seek to do something to make our situation more endurable while we wait for the end.

Indeed, some seem so driven by the frustration of *Time's* "nothing" that they respond by arguing that everything must be done to rid our lives of this threat. Every aspect of our lives must be subjected to the discipline of examination to discern whether we may in fact be unconsciously supporting the continuation of nuclear weapons. For it is argued that unless we eradicate the bomb from our lives, then nothing we do can have meaning, since all is threatened by destruction. People possessed by such passion tend to make the rest of us feel a bit guilty, as we simultaneously suspect they are right and yet continue jealously to guard our right to take the time to enjoy a baseball game.

In this respect the situation we are in reminds me of discussions I heard during the Vietnam War era. During that time, some argued that this war was so immoral, so perverting, to anything we believed as Americans that all normal and everyday activity must stop. To go to a football game, even at Notre Dame, was said to be but a diversion which the power elite used to direct our attention away from the terrible evil being perpetrated in Vietnam. All life, they claimed, was now determined by "the war." Nothing we did was indifferent or irrelevant to the question of how that war was to be ended. Such claims may appear bizarre to us now, but I think that many of the suggestions about our moral responsibility to work for the eradication of the bomb are embarrassingly similar. One is either part of the problem or part of the solution. There are no other alternatives.

This kind of attitude, which is in many ways quite admirable, and even understandable, also just happens to be totalitarian. For it is the character of totalitarian regimes to make every aspect of life a matter of loyalty to the state, the party, or the cause. There are, or there should be, no indifferent actions. Indeed, one of the ways by which totalitarians tend to convince their followers of the righteousness of their cause is exactly to turn what were once matters of indifference into significant political decisions. Sometimes this is done not by a determined leader or party but by the situation itself which seems to force such choice. South Africa may well be such a place insofar as every issue both in and about South Africa is tyrannized by the question of race.

Those who argue that every aspect of our lives must be determined by the bomb seem to be making this kind of suggestion—namely, that we live in a totalitarian situation where the bomb determines every decision we make. Some may object to this analysis, pointing out that most people do not feel our situation is so desperate, that most of us go on living fairly normally, making plans for the future, and generally refusing to let our existence be determined by the threat of nuclear weapons. There are two responses that those arguing for a more radical account of our situation can make. First, it can be suggested that those who appear to be continuing to live normal lives are, in fact, actually hiding from themselves and each other a profound desperation and fear. There is some evidence that this may be the case. Secondly, it can be argued that even if in fact people do not feel so threatened by the bomb, they ought to feel so threatened. In effect, it is recommended that we *voluntarily* tyrannize our lives in the interest of survival.

You may well feel that no one would argue in this way, but in fact the position is constantly put before us by some very serious people. They claim that the bomb has ontological significance requiring a rethinking of human existence. For example, Gordon Kaufman, in his *Theology for a Nuclear Age* argues that our very conception of central Christian "symbols" such as God and Christ must be rethought in the light of this new reality. We must do this, he says, because we are living "in an unprecedented situation, facing a possible calamity the consequences of which we can scarcely conceive and the dimensions of which we have no adequate means of evaluating, a calamity nonetheless, of which we human beings would be the sole agents, a catastrophe for which we would be exclusively responsible. Although this event would obliterate

255

most of what gives our lives meaning, the act of bringing it on is heavy with meaning—and it is all negative. There is no redeeming value, so far as I can see, in any of the human intentions and actions that bring this event about."[4] What is unique about our situation with the bomb is that no longer is it God who will bring this world to an end, but it is "we human beings who are absolutely and fully responsible if this catastrophe occurs, that this is an event which confronts us primarily as an act of human doing rather than of divine will, and that both our actions and our hopes with respect to it, therefore, must be directed toward the transformation of our human institutions and policies."[5] I suppose that we ought to take it for granted that all this will also entail a profound change in our understanding of God.

Although I am extremely skeptical of Kaufman's claim for the absolute uniqueness of our situation and even more doubtful of his suggested theological revision of our basic "symbols," his position at least makes explicit what many feel when they contend that if we live as if the bomb does not matter, we are making a decisive mistake. The bomb presents a spiritual challenge, for it is unclear how we continue to live normal lives in the face of the destruction it can and perhaps will bring. Our task is to transform our lives so that everything we are and do serves to stave off this threatened end. One may well think I am exaggerating when I suggest that this is a form of totalitarianism and tyranny; but even if I am, the case we seem confronted by is a situation that for better or worse threatens to engulf our lives. And in that sense I think it is quite right to think of the bomb not only as a political, ethical, and theological problem, but fundamentally as a question of the spirit.

Yet I am equally convinced, as is apparent by my use of the term "totalitarian," that we will be making a mistake if we allow the bomb to determine our lives spiritually. Put simply, we will not be working for a peace worth having if we assume that peace means only the elimination of the bomb from our lives. One may well ask whether we have an alternative since the bomb does in fact determine our existence and peace does in fact mean lessening the possibility of nuclear war; such is the reality of our lives.

Yet I believe we do have an alternative to the desperation that fuels our fear of nuclear war. That alternative is, quite simply, the need to reclaim the significance of the trivial. For it is my belief that there is no more powerful response to totalitarians than to take the time to reclaim life from their power. By refusing to let them claim every aspect of our life as politically significant, we create the space and time that makes politics humane. Therefore, there is nothing more important for us to do in the

256

face of the threat of nuclear war than to go on living—that is, to take time to enjoy a walk with a friend, to read all of Trollope's novels, to maintain universities, to have and care for children, and most importantly, to worship God.

I must tell you, however, that such a suggestion is only intelligible and moral if God really is the being whom Jews and Christians have affirmed. For it is our belief that God has given us the time and space to be people who can rest and enjoy our creation as creatures. Kaufman suggests that the symbol "God" today can only mean that "which focuses our consciousness and attention on that which humanizes and relativizes us."[6] But such a God as that plainly lacks the power and grace to give us the means to stand against the glorification of human power, which is of course the ultimate source of the bomb. Indeed, on his own grounds, I do not see how Kaufman can avoid affirming the bomb as the ultimate focus of religious devotion, since he knows of no object that more nearly relativizes us.

For us to have the means to live in the face of the bomb, God can be no mere symbol. For us to have the means to live in the face of the bomb, we need the mighty and frightening presence we find in the giving of the law and the cross of Jesus. God is not powerful because we need a God of power, but rather God's power is manifest in those who continue to be drawn to be a people trained in the trust made possible by God's presence. God's power is not the coercive power of the totalitarian but the power that attracts and claims because of its sheer goodness. God's power is manifest in his patience, through which he creates the time for us to learn that our lives are distorted as long as we think we, rather than God, rule this world. God has given us the time to learn that and, as his followers, we would be false witnesses if we acted as if such time were not available. That is why we can and should take the time, even in the face of the bomb, to be at rest—to observe the Sabbath.

I do not wish to be misunderstood. I am not suggesting that those who would be faithful to God should give up trying to make the world safe from nuclear destruction. Let us continue to tie ribbons around Washington. Let us continue to try to find ways to help our political leaders discover the means to end the constant spiral of nuclear buildup. But let us also recognize that efforts like these hold out little chance that nuclear weapons will, as if by magic, be eliminated from the world. More important, however, we need to know that our efforts to eliminate or reduce the number of nuclear weapons cannot help but be hollow if they do not participate in the peace that comes from worshipping a God who has given us the time to enjoy the trivial.

2. The Time that Peace Creates

I suppose I may have done little more in the above argument than confuse and probably frustrate you. I suspect you came expecting to hear another talk about why we should be more concerned about nuclear war and how we should work all the harder to stand against nuclear weapons. You certainly should have expected that from someone like me—a pacifist who is also a theologian. After all, what are theologians good for today, if they are not used to rally the troops around generally agreed-upon good causes? Of course, when theologians urge such action, they too often give the impression that it makes no difference whether what we believe about God is true or not, that it just matters that it have some good results.

But instead of being a call to activism, what I have argued seems to justify being passive in the face of the bomb. I am not sure that I can counter that impression, but let me try. I am not suggesting that the bomb should make no difference for how we live our lives; rather, I have tried to suggest that when we allow it to make *all* the difference, we lose the power to stand against the forces that built the bomb in the first place. For our lives become determined by the kind of urgency that robs us of the freedom to enjoy the time God has given us to make peace possible.

Peace takes time. Put even more strongly, peace creates time by its steadfast refusal to force the other to submit in the name of order. Peace is not a static state but an activity which requires constant attention and care. An activity by its very nature takes place over time. In fact, activity creates time, as we know how to characterize duration only by noting that we did this first, and then this second, and so on, until we either got somewhere or accomplished this or that task. So peace is the process through which we make time our own rather than be determined by "events" over which, it is alleged, we have no control.

By saying that peace takes time I do not mean simply that for a community to be peaceful means that they must take the time to try to reach agreement. That, of course, is not unimportant for helping us understand the significance of living peacefully. But I suspect that one of our difficulties in capturing a sense of how our lives can be peaceful is that we have become too used to the everyday procedures which we use in the name of fairness or the common good, to coerce people into doing what they do not want to do.

For example, I know of a group of Mennonites who had formed a community in which they were committed to supporting one another both spiritually and financially. Most in the group thought it a good idea for them to pool their resources to buy a house in common. They were prevented from doing so for over two years by one member of the group who felt strongly that Christians should not own property. One might well say in such a situation that the majority rules, but that is not how they handled it. Instead, they spent the time studying the Scripture, praying together, and intensely arguing until they felt they could purchase the property as a community. Such a process takes time, but it is also the kind of time that makes peace possible.

Peace not only requires time for us to work out our differences, but peace also is found within our timeful activities. We are often told, with good reason, that we live in a violent society. We know that in this society someone is being killed or injured every minute. I have no doubt that violence surrounds us, but I think we must not overlook the fact that most of our lives are constituted by peaceful and peacemaking activities. Such activities may appear trivial or uninteresting precisely because they are so common, but they are no less morally significant for that. For the willingness to take the time to care for the trivial is exactly the disposition that provides the basis for our learning to be peaceful people capable of finding peace as a community.

We must be careful not to lapse into sentimentality on these matters. I am not suggesting, as the popular song suggests, that all we need to do is take the time to smell the flowers. Smelling flowers is not a bad thing, but it is finally not something that can sustain a life. For the activities that embody peace must also be such that give us a sense of worth, a sense of making a contribution which enriches our own life and those of other people. That does not mean that we have to seek some grand achievement; rather, I am thinking about something as common and significant as enjoying the preparation of a meal and then enjoying the pleasure that it gives others.

Indeed, I think peace is all around us; it is the air we breathe, but we simply fail to notice it because it is so common. But in failing to notice it we are also robbed of the ability to extend it into other aspects of our lives. For example, at Duke we have the largest lemur colony in the world outside Madagascar. They are there because one man is concerned that lemurs are threatened with extinction because of the eradication of the forests in Madagascar. So, taking a few animals from Yale, he started a colony in Durham which now numbers over six hundred and includes every known species. No invasive research is allowed on the animals, though anthropology graduate students spend a good deal of time watching these very social creatures interact and listening to their quite

259

complex language. For the rest of us, it is a sheer pleasure to have the opportunity to see these lovely animals.[7]

The scientist who has created this colony is an internationally famous anthropologist who cares most about the preservation of these primates. It turns out that there is no subject which is not in some way relevant to lemurs. If one talks with him about ecological problems, one soon learns that what is good for the survival of lemurs will also be good for the survival of us all. I feel sure that he would address issues of international relations in the same spirit.

But wait a minute. We are supposed to be talking about peace, not lemurs. Yet my point is that such work is peace. The extraordinary commitment to saving lemurs, to taking the time and resources in a world like ours to do nothing but to learn about lemurs, is a way peace becomes concretely embodied in our lives. This is not because such activity keeps us from the business of war, but because such activity creates the space and time in our lives so that peace can reign there.

It may perhaps be objected that I could not have chosen a worse example to make my point. How can we justify all the care and attention that goes into saving lemurs, when people are starving in Africa? How can a man justify dedicating his whole life to lemurs when our world is threatened with complete destruction? The answer is because lemurs are worth saving. Of course, people in Africa should be fed and we should not have nuclear weapons, but neither of those grim realities will go away if we suddenly ceased trying to save lemurs. Put more strongly, we would have no idea how to deal with either reality if we were devoid of people willing to dedicate their lives to saving lemurs.

These same kinds of questions can, of course, be raised about the very existence of universities as well as our involvement in them. For in a world of such need, in a world that seems on the brink of destruction, how can we justify setting aside the time, resources, and energy to let some people do nothing but read books? Moreover, they are not just "some people"; they are people of privilege from the most privileged society who are simply engaging in leisure-time activity before they have to enter the "real" world.

Perhaps making the university even more questionable is that the threat to our existence we confront in the bomb is in fact the result of the university. Without universities and university-trained people we would not have developed the science that makes our destruction possible. Indeed, no fact more clearly gives lie to the claim of the neutrality or objectivity of the university than that of the bomb. Universities, like politics, reflect and serve the interests of their societies. They will be as good or as corrupt as the people who support them—good reason, it would seem, to doubt their continued viability in a world such as ours.

Some persons concerned with such questions would have us reshape university education. Our task must be to use the knowledge generated by the university to find alternatives to a world at war, they would say. The university must now help to save us from the very world it has created by using its considerable resources in the interest of peace and justice. Therefore, the student can justify the time spent here in terms of the power it gives him or her to do good on leaving the university.

The problem with this account of the university, however, is its failure to see that the university, like raising lemurs, is not a means to peace but is a form of peace. I have been around universities many years and I am well aware that no politics is as dirty or as intense as the politics of the university, but I still maintain that the university is one of our most important institutions of peace. Universities are dedicated to continuing the conversation across centuries of the hard-won wisdom of people who often sharply disagree. The university is committed to exposing those disagreements, believing that by so doing our lives will be lived more honestly and richly. The university, therefore, stands as an activity that thrives on disagreements while believing that such disagreements can never be resolved by violence.[8]

To be invited to be part of that process, even for a little while, is morally important. The university should be committed to the moral formation of its students through development of the skills and virtues necessary to be a people of truth. Therefore, the university does not have to be put at the service of trying to make the world more peaceful. The university is one of the ways in which we believe we and the world are involved in the process of peace. Students need no moral justification for taking the time to be students if the university is, in fact, doing its job.

But let me push the issue one step further. I have suggested that universities are institutions of peace, as they are dedicated to initiating the young into the continuing conversation of our culture about the good, the beautiful, and the true. But without the young, a society's need for the university disappears; so I want to say it is important that we have children, not just for the sake of the university, but because we are convinced that life is worth living and that we have much good to pass on to the coming generations. Yet no activity has been rendered more problematic by the bomb than having children.

How does one justify bringing new life into a world threatened by ultimate destruction or by the cynicism and despair this destruction breeds? It is almost impossible to avoid perverting our children's lives. This is the most profound sense of sickness suggested by Schell, since its destructive process is so imperceptible. For whether many acknowledge the threat or not, its presence invades their lives and seems to render all their activities pointless, even, or perhaps especially, the activity of having children. Since, as *Time* reminds them, they can do nothing about the bomb, they seek to forget or deny its existence and, as a result, its presence is given even greater power over their lives and those of their children. The only alternative, and ironically it seems to be the most humane alternative, is to drink, eat, and make love with no thought for tomorrow, since tomorrow may not come. By so living, their lives lack worth, but at least they do not impose their same hopeless attitude on others.

Even more than I fear the bomb, I fear this attitude. For it is a stance that has much power in our world. Indeed, I am not sure which came first, the bomb or this attitude. I believe not only that we get the politics we deserve, but that our military planning and technology ultimately reflect the kind of people we are. Could it be that the bomb and our fear of it are but the manifestation of our prior sense of lack of worth and correspondingly, the fear of reproducing ourselves? Whether they are or not, we now find ourselves in a vicious circle which will not be easily broken.

Nothing is more hopeful or peaceful than the willingess to open our lives to children. Having children is activity in its most paradigmatic form, as the having of a child is its own meaning. Moreover, having children is our most basic time-full project, not only in the sense that children are time-consuming, but because through children our world quite literally is made timeful. Children bind existence temporally, as through them we are given beginnings, middles, and ends. They require us to take time and, as a result, we learn that time is possible only as a form of peace.

Perhaps I can illustrate this best by asking you to think of the relation of revolutions and children. Revolutions are often conducted in the name of what is good for future generations, even though revolutionaries often do not have children. The reason may be that the business of revolution is demanding and some must devote all their time and energy to it. No doubt children are a drag on revolutionaries, but they also may be necessary if the goals being sought are to be kept humane. For it may be that finally the most radical stance possible for any human is the willingness to have a child in the face of injustice, oppression, and tyranny. Having children is the ultimate defeat of all totalitarians.

If that is right, and I think it is, then nothing can be more important for us in the face of the bomb than to go on having children. That is what we can do. That is a way we work for peace. If the many other ways we work for peace somehow make that activity secondary or irrelevant, then the peace we seek cannot help but be shaped by the same kind of desperation that built the bomb in the first place. For it is through children that we are given the time to be peaceful in a world at war.

One may well ask at this point: "But why call activities such as raising lemurs, sustaining universities, and especially, having children, trivial? At least on your own grounds they seem very significant. Are you not just playing a rhetorical trick by calling them trivial?" I obviously do not have a great stake in denying this charge, but I am serious about calling such activities trivial. I have done so in the hopes of reminding us that peace is a more profound reality in our lives than we think. The primary meaning of "trivial", after all, is not "trifling" but "that which can be met anywhere." To speak of the significance of the trivial is to remind us that some of our everyday activities, e.g., the birth of a child, embody significant moral commitments.

I have also been serious in calling such activities trivial in order to remind us that the most significant aspects of our lives are constituted by the trivial. Put differently, without the trivial life would have no duration, as we keep time by giving the trivial significance through memory. Ultimately, nothing has ultimate significance, not even the survival of the world, but we can be significant to one another by taking the time to learn to be at peace.

It has sometimes been suggested that baseball is the ultimate metaphor of the American experience. I am not sure that is right but I hope it is, for one game of baseball takes quite a bit of time. Indeed, during a game a spectator can even miss a few pitches here or a good play there because he or she is comparing with a friend ways of preparing Polish sausage. Beyond that, one game does not make a season, so one knows that one will not be crushed if one loses a game now and then—there is always tomorrow or, if one is a Cubs fan, next season. "We'll get them next time." Baseball and life are both trivial, but we can only learn how to play and live both by taking the time to do so. And in the process we also learn, if we are attentive, how interesting it is to live peacefully.

3. Peace and the Realities of Our Existence

I suspect I should end on this obscure but winsome suggestion about baseball, but I must tell you that things are not that easy. For I have suggested that the way of peace comes by our refusing to let the threat of nuclear destruction determine our lives. Instead, our task is to take the time to rest in and enjoy the trivial. As I suggested, this is a kind of spiritual counsel about how to live in a nuclear age when we are told either that we must do everything to rid our existence of the nuclear threat or, alternatively, that we can do nothing. I have said we can do something: we can go on living peacefully.

But the realists must have their say, for they remind us that the very activities to which I directed our attention — raising lemurs, going to school, having children, baseball — are made possible only because some are willing to develop and use the military might necessary to protect and sustain those activities. The very fact we go on having children is the reason that we cannot morally cease defending our ability to do so through the agency of the nation-state. We rightly want our children to survive, and such survival can now be assured only by threatening the survival of other people and, ironically, ourselves and our children. So my defense of the need to take time for peace in the end cannot help but justify the status quo.

There is no easy answer to this. But I think there is a response possible which has some force. If I have been right that saving lemurs and universities and having children are not just means of peace but forms of peace, then we have a way to understand our dilemma as well as a response to it. Our current problem is that the means we have used to protect those activities pervert their character. When we use them as justification for violence, we undermine them as activities worthwhile in themselves. As a result, we lose the power they possess to help us live more peaceful lives.

It may be objected that the use of force does not deny that raising lemurs or children are worthwhile activities, that in fact, it is because they are worthwhile in themselves that we are jealous of our ability to protect them. There is no question of the descriptive power of this objection. The only response can be theological — namely, that Christians believe that only as we learn to follow him who is God's peace can we make the peace that surrounds us more fully ours.[9] Such a theological appeal, however, is not extranatural but rather the means through which we come to see the naturalness of peace. Without such convictions our peaceful activities — such as having children — can justify as well as become terrifyingly violent.

Our situation in this regard is not unlike the question of why we should be courageous, just, truthful — that is, virtuous. The temptation is to think that the virtues must be for something — they must allow us to accomplish certain ends. Moreover, it is certainly true that the virtues do give us power we would otherwise lack to secure appropriate goals; in Aristotle's language, they give us a second nature. But the virtues can be perverted. They are not true virtues if they are acquired only in order that we might serve ends not intrinsic to the virtues themselves. Just as a musician cannot be a great musician if he or she become such in order to make money, so the person of character cannot become virtuous in order to secure power over others. That is why Christians have maintained that the "natural" virtues must be formed by charity, for without charity they risk becoming even more powerful forms of the demonic.

There is still another analogy between the virtues and peaceful activities, as the virtues also take time, or, perhaps better put, are timeful activities. This is not just because the virtues can only be developed through habitual formation, but because the virtues bind our past with our future by providing us with continuity of self. Because we are virtuous people, as we are peaceful people, we do not confront just any future but a future of a very definite kind. Just as the fears of the courageous person are not the fears of the coward, so the future of the virtuous person is not the future of those who lack character.

Our task, therefore, as people of peace is to make the activities we care about determine rather than be determined by those forces that claim they are serving our interests by insuring our future. All they are insuring is our survival, not our lives. That is a demanding task indeed, and one that will take all the time and energy we can muster. But we will not even be able to begin that process if we are unwilling to take the time to enjoy those activities through which we learn what peace is like.

That we are able to take the time to be peaceful certainly takes out some very strong metaphysical drafts about the way the world is. At least for Christians, taking the time to be at peace derives from our strong conviction that the "realities" that claim to rule this world and to give us the security to be at peace in fact are not capable of such security. Instead, we believe that God has done all that is necessary to give us the time to learn to be at peace in a world at war. We will not be of service to such a world if we act as if there were no time left.[10]

NOTES

1. Anon., "A Vision of Ourselves," *Time* (July 29, 1985), p. 58.
2. Jonathan Schell, *The Fate of the Earth* (New York: Alfred Knopf, 1982), p. 8.
3. "A Vision of Ourselves," pp. 58–59.
4. Gordon Kaufman, *Theology for a Nuclear Age* (Philadelphia: Westminster Press, 1985), pp. 6–7.

5. Ibid., p. 7.

6. Ibid., p. 37.

7. For an account of the colony, see *Duke Magazine*, January–February, 1985, pp. 12–16.

8. As Michael Oakeshott says, "A university is not a machine for achieving a particular purpose or producing a particular result; it is a manner of human activity" ("The Idea of a University," *The Listener* [March 9, 1950], p. 424). This activity, which Oakeshott identifies as the pursuit of learning, while not peculiar to the university, is the university's particular responsibility because of its commitment to enhancing the conversations with the past and present necessary for us to be civilized.

9. For a fuller defense of this claim, see my *Against the Nations: War and Survival in a Liberal Society* (Minneapolis: Winston-Seabury, 1985).

10. I am indebted to Mr. Greg Jones, Mr. Michael Cartwright, Dr. Harmon Smith, and Dr. Dennis Campbell for their criticism of this paper.

INDEX